THEIR DARKEST HOUR

THEIR DARKEST HOUR

LAURENCE REES

LARGE PRINT

Oxford

First published in Great Britain 2007
by
Ebury Press
An imprint of Ebury Publishing

Published in Large Print 2009 by ISIS Publishing Ltd.,
7 Centremead, Osney Mead, Oxford OX2 0ES
by arrangement with
Ebury Publishing
A Random House Group Company

British Library Cataloguing in Publication Data
Rees, Laurence, 1957–
    Their darkest hour [text (large print)].
    1. World War, 1939–1945 - - Personal narratives.
    2. World War, 1939–1945 - - Atrocities.
    3. World War, 1939–1945 - - Biography.
    4. Large type books.
    I. Title
    940.5'481–dc22

ISBN 978–0–7531–8310–6 (hb)
ISBN 978–0–7531–8311–3 (pb)

Printed and bound in Great Britain by
T. J. International Ltd., Padstow, Cornwall

For Helena

ACKNOWLEDGEMENTS

Recently I interviewed one of the most famous German U-boat captains of World War II and asked him what qualities were required of a submarine commander in action. He replied: "The most important quality a U-boat commander needed during the war was simple — a good crew."

And my own experience of television confirms that his words apply just as much to programme-making as to U-boats. For I owe a tremendous debt to the various production teams that I have been lucky enough to lead over the years.

The people whose historical detective work and journalism helped make the interviews in this book possible include: Martina Balazova, Tanya Batchelor, Saulius Berzinis, Fumio Kanda, Sally Ann Kleibal, Wanda Koscia, Tomasz Lascia, Karen Liebreich, Tilman Remme, Detlef Siebert, Dominic Sutherland, Frank Stucke, Anna Taborska and Elena Yakoleva. I want to ensure that the enormity of their individual contribution to the various television series I have written, produced and directed is acknowledged — and I gladly and gratefully do so here.

But over the last 20 years or so I have worked with other researchers and assistant producers around the world who were also a huge help, and whose names I need similarly to record with gratitude: Ian Affleck,

Friederike Albat, Maria Azarianc, Valeri Azarianc, Maria Belyakov, Marcel Joos, Miho Kometani, Marita Kraus, Adam Levy, Michaella Lichenstein, Sue McConachy, Anya Narinskaya, Maria Razumovskaya, Jon Rees, Stanislav Remizov, Corinna Stuermer, Roksolyana Shumeiko, Taras Shumeiko, Eric Shur, Elena Smolina, Manfred Oldenburg, Hong Quin, Alexandra Umminger, Doris Wong, Jason Wordie and Alicija Zakauskaite.

No one person worked with me continously over the past nearly twenty years, but two came close. Martin Patmore was the cameraman who photographed the majority of people featured in this book. He was a most congenial companion on our travels around the world. And Alan Lygo was the film editor on the vast majority of my programmes. He contributed a huge amount — and often acted more like an Executive Producer than a film editor. I am enormously grateful to them both — and hope that each of them think that their long-term tolerance of my idiosyncrasies was worth it.

If I were also to list all of the other camera crews, post-production personnel, co-producers, secretarial help and television executives involved over these last two decades I would need several more pages. I thank them all. And my thanks are no less sincere merely because reasons of space prevent me listing them all here.

At Ebury Press, Jake Lingwood and Martin Redfern were a great help with this project. Andrew Nurnberg surpassed himself with literary and other advice. My boss at the BBC, Keith Scholey, generously gave me permission to write the book and to use BBC material within it. More than that, he was always immensely supportive and encouraging.

A number of people, including my father-in-law, Professor Derek Brewer, my wife Helena, and Professor Sir Ian Kershaw read this book in draft and I am grateful for their comments.

But my chief thanks, as always, go to the many people who agreed to meet me and answer our questions. Many of them have died in the years since we filmed them — but the history they recounted lives on.

CONTENTS

INTRODUCTION...........................xv

PART ONE — MASS KILLING
1. Paul Montgomery and Bombing the Japanese
   to Destruction......................6
2. Petras Zelionka and the Killing Fields of
   the Holocaust......................14
3. Oskar Groening and a Double Life in
   Auschwitz.........................20

PART TWO — RESISTANCE
4. Alois Pfaller and the Struggle Against the
   Nazis.............................34
5. Aleksey Bris and the Shattered Dreams of
   the Ukrainians.....................42
6. Vladimir Kantovski and Stalin's Penal
   Battalions.........................50

PART THREE — FIGHTING AND KILLING THE "INFERIOR" AND THE "INHUMAN"
7. James Eagleton and Killing the Japanese.......61
8. Hajime Kondo and the Making of a Devil
   in the Japanese Imperial Army.................69
9. Wolfgang Horn and Shooting Red Army
   Soldiers..........................78
10. Masayo Enomoto and Rape, Murder and
    Cannibalism......................85

PART FOUR — PRISONERS

11. Aleksandr Mikhailovski and the Nazis'
    Human Mine Detectors........................97
12. Samuel Willenberg and Surviving a
    Death Camp..................................104
13. Peter Lee and the Virtues of an Englishman
    Imprisoned by the Japanese..................112
14. Tatiana Nanieva and the Revenge
    of Stalin....................................119
15. Estera Frenkiel and Choices in the
    Ghetto 127
16. Maria Platonow and Betrayal by the
    British......................................135
17. Toivi Blatt and the Philosophy of
    Sobibor 145
18. Connie Sully and Rape by the Japanese.......155
19. Lucille Eichengreen and Abuse in the
    Ghetto 162

PART FIVE — SOLDIERS OF BELIEF

20. Vladimir Ogryzko and the Panic in
    Moscow......................................178
21. Suren Mirzoyan and Hand-to-Hand
    Combat in Stalingrad........................185
22. Jacques Leroy and the Mentality of a
    SS Fanatic..................................192
23. Zinaida Pytkina and SMERSH.................200
24. Hiroo Onoda and the Refusal to
    Surrender...................................206

PART SIX — SERVANTS OF THE REGIME

25. Erna Krantz and Living an Ordinary
    Life under the Nazis 221
26. Mark Lazarevich Gallay and the Mind
    of Josef Stalin..................................229
27. Manfred Freiherr von Schroeder and
    Working with Hitler............................238
28. Ken Yuasa and Human Experiments in War...246
29. Fritz Hippler and "The Eternal Jew" 253
30. Nigel Nicolson and Deporting Yugoslavians ...260
31. Karl Boehm-Tettelbach and the Charming
    Nazis...268
32. Kristina Söderbaum and Acting for Hitler.....278

PART SEVEN — MASS SUICIDE

33. Kenichiro Oonuki and the Logic of the
    Kamikaze 292
34. Waltraud Reski and Mass Rape in
    Demmin 300
35. Shigeaki Kinjou and the Death of the
    Innocent 307

Postscript...313

INTRODUCTION

How could Nazi killers shoot Jewish women and children at close range? Why did Japanese soldiers rape and murder on such a horrendous scale? How was it possible to endure the torment of a Nazi death camp? For nearly 20 years I have tried to answer these and many other similar questions by meeting hundreds of people who participated in World War II. I was particularly interested in the motivation of the perpetrators — the people who committed atrocities — though I also met many of their victims and others who faced difficult, sometimes impossible, decisions during the war.

In the course of my work I travelled from Japan to the Baltic States, from Poland to America, from Germany to Borneo and from Italy to China. I encountered rapists, murderers and cannibals. I talked to soldiers who acted heroically; survivors of the worst atrocities imaginable; even a man who shot little children. Each of the hundreds of interviews was filmed, and each encounter lasted several hours. I used some of this interview material in a series of television documentaries I wrote and produced about the war and in the accompanying books, but an enormous amount of historical information remained unpublished. So I decided to study carefully once again the more than 7 million words of interview transcript and write a series of essays about the 35 most extraordinary people I met on my travels. This approach has enabled me to include in the previously published stories information that has not been made public before, and to add several new interviews, which appear here in book form entirely for the first time — notably my encounters with Hiroo Onoda, Nigel Nicolson, Marie Platonow, Fritz Hippler and Kristina Söderbaum. This fresh format also allowed me to offer an insight into my own personal encounters with all of these interviewees, which the previous narrative form prevented.

Over the years, as I questioned people who had been tested in ways that I had never been, I also felt questions asked of myself. And the one question that I believed I had to address more than any other was simple: what would I have done in similar circumstances? Of course, I could not know for certain. Had I been in those circumstances all those years ago then I would not have been the identical person I am today, since we are all shaped so much by the times in which we live. But in order to read any history we have to imagine what the past was like and create once again the circumstances in which historical characters lived. And by a similar act of imagination we can surely place ourselves in history and ask what kind of person we would have become in that situation, and consequently what choices we might have exercised.

The past is not some alien world. They may have "done things differently" there but that is because the circumstances were different, not because human beings and their fundamental needs and motivations were different. The physiology of the human mind has not changed over the last few thousand years (certainly not since World War II) and so the dilemmas and challenges faced in this book were faced by people essentially like us — indeed, by our parents and grandparents. I believe there is consequently a great deal we can learn about ourselves by asking, "What would we have done?"

It was vital, of course, to treat the oral testimony that I and my team were gathering with an element of scepticism — especially when people were talking so long after the event. We researched all the interviewees thoroughly before filming, and checked that the factual details of their story were consistent both internally with their own testimony and externally with documents of the period, like the war diaries of the various military units concerned. If we had any doubts about the fundamental veracity of a potential contributor's testimony, then we did not film an interview.

Unlike some interviews conducted for oral-history projects, I also focused each filmed interview around a handful of specific themes. There were two reasons for this. First, I found we got the most interesting answers when we concentrated on one area rather than trying to cover an entire biography, and, second, it allowed us to check once again with internal references that the story we were hearing was consistent.

Then there is the question of how much we can expect human beings to recall so long after the events in question. Here I think there is an important distinction to make. If you interview people about what seem to them insignificant details, like the exact names of all their comrades years ago, it is likely that their recollections will be unreliable. But if you focus on key emotional moments, then in my experience many people have very powerful and accurate recall. I think we can recognize this from our own experience. I could not tell you, for example, exactly what I had for lunch four weeks ago. But I could tell you precisely the circumstances and emotions around the sudden illness and death of my mother 30 years ago. One event was not very significant to me; the other was a searing, life-changing moment that I can recall in almost photographic detail.

Historians must ask questions of all source material, and oral testimony is no exception to this rule. But, as I discuss later in this book in the story of Nigel Nicolson and the deportation of thousands of Yugoslav soldiers to their deaths, it is important to remember that documents are capable of lying just as much as people.

As for the format of this book, I have chosen to divide it into seven sections. But I appreciate that many of these interviewees could have fitted into several sections: someone involved in mass killing was also subsequently a prisoner, for example. So what I have done is to place each person in the category that was historically the most significant for them. This was, I think, the best way to present this material since it allowed comparisons between nationalities to be made which I believe have not been highlighted before; though I am the first to recognize that the chief value of this testimony remains the detail of the individual experience.

However, it is important that the intermingling in some sections of this book, of essays about former Nazis or soldiers of the Japanese Imperial Army with essays about veterans from the Allied side, is not taken to imply any moral equivalence between the different political systems involved. No one with my family heritage — a father who fought in the RAF during the war and an uncle killed on the Atlantic convoys — could ever forget that the Western democracies were fundamentally on the side of righteousness during the conflict. Though the testimony in this book does reveal that there are occasionally some surprising similarities of personal experience across national boundaries.

Meeting these people has changed the way I think about the world. Whilst they may have talked about the past, I believe that what they said is of value for the future.

Laurence Rees
London
JULY 2007

PART ONE

MASS KILLING

Over 60 million people died in World War II — more than in any other conflict in history — and one of the chief reasons this level of carnage was possible was the power of modern methods of killing. Two of the three personal histories in this section illustrate how easy it had become — both technologically and psychologically — to kill people in large numbers by the middle of the twentieth century. Oskar Groening talks of the modern killing techniques of Auschwitz allowing him to "separate" himself from the murders during his time working in the camp. And Paul Montgomery speaks of the "distancing" effect of bombarding civilians from the air.

It is troubling material for many reasons, not least because this testimony forces us to confront an important issue about the human capacity to kill. What if all it took to remove your greatest enemy, your biggest threat, the person who you believed threatened your own life, was merely to press a button in front of you? You simply wouldn't see them again. No bad memories, no post-traumatic stress. In fact, you wouldn't really feel you had "killed" anyone. After all, you would only have pressed a button. Paul Montgomery put the issue succinctly during his interview when he revealed that he felt destroying people by dropping bombs on them was like playing "a video game".

And these modern methods of killing didn't just allow more people to be destroyed than ever before, and with less personal involvement from the killers; they also raise difficult questions of guilt and innocence. It is easy to see how the third person included in Part One, Petras Zelionka, was guilty of murder: he stood in front of his victims and pulled the trigger. As a result he was sentenced to 20 years in a prison camp after the war. But what about Oskar Groening? He worked in an office sorting money and never directly killed anyone, yet he clearly helped the smooth functioning of the murder factory that was Auschwitz.

Along with thousands of other members of the SS who worked at Auschwitz, Groening was never charged with any offence — 85 per cent of the SS who served there escaped all punishment. This was primarily because the legal authorities in most countries decided that the majority of SS men in Auschwitz had not personally killed anyone — it was chiefly the technology that was guilty. And you can't put gas chambers on trial. All of which begs this question, of course: does that mean that if in the future a state organizes an entirely mechanized system of extermination, no one will be guilty of any crime?

Then there is another question of guilt and innocence that this testimony raises. Both the Nazis at the time, and a number of people since, have argued that there is some kind of equivalence between the extermination of the Jews in the gas chambers and the mass killing of the Japanese and Germans by Allied bombers. Oskar Groening himself implies this comparison (see page 25). It's an extraordinary idea — especially given that American flyers like Paul Montgomery came from a democracy and had been forced into a war to defend themselves against blatant aggression — but it is important to address the question, and I discuss it towards the end of my essay on Groening.

None of these issues is easily resolved. But the questions they raise are fundamental to any judgements we form about the legality and morality of war.

PAUL MONTGOMERY
AND BOMBING THE JAPANESE TO DESTRUCTION

I have probably met more people who were responsible for mass killing during World War II — from Japan, Germany, the former Soviet Union and the USA — than any other living person. It is a dubious distinction and was not one of my life ambitions. But it does offer me the opportunity to make some comparative judgements. And one of my most surprising findings was that the vast majority of the people I met who were involved in killing large numbers of men, women and children seemed relatively untroubled by their actions. Take the case of Paul Montgomery for example.

I interviewed him in 1999 at his ranch in the heart of the Mid-West. The setting was idyllic. His house nestled peacefully in green pastures, and was reached down a long country road. He and his wife had been happily married for years, and were at the heart of a large extended family of children, grandchildren and great-grandchildren. His home was a calm and happy place to be. Paul Montgomery himself had been raised near by as a teetotal, model citizen. So the idea that this man had participated in the killing of thousands of people was almost unimaginable. It was the war, obviously, that allowed him the opportunity to commit these acts. In particular, it was the branch of the armed forces that he chose to join that made it possible, because he was a flyer in the United States Air Force (USAF).

He joined shortly after Pearl Harbor, and the memory of that "sneak" attack conditioned his attitude throughout the war. "I began to develop a hatred for the Japanese for what they had done in such an underhand manner," he told me. "The Japanese had surely damaged our property ... and I wanted to confront the Japanese much more than I did the Germans. I had lost some friends in Pearl Harbor and so I felt a responsibility to them." The bombing of Pearl Harbor in Hawaii before declaring war on the United States was a catastrophic misjudgement by the Japanese. Of course, any country would have reacted to such an attack with outrage and fury, but with the Americans there was an added intensity to the response. It touched something deep in the American psyche — something to do with an almost mythic notion of "fair play" or "straight dealing" that was central to how many Americans saw themselves and their country. It drove Montgomery and millions of his compatriots to sign up for the war effort with vengeance in their hearts. He had always wanted to fly, and his chosen weapon of retribution was the four-engined bomber.

Initially he joined the USAF pilot programme, but after being told there were too many pilots he transferred to train as a radio operator. Eventually he was posted to a base on the small island of Tinian in the Pacific as part of the crew of a Boeing B29

Superfortress, the biggest and heaviest bomber of the war. His job was to help guide the plane over Japan to the general vicinity of the target and assist the bombardier in ensuring that the bombs fell where they should. His first raid was on the refineries at the port of Yokohama: "After we rolled off the target we could look back, see the refinery ablaze, and finally I felt some sense of accomplishment." A number of industrial targets followed, like the Mitsubishi heavy machinery complex at Osaka, but soon the overwhelming size of the USAF meant that Americans quite simply ran out of factories to bomb.

So now Montgomery and his crew participated in one of the most controversial military operations of the war — the fire-bombing of Japanese cities: "It was felt that we had to reduce not only their ability to wage war, but their desire to wage war. And so that brought about the fire-bombing missions of the major targets. We started with Osaka and Tokyo and Nagoya, and all the major cities, and they were fire-bombed to nothing left except steps and chimneys. Complete one hundred per cent obliteration." Within their bomb clusters the Americans dropped special "fire-fighting bombs" that exploded at unspecified intervals to prevent firemen from dealing with the blaze. "Not that these bombs were strictly necessary because the Japanese had virtually no ability on the ground to deal with these attacks. The few who survived the mass bombing speak of "blizzards of fire" and of "living people burnt alive".

The wooden and paper houses of the Japanese instantly combusted, and fire storms engulfed whole communities. Around 100,000 Japanese died in the fire-bombing of Tokyo during the night of 9–10 March 1945 — more than were initially killed at either Hiroshima or Nagasaki by the first atomic bombs.

"I didn't have any regrets, to put it bluntly," said Montgomery. "I was twenty-one years old that summer of the fire-bombing. And I really was wanting to get the war over and I wanted to go home. And if they told me to go bomb some cities, I went and bombed cities." He admitted that below him, suffering in the fire storm, "it must have been women and children, yeah," but he still felt that "it's just what I was told to do as part of the war effort."

These words on the page make Paul Montgomery sound like an unthinking man. But he wasn't. With each of my questions he tried to search his own emotions and respond honestly. In a way, it was still hard for him to realize, emotionally, that he had been a part of a military operation that had brought death to thousands and thousands of women and children. One reason he felt that was because he had been just one of the aircrew in his plane, which itself was part of a larger unit. So itemizing out the number of people that each individual had personally killed was impossible. But he himself articulated another, more important, reason why he felt so little about the destruction he had helped create: "It's not like going out and sticking a bayonet in somebody's belly, OK? You kill them from a distance and it doesn't have that demoralizing effect upon you that it did if I went up and stuck a bayonet in somebody's stomach in the course of combat. It's just

9

different. It's kind of like conducting war through a video game."

This "distancing" is, I believe, one of the keys to understanding why such a seemingly "normal" man can participate in the killing of woman and children in large numbers. Modern methods of killing have not just allowed more people to be killed than ever before, they have made the task psychologically easier for the killers. It was almost certainly harder for our ancestors to kill one person with a stone axe than it was for Paul Montgomery and his comrades to kill thousands via aerial bombardment from six kilometres up in the sky.

This ease of killing combined powerfully with the immense sense of justification that the US bomber crews felt in pursuing "vengeance" against the Japanese. The Americans had not started the war, had not coveted anything the Japanese possessed, and felt they had been placed with no option but to fight. At Pearl Harbor the Japanese had sown the wind — now they would reap the whirlwind. In addition, a number of the US servicemen in this war believed they were fighting racially inferior people — American cartoons even portrayed the Japanese as "monkeys". But Paul Montgomery denied that racism formed part of his own motivation. "One of my sons married a Japanese — she's from Hawaii," he told me, "and she's the greatest thing that ever happened to him. I have no animosity towards the Japanese people at all. I just, at the time, had an animosity towards the German or the Japanese war effort . . . And I was determined, as we all were, that we were gonna end the war . . . And if it took bombing civilian cities, so be it."

But during one mission — and one mission only — Paul Montgomery felt a connection with the people down below him. It was during a raid on the city of Kure on the southwest coast of the island of Honshu. His plane was one of the last to make its bomb run, and below him the city was ablaze: "Kure was burning with such intensity, and we were at such low level, we had obnoxious odours from the incineration coming up to the airplane. We could see sheets of metal from out-houses and what have you coming up almost to our altitude . . . I was gagging . . . that odour struck me as an odour of indescribable stench. It was somewhere between burning urine and human waste . . . It was a nauseating experience."

"What did it make you feel," I asked, "when you smelt that?"

"I don't know. I felt everything except mercy for the people, for some reason. I was not obsessed with any feeling of sympathy. I just wasn't. I was young and I was case-hardened."

Despite his statement that he felt "no mercy" for the people below him, the smell of human waste coming up from the fire storm did affect Paul Montgomery. As he told the story of the raid on Kure he looked uncomfortable for the first time in the interview. It was as if he were still fighting to eliminate the message his senses had given him: this is the consequence of what you have done, the intense heat, the destruction of metal and wood, and the elimination of human beings so that all that is left is the smell of their excrement. The circumstances of the raid over Kure must surely have created all of these feelings somewhere deep within him — feelings that the "distancing" of previous raids had prevented.

Clearly his superiors were aware that there was a danger the American bomber crews would suffer psychological problems because as soon as they landed back on their home base of Tinian and their debriefing had been completed a flight sergeant offered each member of the crew a shot of powerful liquor. "I said, 'I don't drink.' He said, 'Drink it anyway.' And so I drank it. And what I'm saying is it masked or tranquillized me almost to the point I couldn't get back to my barracks. I went right to sleep. And he [the flight sergeant] said, 'This is to prevent you from having any nightmares or failing to go to sleep.' And I went right to sleep. I was knocked out. And that's the only time I ever drank any alcoholic beverage in my life."

So concerned were the medical authorities for the psychological welfare of the bomber crews that a "medical man" patrolled the rows of resting airmen to check that everybody was asleep. "He explained to us later that it was necessary — vital — that you get to sleep right away. That you not start this traumatic afterthought. And it worked. I didn't feel any sympathy for the Japanese at any time."

As I said earlier, these sort of words — "I didn't feel any sympathy for the Japanese at any time" — appear harsh. But I would defy anyone to meet Paul Montgomery and not like him. It was typical of him that as I left he pressed me to take a jar of home-made preserve back to London for my family. This was an intriguing person to meet. He freely admitted that he had participated in the mass killing of thousands of Japanese civilians — men, women and children. He had managed to do all that and yet he remained an apparently "normal" man, full of kindness and generosity.

PETRAS ZELIONKA
AND THE KILLING FIELDS OF THE HOLOCAUST

In the summer and autumn of 1941, when he was a young man of 24, Petras Zelionka participated in one of the worst crimes in history: the shooting of Jewish men, women and children in the murders that occurred in the wake of the Nazi invasion of the Soviet Union.[1]

I filmed an interview with him in the mid-1990s at the site of one of the massacres — the Seventh Fort in Kaunas, Lithuania. He was able to spare us an hour or so of his time, he said, as his wife had gone shopping and he was waiting for her to return before travelling back to their home in the countryside. We were fortunate — and we knew it — that he had been persuaded to be interviewed at all.

What I wanted was to see how far it was possible to understand why he had taken part in the crime. And it was clear that an understanding of the background to

[1] It is important to remember that the Germans initially invaded the Soviet Union, not Russia, on 22 June 1941. In fact, they didn't reach Russian territory for some time since they had first to fight across the territory of the Ukraine, Belarus or the Baltic states (all, at the time, part of the Soviet Union) in order to get Russia. In addition, large numbers of Red Army soldiers were not of Russian, but of Soviet origin (i.e. from one of the Soviet republics other than Russia).

the killings was crucial in any attempt to penetrate his mentality.

There was long-standing "traditional" anti-Semitism in Lithuania, based in part on jealousy of the (often imaginary) wealth of the Jewish population, and events in the year before the Nazi invasion had strongly reinforced this prejudice. In 1940 Lithuania, along with the other Baltic states, had been occupied by the Red Army and there was a widespread (though false) belief amongst Lithuanians that many of the worst atrocities subsequently committed by Stalin's men had been perpetrated by Jews. "In general," says Zelionka, "there was the greatest indignation when the Russians came. Many Lithuanian Jews became the political leaders, joined the police . . . and everyone was saying that in the security department people were mostly tortured by the Jews. They used to put the screws on the head and tighten them, thus torturing the teachers and professors."

Now, after their invasion of the Baltic States and the rest of the Soviet Union in June 1941, the Nazis wanted to murder first the adult male Jews and then, soon afterwards, the women and children as well. The Nazis were driven in their task primarily by ideological fervour — how could the "Garden of Eden" that their Führer, Adolf Hitler, wanted for the Germans in the East be created if any Jews still lived in it?

Jews were driven out of their homes by the Germans and Lithuanian collaborators like Petras Zelionka to the nearby countryside, where large pits had been prepared. Often many curious villagers followed this sad procession. The Jews knew they were going to die so they ripped up the paper money in their pockets and threw it to the ground in order that their killers would not profit. Standing by the pits, the Jews were then ordered to take their clothes off. Just before they were shot, they would sometimes try to throw a treasured coat or jacket to one of the non-Jewish bystanders from the village in a last act of generosity.

Zelionka admitted that he and his comrades took the Jews out from the villages or the city ghettos to the freshly dug pits, stripped them of their clothes and pulled the trigger: "Everything short and clear. Without any ceremonies — nothing. We used to give them up for lost and that was it." Sometimes, he remembered, just before they were shot, "At the edge of the grave, some of them used to say, 'Long live Stalin!' Only that kind of 'prank' . . . Sometimes when I think about the story of my life — you could write such a book. You would read without stopping . . . Maybe [people] would understand, but maybe it becomes worse [and they don't]."

Zelionka also revealed that he and his comrades were often drunk when they shot the Jews — alcohol played a big part in the killing process. "After you have a drink," he said, "everyone is braver then." At the end of a day's shooting he and his comrades returned to their Lithuanian army base: "When you came back to the barracks, no one used to pay any attention. They used to bring us vodka; we could drink as much as we wanted . . . If they give me, I drink." Zelionka drank after the killing partly, he said, to "throw out" of his head the "unpleasant" pictures in his mind from the day's events.

But the fact remains that Petras Zelionka chose to take part in the killings — he was a volunteer. And though he was too careful to express virulent anti-Semitism more than 50 years after the murders, he admitted that amongst his fellow killers, "Some people were saying that they [the Jews] deserved it, that they tortured other people or helped torture them . . . there were many men who became indignant with the Jews. We were told what they have done, how they used to kill even the women . . . others did it because of their indignation. The Jews are very selfish."

And even though he tried, I believe, to conceal his own personal hatred towards the Jews during our interview and to distance himself from the views of these "other" people who took part in the killing, there were moments when what I took to be his genuine emotion came through. He described himself as a "real Lithuanian" and was quick to point out that he had not shot other Lithuanians, "only Jews" (even though, of course, the Jews he shot were of Lithuanian nationality). And when asked if he would have been prepared to shoot non-Jewish Lithuanians, he instantly replied, "I would not shoot." He also confessed that he was worried that he might have been asked to shoot someone who was "innocent" (by which he meant non-Jewish; he therefore did not consider Jewish women and children, even Jewish babies, "innocent").

Fuelled by their "indignation" against the "selfish" Jews these killers went about their work, driven on chiefly by their hatred of the Jews. But another motivation was greed: "They [the Germans] used to search them [the Jews] and take all golden things from them, watches etc., everything made of gold . . . Our former warrant officer also had a suitcase where he used to put those things." And though Zelionka denied that he personally benefited from this theft, it is clear that the killers had the opportunity to share out some of the belongings of the dead Jews amongst themselves — despite the fact that, according to Heinrich Himmler, commander of the SS, all "profit" from the killings should have gone to the Nazi state.

As our interview neared its end — and he was worried that he might be keeping his wife waiting on her return from her shopping expedition — Zelionka gave two final clues as to his own motivation for the murders. First, he revealed that he had possessed a kind of "curiosity" about what he would see after he had pulled the trigger. Curiosity is, at first hearing, perhaps too weak a word to describe a killer's motivation to shoot a child at close range. But curiosity is clearly a powerful force in our lives. It is the basis, surely, of much human development. Children want to crawl because they are curious about what is on the other side of the room, just as Columbus set sail on his voyage of discovery across the Atlantic because he was curious as to what lay on the other side of the ocean. And curiosity can be a very dark force indeed. For thousands of years myths and fairy stories have focused on the power of curiosity to overcome good sense. In Ancient Greek legend, for instance, it was Pandora's desire to see inside a box given her by the gods, which she had been forbidden to open, that brought suffering into the world.

The second additional clue Zelionka gave to his motivation was an almost throwaway remark that "youth is foolishness" and "whilst you are young, you do a lot of stupid things". It was an important reminder that these killings were committed when this grey-haired grandfather was a vigorous young man in his twenties. Indeed, the reality is that the majority of violent crime in most countries is committed by young men between the ages of 18 and 25 — precisely the age range that Petras Zelionka and many of his fellow killers fell within.

After the interview was over Zelionka was hailed as something of a hero by one of the Lithuanian army officers who had helped us to arrange the filming at the Seventh Fort. "You're a journalist," this man in his mid-twenties said to me, "and you're missing the big story. The story isn't what we did to the Jews. It's what the Jews did to us." Then he looked across at Petras Zelionka, now happily reunited with his wife, and smiled.

OSKAR GROENING
AND A DOUBLE LIFE IN AUSCHWITZ

One of the few certain conclusions I have come to as a result of my work is that people rarely conform to your preconceived ideas about them. Take the kind of person who might have worked in Auschwitz, for example. Try to imagine someone who was a committed supporter of the Nazis whilst he was growing up in the 1930s, volunteered for the SS during the war, and then participated in a killing process that made Auschwitz the site of the largest mass murder in the history of the world. Who do you see? Well, whoever it is, I doubt if your creation corresponds to Oskar Groening.

He was one of the calmest people I have ever encountered. He wore spectacles and was rather mild-mannered. After the war he became a personnel manager in a glass works. And he doesn't seem to have lost a moment's sleep as a consequence of his time at Auschwitz. When I met him in Hamburg a couple of years ago I thought he resembled one of my Scottish uncles who had spent his working life in a bank. Like my uncle, Oskar Groening was upright, well turned out and apparently exceedingly respectable. And I soon discovered it wasn't surprising that he reminded me of my relative, as Groening revealed he had also worked in a bank before the war. Groening had never been a man of action — had never wanted anything more for himself than to be considered a useful member of society. But, of course, the society he lived in during his formative years was the one created by the Nazis, and he unquestioningly accepted their values as his own.

When war broke out he was 18 years old and, much influenced by stories of his grandfather who had been a trumpeter in a cavalry regiment, he craved to be a member of an "elite" unit of the German armed forces. So, despite his poor eyesight, he applied to join the SS. He was successful, and was assigned to administrative duties in southern Germany. Then, in 1942, he received news of a different posting, to a concentration camp in the east called Auschwitz. He had never heard the name before, but he knew, of course, that concentration camps existed in the Nazi state to control and punish the "internal enemies of the country".

When he arrived at Auschwitz main camp by the Sola river in the south of Poland he thought he was entering a "normal" concentration camp. He was assigned to the "economic department" of the camp and started sorting the cash that had been taken from the inmates on arrival and that he thought would be handed back to them on their eventual release. It was only when he was told that the money taken from the large numbers of Jews arriving at the camp "was not going back to them" that he realized that Auschwitz was not an "ordinary" concentration camp at all. It was explained to Groening that Jews who were not capable of work in the camp were "being diminished" and "got rid of". When he asked what being "got rid of" actually meant and was told the truth — extermination — he just "couldn't imagine it". It was only when he witnessed the arrival of a transport of Jews to the camp and saw first hand the selection process by which some were picked to work and others were chosen to die at once in the gas chambers of Auschwitz/Birkenau that Groening fully grasped what was taking place.

Learning the true function "was a shock", said Groening: "But you mustn't forget that not only from 1933 onwards but before that, in the propaganda I received as a boy in the media, we were aware that Jewishness — especially in Germany — was the cause of the First World War and the 'stab in the back' legend [by which German Jews behind the lines were falsely blamed for betraying the troops at the front]. [The Jews] also ensured that the Communists had a revolution in 1918–19, and it spread. The Jews were actually the cause of Germany's misery . . . and we were convinced by our world view that there was a great conspiracy of Jewishness against us. And that was expressed in Auschwitz in the idea that said, 'Here the Jews are being exterminated . . . what happened in the First World War — that the Jews put us into misery — must be avoided. The Jews are our enemies.' So we exterminated nothing but enemies."

But whilst he might have agreed in a theoretical way with the collection of lies that constituted the Nazi propaganda against the Jews, it was quite another thing to be involved in their mass murder. And crucial to the way Groening adjusted to Auschwitz was his immediate decision to separate method from theory. When he saw SS "sadists" brutally clearing the arrival ramp of lost children, the sick and the elderly, he went at once to complain to his superiors and asked for a transfer (which was denied). But he didn't think of complaining about the fact that mass murder was taking place — instead he complained only about the way it was happening. He said to his boss that "if there was a necessity to exterminate the Jews, at least it should be done within a certain framework."

Groening accepted the decision of the Nazi leadership that the Jews were a threat and had to be "diminished"; I suspect he even agreed with the policy. So he concentrated his efforts on ensuring that, on the rare occasions he witnessed it, the process was completed in as ordered a way as possible. And in this respect Auschwitz was the ideal place for him to work.

Only a handful of members of the SS at Auschwitz were directly confronted with the murder of the Jews. Each of the four combination crematoria/gas chambers of Auschwitz/Birkenau, capable of killing 4700 people per day between them, was manned by fewer than half a dozen Germans. The work of cleaning the gas chambers of bodies and human waste, of burning the corpses and of sorting the belongings of the murdered victims, was all carried out by other prisoners, forced to participate in the killing process or else face immediate death themselves. (These Sonderkommando were, of course, by their actions only postponing the moment of their own murder.) This meant that a member of the Auschwitz economic department, like Oskar Groening, only rarely had to face the reality of the killing. For most of the time he could sit in his office sorting out money, or rest in his barracks drinking liquor stolen from the latest transport of Jews to the camp.

Auschwitz main camp, where Groening worked most of the time, was about 2.5 kilometres from the killing factory of Auschwitz-Birkenau, so he felt removed from the process of murder physically as well as emotionally. As a result he came to feel that the main camp was like "a small town. It had its gossip . . . There was a cinema and a theatre with regular performances." There was even an Auschwitz "Sports Club" of which Groening was a keen member — he revealed during his interview that he "specialized in the high jump". And it was not just the social structures that allowed Groening to form the opinion that, from his perspective, Auschwitz was a "wonderful" environment in which to exist; that view extended to the people who worked alongside him. "Apart from the fact that there are pigs who fulfil their personal drives — there were such people — the special situation [at Auschwitz] led to friendships which I'm still saying today I like to think back on with joy."

It was thus a combination of his own personality and the structure of Auschwitz that allowed Groening to "separate" himself from the reality of the killing. "It's a quality of human beings," he said, "even a good quality, that they separate pleasant things from unpleasant things in such a way that they don't begin to suffer in such a situation." Groening shifted knowledge of the details of the killing process into a distant part of his brain and locked the door. But this technique of "separation" only worked so long as he could turn his back on the suffering. Groening felt that if he had witnessed the killing in front of his own eyes on a regular basis then he would probably have gone "mad". And so he came to the conclusion that "it is easier to throw a hand grenade behind a wall than to kill a man who is in front of a wall."

Like many of the people I have filmed over the years — not just former Nazis but veterans from all sides — Groening was a believer in the "life is about looking after Number One" school of philosophy. "Everyone puts himself first," he said. "So many people died in the war — not only Jews. So many things happened. So many were shot. So many were burned. If I thought about that, I wouldn't be able to live one minute."

Groening would even like us to believe that there is a legitimate comparison to be made between the Allied bombing campaign during the war and the extermination of the Jews. He put it this way: "We saw how bombs were dropped on Germany and women and children died in fire storms. We saw this and said, 'This is a war that is being led in this way by both sides.'" Other Nazis took the same view. Rudolf Hoess, the commandant of Auschwitz, directly compared himself with a bomber pilot who was ordered to drop bombs on a town that he knew contained women and children. Just like the SS in Auschwitz, so that argument made by the Nazis and their supporters goes, the bomber crews participated in the mass killing of non-combatants. And it is correct that the Allies deliberately targeted enemy civilians. Towards the end of the war, one criterion used in target selection was the "burnability" of German towns — something that led to the destruction of ancient cities like Würzburg.

But though all that is true, there are important conceptual differences between the mass bombing of German and Japanese cities and the Nazi extermination of the Jews. The bombing campaign was authorized by democratic governments in pursuit of one simple aim — to defeat anti-democratic regimes that had initiated the war out of a desire for ruthless conquest. Nor did the Allied bombing campaign target a specific group of the German or Japanese population, and nor was it motivated by a desire to exterminate all of the enemy. The killing of the Jews, on the other hand, was eventually part of a wider plan of annihilation that would not have stopped had Germany won the war. Nazi plans for the Soviet Union envisaged mass starvation and the elimination of tens of millions of people. Extermination was not a device to try to end the war; it was partly the *point* of the war in the east, at least from the Nazi ideological perspective. And unlike the German or Japanese leadership who could have prevented the bombing in an instant by surrendering, there was nothing the Jews could have done to stop their own extermination. No discussion, no negotiation, no surrender was possible.

None the less, many people still legitimately feel uneasy about the mass bombing campaign mounted by the Allies. And the fact that there are conceptual differences between the bombing campaign and the extermination of the Jews would have been of little comfort to the German women and children who died in the bombing of Dresden and Hamburg, or the Japanese women and children who were incinerated in the fire storms of Tokyo and Osaka. But we must always remember that the moment the war was over the bombing stopped; whereas if the Germans had won the war the destruction of the Jews would surely have continued.

The idea that they were doing no more right or wrong than an Allied bomber pilot was clearly a sustaining idea for a number of the SS in Auschwitz. And in addition to this comforting thought, Groening cultivated his lack of emotional connection to the killing. Indeed, his whole anti-Semitism was "unemotional". Whilst the Nazis "recognized" that the Jews were a "problem", he maintained that "this didn't lead to one becoming involved in such a way that if I found a Jew I'd hit him in the street."

But in a strange way the lack of connection — coldness, in effect — of his approach to the killing of the Jews made Oskar Groening a particularly disturbing figure to meet. He was a "reasonable" perpetrator. And this meant that he was capable of giving this calm explanation when asked why the Nazis considered it legitimate to murder more than 200,000 children at Auschwitz: "The children are not the enemy at the moment," he said. "The enemy is the blood in them — the [capacity] to grow up to be a Jew who could become dangerous. And because of that the children were also affected."

As our interview came to an end, Groening chillingly revealed that he didn't feel "ashamed" to have been part of Auschwitz. Rather, he confessed to feeling "ashamed" only that he had fallen for Nazi propaganda about the Jews, and so carried on working at the camp for so long: "I find it terrible what happened, and the fact that I had to be there disgusting. But guilty? No."

PART TWO

RESISTANCE

The stories gathered here represent the two different sides to resistance during World War II. On the one hand there were people like Alois Pfaller and Vladimir Kantovski who decided early on, out of deeply held principle, that they would not tolerate the injustice around them and, on the other, there were those like Aleksey Bris whose decision to resist was not entirely selfless and influenced in part by self interest. It is my belief that the first type of resistance was rarer than the second.

Take the "French Resistance", for example. Contrary to popular myth, there was little resistance in France to the German occupation in the early years of the war. It was only when the tide turned against Germany after the loss of the battle of Stalingrad in January 1943 that mass resistance began in earnest. The war career of François Mitterrand, later president of France, is instructive. He served Vichy — the government that collaborated with the Nazis — but also kept his options open by spying for the Free French. Only in 1943 when he finally saw which way the war was going did he commit himself wholeheartedly to the Resistance. He played his hand carefully and pragmatically: if the Nazis had triumphed, he could have carried on and risen up the ranks to become a senior figure in the Vichy government; if the Nazis faltered, he could — as indeed he did — claim that he had been a devoted member of the Resistance.

It is not so surprising that human beings behave in such a way — it is something that most of us witness in our own lives, though on a much less heightened scale. For example, who hasn't seen an employee suddenly criticize the previous regime in a company when a new boss arrives with a different approach? And perhaps, if we are honest, most of us will admit to having behaved in a not too disimilar way ourselves at some point in our lives. In the last of these three stories, it is significant that it was only after Aleksey Bris had been thwarted in his ambition to become a doctor that he turned against the Nazis.

Which is why the stories of Alois Pfaller and Vladimir Kantovski are particularly intriguing. They don't seem to be acting in their own best interests at all. Despite all kinds of pressure, despite moments when the "sensible" course of action was to choose personal safety, these two stayed true to their beliefs. They are the rare stuff of which saints and revolutionaries are made. Although they were of different nationalities, I thought it was no accident that neither of them was an easy-going person. I got the impression that after the war they were just as likely to tell their boss they were not doing something because it was "unjust", or deliberately to put themselves in danger by trying to prevent a stranger on the street being attacked by a group of yobs. Their kind of outlook is not something you can switch on and off.

My own view, having met so many people who enthusiastically served various repressive regimes out of straightforward self-interest, was one of gratitude that there were *any* people like Alois Pfaller and Vladimir Kantovski in the world.

ALOIS PFALLER
AND THE STRUGGLE AGAINST THE NAZIS

To resist the Nazis was to put oneself in immediate danger of torture and death. The Nazis imprisoned over 100,000 of their political opponents before the war, and sentenced thousands more to death for "high treason" once the conflict started. To stand out against this regime — at any time — took immense courage. Which is why, meeting Alois Pfaller in the mid-1990s made such an impression on me. For here was a man who had unquestionably resisted the Nazis from the very first.

I vividly remember the small, rather run-down house he lived in just outside Munich. It was in dramatic contrast to all the other properties I had visited on that filming trip. They had been luxurious — and they had all belonged to former Nazis now prosperously integrated into post-war Germany. It was obvious that Alois Pfaller's resistance and subsequent suffering had not brought him material reward.

He was born in 1910 near Ingolstadt in Bavaria in southern Germany. His father owned a small farm and he was one of five children. His mother died when he was three years old, and when his father married again, his stepmother brought her own four-year-old daughter into the family. This was a formative moment in Alois

Pfaller's life: "I got a sister," he said. "That was the competition. I often envied her — the mother is the mother, after all, and I was someone else's child."

One of his elder brothers took an interest in the local Communist youth movement and when he was old enough Alois Pfaller started to go along to meetings with him: "There were discussions about the role of the trade unions, and the interests of the workers." This became of particular relevance to Alois when he went to work as an apprentice to a local painter and decorator. He felt "exploited" by his boss and tried to organize the other apprentices into a union. He then went on strike — and his boss summarily sacked him. So he left to get a job as a painter in Munich where he "earned double". His hopes were clear — "that socialism would be coming, that unemployment would be vanquished, that you would have a right to a job, and that you would be paid more." In pursuit of this vision he became a Young Communist himself. And there was the added benefit that "we didn't just engage in politics, we also played games, had dances and so on. We even went to villages and performed popular theatre."

At the same time as Alois Pfaller was enjoying membership of the Communist Youth section, he could see that thousands of other young Germans were joining the Nazis. "I've wondered — why didn't I just join the SA [the Nazi Stormtroopers]? Because there was a bakery next to our house and there were two young lads and they were with the SA. So we saw the uniforms and we talked to them. But, well, we discussed it in the group and they convinced me that 'It gets us nowhere. They only support business and not the workers — it's just rubbish.'" He also couldn't understand the Nazis' attitude to the Jews: "I knew Jews and I had [Jewish] friends with whom I used to spend time, and I absolutely didn't see what difference there was supposed to be — we were all humans . . . I'd seen they [the Nazis] wanted a Jew-free society. Well, that was not my thing. I have always stood up for justice, for what is just and reasonable — that was my problem. And also fighting injustice — that was my problem — and not somehow persecuting other races or other people."

As the economic situation worsened in Germany in the wake of the Wall Street Crash and the agricultural depression, Alois Pfaller started taking on the Nazis in the streets. He noticed that the police always seemed to side with the Nazis, but that only spurred him and his friends on. There were memorable fights in beer halls with glasses and chairs flying through the air, and once, his face bloodied, he had to make his escape through a toilet window into the night.

But as soon as Hitler became chancellor in January 1933, Alois knew that the street fighting was over and state persecution of Communists would begin. So he fled to Moscow in order to escape imprisonment: "And my brother didn't come with me. That was his mistake — it cost him his life. He was sent straightaway to Dachau [concentration camp] in '33 and he was let out after eight years, mortally ill, and he died a few years later." Although safe in Moscow, Alois was unhappy.

News of the mass arrest of Communists in Germany didn't make him feel lucky to have escaped so much as inadequate because he hadn't stayed and fought: "I told myself I had to go back — they had almost nobody left. So I announced that I wanted to go back to Germany."

Alois had made a life-changing decision. If his were a fictional story, this would be the point in the narrative when his character might spend days carefully deliberating this momentous choice. But that is not what happened. He decided to go back almost on an impulse, because he knew somewhere inside himself that this was simply the right thing to do.

And so, in 1934, Alois Pfaller returned to Germany with a "false passport and a false name". He travelled to Frankfurt and Offenbach in order to "get the youth group back together — what was still left of it". But, not surprisingly given that Communists were considered especially dangerous by the Nazis, there were few people who would now risk their lives and associate with him.

Eventually he went to Leipzig where he printed leaflets critical of the Nazis. There he met a woman, whom he knew had once been a Communist, who offered to help by organizing a meeting with someone she said was a "contact" at one of the factories. But in fact she had been "turned" and was now a Gestapo agent. Despite subsequent events Alois Pfaller bears no grudge against her, "because as a woman, the way she looked, she couldn't have taken a beating". When he arrived for the rendezvous, "some people suddenly appeared and they said, 'Could you show us your papers?' And then I said, 'Listen, you come to Germany to have a look at the accomplishments of the Third Reich and quietly hoping to get some work, and then you get arrested on the street — what's going on?' And the officers had a strange expression on their faces, so I continued to talk and one said to the other behind my back, 'I think we got the wrong one.'"

But Alois had a problem — the anti-Nazi leaflets he had printed were in the pocket of his coat. So he decided to chuck them away down an embankment when he thought the Gestapo men weren't looking. But they spotted him. "And suddenly someone shouted, 'He's thrown something away! He's thrown something away!'" The Gestapo found the leaflets and then dragged him off to the police station where a reception committee was waiting: "I opened the door and I was going to go in, but suddenly I got a punch in the face, and my nose got broken. Then they just pitched into me and beat me up."

When Alois denied that he had been involved in the production of the leaflets, it earned him another beating. Then the police made him turn out his pockets, and found his diary and a series of coded messages. And so the beatings resumed. One of the policeman took off his uniform belt with a solid metal buckle and started thrashing Alois with it: "I was quickly unconscious — it didn't last long. Then I came to again and then they did it a second time, again unconscious, the third time, again unconscious, the fourth time, again unconscious, then they stopped because I hadn't told them anything."

But, according to Alois, "That wasn't the worst — the worst was when they hit me in the face. For three hours! Always at my face. In the meantime my eardrum had split, so then I heard an incredible racket. It was a roaring, as if your head was on the sea bed, an incredible roaring so you couldn't understand anything properly any longer." Alois decided to try to fight back. At least, he felt, if he were going to die he could take one of the policemen with him. But before he could mount his attack he suffered a massive haemorrhage: "So the policeman stopped [beating me] and I was given a bucket with a cloth and I had to clean the whole desk and the floor, had to clean off all the blood, and then I was handed over to another officer to get me back to my cell."

Throughout his imprisonment Alois Pfaller was never tempted to betray his comrades: "It's a question of honour. I would rather have died miserably and I'd have let them beat me to death, but I would never have done that." Alois knew, deeper even than his conscious mind, that it was wrong to grass on his friends; so he wasn't going to do it. No moral crisis, no weighing of the options, no inner torment. And the intensification of the beatings only served to increase his determination not to reveal the information his torturers wanted.

After the failure of the interrogators at the police station to gain the information they desired, Alois was sent to a concentration camp — initially Sachsenburg in Saxony. Paradoxically, once he was in the concentration-camp system Alois Pfaller felt "secure" because he believed that he wouldn't be beaten as harshly as he had been at the police station. And some of the SS guards seemed almost to admire him for his resistance.

There were many cases in the 1930s where prisoners were murdered by the SS in concentration camps, and the harsh conditions were designed to break the spirit. But the extermination camps of Auschwitz and Treblinka were not yet born, and most political prisoners sent to German concentration camps in the 1930s were released after a stay of between six and eighteen months. But Alois Pfaller was not released after a year and a half, or even after eight years like his brother. He was one of the few prisoners considered so dangerous by the Nazis that he was imprisoned from 1934 until he made his escape in the chaos at the end of the war in 1945.

When I met him he still railed against the injustice of it all — and now that injustice had a particular focus: "The SS people get their pension — it pisses me off — and I was in the Communist party, I had the wrong party card. I don't get it. It pisses me off, not because of the money, but I was brought up like that, or I brought myself up, who knows, [to believe] that injustice remains injustice wherever it comes from. You have to fight against it, and if we don't do that, if we won't change things, then God have mercy on us."

Having heard Alois Pfaller's lengthy story of resistance, I was keen to try and gain a greater insight into why he in particular had been able to stand out against the Nazis. And at the end of the interview he gave this explanation: "I told you I had a stepmother and she preferred my stepsister. And I knew that, and I found it impossible. And then I swore to myself, when you grow up, you have to fight against injustice, never mind against who, you always have to fight injustice. And I internalized this, and with this I had the ability to resist, and the ability to get through it — nothing else."

ALEKSEY BRIS
AND THE SHATTERED DREAMS OF THE UKRAINIANS

Part of the difficulty in understanding history is that events lie inert in the past, certain, unchanging, as set as concrete. The Red Army won at Stalingrad; Churchill became a national hero; Hitler lost the war: these factual statements appear as sure as the air we breathe. But in order to try to penetrate the minds of people at the time, we have to envisage a moment when the facts were not certain — when individuals were faced with decisions that could have gone either way. Thus we need to imagine that the Red Army might have been defeated at Stalingrad; that Churchill's career could have ended in ignominy; that Hitler need not have lost the war. And it struck me, listening to a silver-haired old Ukrainian called Aleksey Bris, that his dramatic story particularly demanded this approach. For as an 18-year-old student, back in the summer of 1941, he had initially thought the German invasion might bring positive benefits for the Ukraine, believing — mistakenly as it turned out — that "any war against the Soviet Union was a good war".

The Ukraine had suffered massively under Stalin. During the 1930s and the era of forced collectivization around 7 million Ukrainians had died amidst scenes of horror that still disturbed the collective consciousness of the nation. "These repressions made people angry," said Bris, "made them fear, and this feeling of terror — those who haven't felt it, can't imagine it. That's why, when the war broke out between Germany and the Soviet Union, the population thought that things would change for the better."

Allied to this belief that the Germans had to be an improvement on the Soviets was the conviction that Stalin and his men were not coming back: "Everybody thought in the very beginning that the war will result in the complete defeat of the Soviet Union," said Aleksey. "There was a feeling that the Soviet Union might collapse — the collapse which happened in the 1990s could have happened at that time."

He revealed that during the early days of Nazi occupation "Ukrainians could see a different way of life. They saw they could go to dances and have different clothes and that there was free communication between people."

When I heard Aleksey Bris say those words, sitting in his small house just outside his home village of Horokhiv, it opened up a whole vision of what might have happened. Perhaps he was right; perhaps the whole edifice of the Soviet Union could have tumbled 50 years earlier than it did. After all, it had been Hitler's most important military adviser, Alfred Jodl, who had said just before the invasion, "The Russian colossus will prove to be a pig's bladder — prick it and it will burst."[1] Jodl was wrong, of course — the

---

[1] Laurence Rees, *War of the Century* (BBC Books, 1999), p.30

"Russian colossus" did not "burst" like a "pig's bladder". And one crucial reason why it failed to do so was that the Nazis did not capitalize on the hatred the various nationalities within the Soviet Union had for Stalin — because Nazism was one of the most inherently exclusive ideologies that has ever existed.

From the very beginning, in the days immediately after World War I, the Nazis chiefly defined themselves by those whom they excluded — notably the Jews.

Adolf Hitler, who became leader of the fledgling Nazi party in 1921, understood that it was much easier to create a coherent party policy via a series of negatives — hatred of the Jews, hatred of the Communists, hatred of the Versailles Agreement, hatred of the socialists — than by defining exactly what the Nazis actually stood *for*. This turned out to be an effective strategy for the times, because whenever the Nazis met to agree the precise detail of their economic or social policies they squabbled like children. No, Hitler realized, far better to keep the "positive" policies as vague as possible — a call for a "strong, united and racially pure" Germany, for example — and to concentrate his efforts on itemizing in detail only the negative ones.

Hitler became popular during the early 1930s partly because he made many Germans feel good about themselves after years of perceived humiliation, as he preached that "Aryan" Germans were a superior people (excluded, of course, were the German Jews — who constituted less than 1 per cent of the population). As the Japanese had discovered hundreds of years before, so long as there is no expansion beyond the borders of the existing state, and so long as the vast majority of the population are of a single national or ethnic group, this policy of exclusion can be effective. But the strategy of defining who was a "true" German by who was excluded began to become a problem for the Nazis once they tried to create an empire.

Hitler believed to the very core of his being in excluding the Slavic inhabitants of the countries of the east from citizenship of the new Reich: he saw the Slavs as "slaves" who "bred like vermin". Looking to the East, and the valuable agricultural land of the Ukraine, he said, "It's inconceivable that a higher people [i.e. the Germans] should painfully exist on a soil too narrow for it, whilst amorphous masses, which contribute nothing to civilisation, occupy infinite tracks of a soil that is one of the richest in the world."[1] Erich Koch, one of Hitler's oldest and most loyal followers, was made Reich commissioner for the Ukraine and eagerly put his Führer's dream into practice. He stated his policy to the city administration in Kiev, the capital of the Ukraine: "We are a master race that must remember that the lowliest German worker is racially and biologically a thousand times more valuable than the population here."[2] In practical terms this meant

---

[1] *Hitler's Table Talk 1941–1944*, 23 September 1941, introduced and with a new preface by Hugh Trevor-Roper (Weidenfeld and Nicolson, 2000)

[2] Koch speech of 5 March, 1943, quoted in Timothy Patrick Mulligan, *The Politics of Illusion and Empire* (Praeger, 1988)

45

that Koch imposed a number of draconian measures, including the withdrawal of education. "Ukrainian children need no schools," he announced. "What they have to learn will be taught them by their German masters."[1]

This all had a dramatic impact on the life of Aleksey Bris who had taken a job working for the Nazis as a translator. He even started a friendship with one of the German women who worked in the local party administration. But soon he noticed "an edge" growing between himself and his new employers. His friendship with the German secretary fizzled out when it became clear that any kind of intimate relationship between Germans and Ukrainians — even Ukrainians who were faithfully serving the Nazi state — was dangerous. But it was a conversation that Aleksey had with his boss, Ernst Erich Haerter, the commissioner for Horokhiv, that was decisive. He asked if it might be possible for him to continue his studies and become a doctor, anticipating that the Germans would approve of his ambition — after all, he reasoned, he would be better placed to serve the Nazis as a doctor than as a translator.

"We don't need you Ukrainians as doctors or engineers," replied Haerter. "We need you as people to tend cows."

Aleksey was shocked at Haerter's words. He was a bright and ambitious young man, and cow-herding was

---

[1] Quoted in Robert Wistrich, *Who's Who in Nazi Germany* (Routledge, 1995)

not for him. But since the Germans were in power what could he do?

His fury at the injustices to the Ukranian people, including his own dashed hopes and dreams, suddenly broke through in a dramatic way one autumn day in 1942 in Horokhiv. A group of locals were queuing to buy pots and pans. Suddenly the German policeman who was supervising the queue started hitting one of them with his cane. As Aleksey watched the beating it triggered something inside him: "Little by little my feelings of anger were growing and I was feeling that I was on the edge of mental collapse . . . the emotions come first and you don't think about the consequences . . . a feeling came to me, that I just hated that our nation was brought to slavery. When you feel that the whole nation is being humiliated you have to do something whether you like it or not, so I was ready to strike them." Consumed with rage, he rushed forward and grabbed the policeman's arm, preventing him from continuing the beating. Other Germans near by moved to unholster their guns and pursue him, but Aleksey was too quick for them and ran off into the woods. Once there he joined the Ukrainian Nationalist Partisans — the Ukrainska Povstanska Armiia.

For the next two years Aleksey participated in a brutal partisan war. The Ukrainska Povstanska Armiia were fighting not just the Germans but Stalin's own partisans as well. No prisoners were taken on either side. Stories of how the Red Army partisans treated the Ukrainians when they were captured — tongues were cut out and ears removed — were legion. By comparison Aleksey remembers that the Germans were relatively mild — they "just" hanged people and didn't indulge in torture beforehand.

The journey that Aleksey Bris took — from hope that the Germans would bring independence, to anguish at their policy of turning the Ukraine into a slave state — was replicated in many other Ukrainians. And without question the policy of the Nazis directly hindered their fight against the Soviet Union. Their racism first excluded the possibility of Ukrainian help and then eventually turned Ukrainians like Aleksey Bris into an additional enemy. So why didn't Hitler do the "sensible" thing and order a more lenient occupation of territories like the Ukraine? In this matter, as in so many others, the Führer was incapable of acting "sensibly". So deeply held was his conviction that the Germans were a master race sent to turn the Slavic people into slaves, that for him to change this one belief would have been like asking him to stop breathing.

We are lucky that the Nazis had not learnt from history. Nearly 2000 years before Hitler's occupation of the Ukraine, another European army was fighting its own war of conquest. But unlike the Nazis, the Romans were to create one of the most successful empires in history. And they built it on precisely the reverse principle to the one that the Nazis employed. Instead of excluding the peoples of the lands they invaded, they sought to bring them over to their side. Alliances with local chiefs were fundamental to the stability and growth of the Empire. It was even possible for foreigners to become full Roman citizens. The emperor

Caracalla, who reigned between AD 211 and 217, conferred Roman citizenship on all inhabitants of the Empire who were not slaves. And the consequence of Hitler's decision to pursue a very different policy and exclude whole ethnic groups from citizenship of the German Reich can be expressed in one telling statistic: the Roman Empire lasted more than 500 years, the Third Reich just 12.

VLADIMIR KANTOVSKI
AND STALIN'S PENAL BATTALIONS

In early 1943 Vladimir Kantovski, a 19-year-old Red Army soldier serving in the 54th Penal Company, stared out from behind Soviet fortifications towards a wood occupied by an unknown number of German troops. He knew that in a matter of moments he would be ordered forward, along with others in his battalion, to take part in "reconnaissance through combat". They would walk towards the German line and attract their fire, so that watching Soviet officers could learn the position and nature of the guns ranged against them. Kantovski knew he faced almost certain death. For the vast majority of his comrades this was to be their first and last military action — and their final day on earth. And yet Kantovski had chosen to be in this position for his character had demanded it.

No human being can exist out of the time in which they are born and everyone is shaped by the events around them. But a rare few, like Vladimir Kantovski, use the harshness of their time to define themselves and to defy the injustice ranged against them.

Kantovski was born in 1923, and to be born into that generation in the Soviet Union was to be destined for a life of almost certain anguish. The Stalinist purges of the 1930s devastated not only the ruling elite but ordinary Soviet citizens as well. In 1938 both of Kantovski's parents were arrested and sent to a labour camp. His father was a Latvian and so, as a non-Russian, had been particularly vulnerable to arbitrary arrest. "Somewhere at heart," Kantovski said, "we felt that sooner or later one would get arrested and that it was unavoidable — that we were doomed to be arrested at some point." Despite the Stalinist rhetoric that this was a land of equality and justice, the reality was that to grow up in the Soviet Union before World War II meant growing accustomed to fear, hunger and arbitrary suffering: "We realized that Stalin's power was not the Communism in which we believed and which we wanted to achieve. We knew that Stalin's power was not proletarian dictatorship but it was dictating to the proletariat . . . and it was a cruel dictatorship." And then in June 1941, when Kantovski was 18, came the Nazi invasion of the Soviet Union. This was not just the biggest land invasion in the history of the world; it was conceived from the beginning by the Nazis as a war of "annihilation".

But as this massive invasion took place Kantovski was not fighting on the front line but in prison for criticizing the actions of the regime. Just weeks before the outbreak of war, Kantovski and his friends had protested at the arrest of their history teacher who had been heard making "inappropriate" comments about Josef Stalin and who had been arrested and taken away by the NKVD — the secret police. The arrest drove Kantovski and his fellow students to action: just hours later they began to hand out leaflets condemning the authorities for taking their teacher away. "We didn't take Stalin and his henchmen seriously," Kantovski said, "but at the same time we remained patriots and in essence Communist — although not Communists in the way Stalin understood it." The NKVD went to Kantovski's flat and arrested him. He was sent to Omsk prison, where conditions were appalling. He was one of 60 people crammed into a cell intended for nine prisoners, and he was only allowed out of it twice a day to go to the toilet. Other than that there was no respite — no exercise, no fresh air, nothing but life in the gloom of his cell, and the fight to survive in its fetid, disease-ridden atmosphere. For the "crime" of writing the pamphlet protesting at his teacher's arrest Kantovski was sentenced to 10 years in a gulag, one of the Soviet labour camps that flourished under Stalin. But then, destined as he thought to languish — probably die — in a gulag, Kantovski found that his fate was now affected by a factor entirely outside his control: the Soviet Union was losing the war.

In September 1941, at Kiev in the Ukraine, the Germans trapped 600,000 Red Army soldiers in the largest single encirclement action in modern times. A few weeks later, in October, at the twin battles of Vyasma and Bryansk, German Army Group Centre took another 600,000 prisoners and the road to Moscow lay open. Terrified by this appalling turn of events, Stalin ordered the toughest measures imaginable to keep the capital from collapsing in panic. Fresh troops were drafted in from Siberia, and special units were stationed behind the Red Army lines to shoot any soldier who retreated. But even these actions were not enough. Stalin knew that the Soviet Union faced a moment of crisis unlike any in its history, so he decided to tap an unlikely source for new recruits for the Red Army — the prison camps.

The Soviet authorities called for "volunteers" from the gulags to fight the German invaders. But the prisoners who came forward were not to be sent to an ordinary prison unit — no, their destination was altogether more deadly. It was a "shtrafbaty" — a penal battalion. Composed of people who had committed political or criminal offences, these units were given the most dangerous tasks in battle. They were often the first wave in any attack, and performed virtually suicidal tasks like clearing enemy minefields by marching over them. Around 440,000 Soviet citizens served in penal battalions during World War II, and only the merest handful survived.

Kantovski volunteered for one of these units even though he knew that his only real hope of survival was to be severely wounded in battle — for his "old sins to be pardoned" through his "blood", as the Soviet authorities put it. But he was a patriot, his country had been invaded and he wanted to fight. He "never regretted" that he chose to join the penal battalions: "It's in my nature. I don't like to muse over decisions I've taken — I never do it, on principle. And in spite of everything some opportunities were opening up for me. There was a small chance of survival — even if ten people survived out of 250 it meant you had a chance." He even found that his life improved: "Although when you arrive at the penal battalion the routine is as strict as the camp, there is no barbed wire around you and the strict routine is not specific to the penal battalion but is similar to the routine in other army units. And it's less depressing because it's not prison. What you have at stake is either life or freedom . . . For me, the little freedom I had in the penal battalion meant a lot. Can you imagine, understand, what freedom is? For that you have to spend half a year in Omsk prison being completely immobile in the cell, and you can only look into the sky through a slot in the window. Of course, you can't compare a penal battalion with it. And also we were patriots, in the best sense of the word."

At the start of 1943 Kantovski found himself on the front line near the town of Demyansk, south of Leningrad, as a member of the 54th Penal Company. As he prepared to walk forward towards the German guns in his first military action as part of "reconnaissance through combat", knowing that he was either about to die or to be seriously wounded, Kantovski felt "fatalistic": "I don't think you can feel any patriotism when you are participating in such an attack. I think the over-riding feeling is one of bluntness — your feelings are blunted . . . You know what is happening is unavoidable, fatal and it's like a game of Russian roulette. Well, what's your lot going to be? . . . As soon as we showed ourselves the enemy began firing . . . our officers shouted, 'Onwards! Onwards!' The Germans carried on the machine-gun fire. We got support from four or five tanks. Obviously our officers wanted to find out whether the Germans had any anti-tank weapons. The Germans were firing from the wood, perhaps 400 metres away. The tanks only advanced 60 or so metres before they were destroyed. And the first victims were the officers who encouraged us to move forward."

After advancing a couple of hundred metres, Kantovski discovered exactly what his own "lot" was going to be. He felt machine-gun bullets smash into his shoulder and arm and he fell down in pain. But as he lay there, his blood flowing freely on to the ground, his immediate thought was not whether he would live or die. Rather, he was uncertain as to whether the wound was serious enough to save him from further punishment. Because if a member of a penal battalion was believed to have stopped advancing as a result of only a minor injury, he would be shot for cowardice. Kantovski was fortunate — after he returned to the Soviet lines he learnt that his wound was considered severe enough to save him from being executed by his own side. But while he survived, the vast majority of his unit died that day.

Kantovski was patched up, and then in 1944 sent back to the gulag to complete his sentence. He was not released until 1951. Even after his return from prison camp he had to endure persecution: he was held back in his career and was never paid as much as others who did similar work. "I didn't query whether Stalin was just or unjust," said Kantovski. "He was simply a tyrant. All of it rested on fear, on cruelty, on informing — on sticks without any carrots."

In the late 1990s, when I met him, Kantovski was living in a tiny flat in a concrete block in the outer suburbs of Moscow. There was little inside the flat — a threadbare carpet, some wooden chairs and a rickety table. On the walls were a couple of pictures torn from newspapers, and wafting through the whole building was the smell of stale cabbage. Rats lived in the lift-shaft and scurried up and down the communal stairs at night. Yet Kantovski told his extraordinary story in a calm, matter-of-fact way. Not once did he betray an ounce of self-pity — not a second of bitterness at the injustice piled on injustice he had been forced to suffer.

I asked if he regretted protesting at the arrest of his teacher. What had he achieved? His teacher hadn't been saved and his own life had, in many ways, been destroyed by this one action.

He considered the question for a few seconds. Then he answered that he didn't regret having protested. "Not everyone could say at the time that he had the liberty to express himself. My personality grew stronger." Then he was silent for a moment, before adding, "I don't regret it, because it gives me self-respect."

PART THREE

FIGHTING AND KILLING THE "INFERIOR" AND THE "INHUMAN"

Cultural differences dominated many people's thinking about the war. And here are four former soldiers — two Japanese, one American and one German — who, though I met them on three different continents and several years apart, certainly subscribed to the belief that the enemy they were fighting were "not like they were". The two Japanese veterans, Masayo Enomoto and Hajime Kondo, both thought that their opponents, the Chinese, were "lower than animals"; Wolfgang Horn, a German soldier, believed that his enemy, the Soviets, were on a "lower level" than the rest of Europeans; and James Eagleton felt that the Japanese were "an inhuman race".

Indeed, a common theme running through many of my encounters with former soldiers of World War II was this belief that the enemy they were fighting was beneath them: the Germans thought the Soviets inferior, the British and Americans thought the Japanese inferior, the Japanese thought the Chinese inferior and so on. And this conviction that they were killing in battle not human beings like themselves, but lesser creatures who probably did not even possess the "normal" capacity for pain, was crucial in allowing combatants to act as they did. This reality came home to me with greatest force when I interviewed a former Panzer officer who had fought first on the Eastern Front against the Red Army and then on the Western Front against the Americans. In the East he and his unit had shot Soviet prisoners and perpetrated a variety of other crimes, whilst in the West they had battled against the Americans within the established rules of war. To a large extent their perception of their enemy had determined how they behaved.

But though there were a number of similarities across different nationalities in the behaviour of many veterans I met, there was one respect in which the former German soldiers — as a general rule — tended to stand out amongst the veterans of non-democratic regimes. They were more likely to explain their actions by saying "I felt I acted the right way at the time," rather than by announcing, "I was acting under orders." In addition they often did not regret any atrocities they had perpetrated.

However, despite the obvious cultural and political differences amongst the various governmental systems to which each of the people in this section subscribed, I still believe that there is an important thread linking their testimony. Together they show in graphic terms just what happens when you believe that the enemy you are fighting are very different from "the people back home".

JAMES EAGLETON
AND KILLING THE JAPANESE

As I checked into my motel in the centre of Tulsa, Oklahoma, I heard the horn of a railway engine as a train clanked through the city. It was a typically American noise, the sound-track to a hundred Hollywood B movies about the West, but I found it unsettling. I had just finished filming in the jungles of Okinawa where many young men from Oklahoma had fought during the war, and it was impossible to imagine a greater contrast between two places. For the Americans from Oklahoma who had travelled to the Pacific to fight — like James Eagleton who I was to film the next day — it must have been like journeying to the moon.

The small city of Tulsa, along the Arkansas river in the foothills of the Ozark Hills, is almost as remote from the great, sweeping events that shape the world as it is possible to get — so much so that the place revels in the one single epithet that is code in America for somewhere far from the action. Tulsa, they say, is "a great place to bring up your kids".

The following morning, when I met James Eagleton in his comfortable house in a prosperous suburb, he looked exactly what he was — a third-generation Tulsa lawyer. His grandfather had come to the town at the end of nineteenth century, just before the oil boom, when it was a collection of wooden buildings around a series of dirt tracks, and eventually he rose to become the probate judge of Pawnee County. And Eagleton's own three sons had also followed the family tradition by studying the law. This was about as solid an American family as you could imagine — happy just to swim in this charming backwater of the Mid-West and "bring up their kids". Yet one event had entered James Eagleton's otherwise unremarkable existence like a hurricane. World War II had offered him a chance to fight for his country, test his character and discover just what he was capable of doing: in his case that meant killing the Japanese in very dark circumstances indeed.

He had decided, on leaving high-school during the war, to join the US Marines. Having been high-school wrestling champion, he wanted the chance to be with like-minded people who were keen to see action. He showed me a photograph of himself back then, stripped to the waist with rippling muscles, a grin on his face and a full head of hair. It was almost impossible to associate the portly, bald old grandfather in front of me with the devil-may-care youth in the photograph.

So tough did James Eagleton believe himself to be at the time that he applied to join the Raiders — the US Marine equivalent of the British SAS. After specialist training in New Caledonia in the Pacific he prepared to go into action, armed with one belief about his enemy that would condition the whole of his time in the Far East. "They [the Japanese]," said James Eagleton, "were an inhuman race."

Just as German troops had been told time and again that the Soviets were an "inferior" people, and the Japanese were taught that the Chinese were "beneath dogs", so the pervasive American propaganda of the times — the caricaturing of the Japanese as slit-eyed apes, for example — also helped create the racism that was behind the judgement of many Marines that the enemy they faced was not worthy of civilized treatment. But regardless of their opinion about the humanity of their opponents, Eagleton and his unit discovered that the Japanese were every bit as determined fighters as they were.

In April 1945 Eagleton and his Raider comrades were shipped to the island of Okinawa where they participated in some of the fiercest fighting in the whole of World War II. Initially it seemed as if the Japanese had simply given up Okinawa as the Marines, who had expected to face resistance on the beach, walked up unopposed: "We were very surprised that there wasn't cannon fire, mortar fire, small-arms fire, meeting us. We were very pleased." But the Americans soon discovered that the Japanese hadn't run away; they had simply changed tactics. Instead of fighting on the beaches, they had regrouped inland and were ready to mount fanatical resistance from a series of carefully prepared fortifications. It was as if they had built themselves into the very fabric of the island. Suddenly, Eagleton and the rest of the Americans came under heavy attack.

The fighting was so intense that there was a high rate of battle fatigue. Eagleton recalled one instance when eight Marines were ordered forward at dusk to set up an advance defence post about a 100 metres forward of the main unit, in order to give warning of any Japanese attack during the night. "That night there wasn't any firing," he said. "When they came back seven of them had battle fatigue. They were crying and unable to function as Marines for a day or two. The one that didn't have battle fatigue, he was a dairy man from New York and I always thought he was too dumb to know what they were out there for." On Okinawa, Eagleton himself began to hallucinate: "You would see things that didn't exist. One time I saw Japanese attacking our position . . . Next morning there weren't any Japanese. Mentally I saw the Japanese. I never had that experience before or since." The Raiders were not taken out of the line for rest as often as other American troops, and this contributed to the amount of battle fatigue their units suffered.

What intigued me, hearing James Eagelton talk about the fierceness of the conflict in the Pacific, was that he simultaneously held the view that the Japanese were powerful fighters and that they were "inhuman". There was even evidence that he admired his opponents. On the island of Guam he had witnessed a single Japanese officer attacking two or three hundred Marines. The officer had suddenly charged out of a cave in full dress uniform, armed with just his sword, and sent seven Marines to hospital, three of them very seriously injured. After his body was stripped by the Americans they found that he'd previously been severely wounded in battle and would have shortly bled to death. Yet he still possessed the fighting spirit to attack the Marines in one last desperate demonstration of fealty to his emperor and his country.

Eagleton seems to have seen in the suicidal attacks of the Japanese evidence of their very "inhumanity". Thus they attacked fanatically, they fought violently, they were prepared to die dramatically, all precisely because they were "inhuman". But one can imagine that had the Japanese possessed the opposite qualities — cowardice and fear — then these too would have been evidence that they were "not like us" and "inhuman".

And since they believed that the Japanese were "inhuman" the US Marines had no problem in taking intimate "souvenirs" from the defeated enemy. On the wall of Eagleton's own house in Tulsa was a framed Japanese flag, tattered and worn from battle. Other American servicemen would kick the gold teeth out of the Japanese in a grotesque search for valuable mementoes of the war.

Marines didn't just commit reprehensible acts of violence against dead Japanese — they committed them against the living. "We did not ever take a Japanese prisoner," said Eagleton simply. "In the two years that I was overseas I saw no prisoner ever taken . . . Once thirty or forty of them came out with their hands up. They were killed on the spot because we didn't take prisoners."

James Eagleton sat there in front of me, contented and self-assured, as I questioned him further on the reasons why he and his comrades had shot Japanese troops who were trying to surrender. And in so far as he had reasons for his actions, he told me they were these:

first, he believed that this was an act of simple revenge, since the Japanese had, he claimed, brutalized, murdered, and tortured US Marines whom they had captured; second, he said that there had been a number of instances when "the Japanese would come up purporting to surrender and would fall down with grenades under their arms and blow people up. We'd call 'em 'Tricky Nipper'. We had a Lieutenant James and he was always talking about Tricky Nipper and 'Don't let that little rascal get close to you.'"

"When you yourself were shooting these prisoners who were trying to surrender," I asked, "what was in your mind?"

"We were just defending ourselves."

"But they had their hands up."

"That's right."

What struck me at the time, as I sat there in a plush armchair listening to this elderly lawyer incriminating himself, was not just the incongruity of the setting, but how similar his remarks were to those of German veterans I had heard describing their actions on the Eastern Front. During the brutal war against the Soviet partisans, the fact that there might have been a handful of cases of women hiding grenades in their skirts and then detonating them as the enemy came close was used by some Germans as a justification for the indiscriminate killing of all women and children they came across. "Why, a child might also be hiding a grenade!" one German veteran said to me.

But it became clear that, at least as far as one of James Eagleton's company commanders was concerned, this idea that surrendering soldiers might harm their captors masked another truth: that Japanese prisoners were not to be taken under any circumstances. This was evident from a story James Eagleton told of what happened to an unfortunate Japanese soldier who had accidentally been captured: "Two fellows running a telephone line across country came across a Japanese who surrendered to them. They took him to company headquarters and the captain just blew his top. 'You've ruined our record!' [of not taking any prisoners], he said. 'Sergeant, take this prisoner to battalion headquarters and I will see you at eleven fifteen.' Well, it was eleven o'clock and the headquarters was five miles away. They took him out and killed him."

Not all American units behaved this way. On Okinawa several thousand Japanese prisoners were taken (Japanese who were, of course, breaking their own oath to their emperor not to surrender). And film archive clearly shows how these American units circumvented the risk of the surrendering Japanese being armed and dangerous. The Americans made the Japanese strip to their underwear while still a safe distance away, so that they could check their potential prisoners were unarmed before allowing them to come forward and surrender.

But such was the intensity of his feeling against the Japanese that as our interview came to an end James Eagleton asserted that he believed that the dropping of nuclear bombs on Hiroshima and Nagasaki was probably a positive event in the history of Japan. He justified this remark with the view that the Japanese had therefore been spared even greater suffering: "We had no concern about killing the Japanese. [If] we'd gone to Japan we'd have probably killed a thousand to one [i.e. 1000 Japanese for every American], but we would've killed 'em without regret."

After the interview was over, and I had thanked James Eagleton for speaking so frankly, I walked out of his house into the sunlight of a clear day in the American Mid-West. I heard the happy shouts of a little boy playing with his mother in a garden across the street, and saw a few doors away a middle-class American housewife getting groceries from her car after a trip to the mall.

Did they know they lived alongside a respectable lawyer who had committed such dark acts during the war? And, since the violence had been perpetrated long ago and far away, did they care?

HAJIME KONDO
AND THE MAKING OF A DEVIL IN THE JAPANESE IMPERIAL ARMY

"I was a human being, and I became a devil," said Hajime Kondo. "But I was made into one."

Sitting in front of me, in a hotel in central Tokyo, Hajime Kondo scarcely resembled the conventional image of Beelzebub. He was an 80-year-old Japanese grandfather, and possessed neither horns nor a forked tail. But having heard his story I was inclined to agree with him — he had become a devil, and he had been made into one.

He had taken part in a conflict that, here in the West, is a little-known part of World War II — the fearsome Japanese struggle against the Chinese. Whilst the massacre by Japanese soldiers at Nanking in 1937 at the start of their war against the Chinese has received some publicity, the reality of the continuing conflict — which carried on in parallel to the Pacific War and the war against the Nazis — has not. Partly that's because it was a conflict that only involved the Americans and Europeans tangentially, but it's also because neither the Japanese nor the Chinese authorities want the world to know all the details.

In 2000 the Chinese authorities were prepared to let me and my film crew come to China to interview a survivor from the Nanking massacre, but they were much less cooperative about allowing us to extend the research and filming to include the investigation of subsequent Japanese actions in the north. The current relationship between the Chinese and Japanese is complex, and whilst, on the one hand, the Chinese berate the Japanese for not admitting the extent of their crimes during this war, on the other hand they also want to have positive economic relations with their technologically advanced neighbour. "Put it this way," our Chinese government minder told me one night after he had been drinking. "We want the Japanese to build a big DVD factory somewhere around here." As for the Japanese, there are even academics who seek to deny or minimize the crimes at Nanking — let alone the subsequent less well-known atrocities. One Japanese history professor spoke to me about Nanking in dismissive tones that would never be tolerated if a German academic had referred to a key event of the Holocaust in the same way.

The result is that this is an area of history that has not received the level of attention it deserves. No one even knows the exact number of Chinese the Japanese killed in the war. Estimates vary from between 15 million to in excess of 20 million. And this black hole of historical knowledge is compounded by the fact that the survivors on both sides are mostly dead or dying — and the vast majority have left their stories untold.

Hajime Kondo is a rare exception — a soldier of the Japanese Imperial Army who is prepared to speak for the record about his experiences. Son of a poor provincial farmer, he was conscripted into the army in

1940 and subjected — like all recruits — to a systematic regime of brutal bullying. "The training was so severe that even dying is better," he said. "I was beaten with fists until I saw stars in front of my eyes." This bullying wasn't the unauthorized "hazing" tolerated in many other armed forces, but a carefully planned and authorized method of mind control. The few other former soldiers of the Imperial Army who were prepared to talk to us recounted similar stories of calculated brutality, one saying that recruits were told to practise "self-punishment" and beat up each other when the instructor's arm got tired with hitting them. The Japanese military instructors also punished the whole group if one of them committed an offence. One person in Hajime Kondo's unit of a dozen or so recruits had eaten a sweet without permission. He didn't own up to this "crime" and so the entire unit was punished. "In the military there is no individual responsibility," said Kondo, "but rather group responsibility . . . so you're often punished not due to your own crime." This method of training created soldiers who possessed an overwhelming predisposition to follow orders immediately and to the letter.

Once he was in China, Kondo completed his basic military education by attacking captured Chinese. "The boss said, 'You are going to do bayonet training.'" In front of the recruits were Chinese men tied to trees. In turn, each of the Japanese soldiers was ordered to run at one of the Chinese men and bayonet him. "I was shaking," said Kondo, "and I ran and I stabbed and it was easy. Before the stabbing I was scared, but after the stabbing I realized I could do it. You can kill a person so easily."

Kondo admits he felt no guilt at killing that defenceless Chinese man. Again he is typical of other recruits I met who participated in similar bayonet "training". One even confessed that when he was praised for his stabbing technique he felt "good". A large part of the reason the recruits felt no remorse at the killing of these Chinese men was, no doubt, the brutality of their own training. But another element played an important part too — the fact that from their earliest days they had been taught that the Chinese were beneath them. "We were told from elementary school," said Kondo, "that the Chinese were poor and that they were an inferior race . . . But the Japanese people — a divine people — are the most superior race in the world. But the Chinese were below pigs. That was the mentality we had."

Worryingly for us British, a number of the Japanese veterans also told me that they were inspired in their conquest of China by the British occupation of India. Japan, like Germany, was a nation that had come late on to the world stage and, also like Germany, wanted that badge of self-respect that any great nation was then presumed to require: colonies. "We heard that from Manchuria we got beans and then from northern China cotton and coal are procured," said Hajime Kondo. "In this way Japan will become more wealthy." In pursuit of their colonial ambitions, the Japanese Imperial Army moved north from Nanking and pursued a war of conquest that, by the time Kondo joined the fight in 1940, had already cut a swathe through the Chinese countryside. He was posted to a unit in Shaanxi Province and often took part in punitive operations in the occupied areas of Henan and Hebei: "In the enemy area [of China] you could do anything," he said. "We unconsciously thought this — we weren't officially taught we could do anything but we learnt it from senior colleagues." Kondo confessed that "individual sin" did not exist for him and his comrades because "we do it as a group" and "Communists should be killed for the emperor. That was the thinking of the ordinary soldiers. So during that operation you can do anything. If you kill a person, then that was good for the emperor." In addition, just as the Germans in the war against the Soviet Union became mired in a series of so-called "revenge" attacks against the Red Army, so Kondo revealed that the Japanese Imperial Army created an atmosphere of almost constant "revenge" against the Chinese — motivated by the fact that the Chinese had, on occasion, dared to fight back.

All of this — the belief the Chinese were "below pigs", the desire to possess a gigantic colony, the sense that the emperor sanctioned any atrocity and the constant spirit of "revenge" — mixed into a powerful and dangerous cocktail of motivation. The result was not just Nanking and a series of other atrocities, but a Japanese army in China whose actions were built around a philosophy of cruelty.

Kondo described how the whole process of subjugating the Chinese countryside involved calculated abuse. First, his unit would seek intelligence reports about a village or town that lay ahead of them by capturing locals and questioning them — and the use of torture was commonplace. Once the villagers had been "questioned", they were killed. But "it was too good to kill a Chankoro [slang for someone Chinese, meaning "pig"] with a gun or a sword — just a stone is OK for Chankoros." Having obtained information about the target ahead, the troops moved forward. The routine was always the same: "The soldiers would first enter the village and go into the houses and steal money and food. Then they would search for women. Then came the gang rapes — around ten to thirty men per woman."

Unlike the German war against the Soviet Union, in which rape — though it occurred — was not the norm, for the Japanese sexual violence was almost commonplace. The Germans had been taught that to rape a Slav was to commit a "race crime" — the fact that they were "subhuman" in Nazi eyes meant that these women were supposed to be beyond the pale. But the Japanese processed the information they had been given — that these Chinese women were "below pigs" — differently. For them, the perceived inferiority of the Chinese was the key that permitted their sexual abuse. But, as Kondo revealed, we would be wrong to imagine that sexual desire, at least as we normally understand it, was the only motivation for these attacks. Something else often lay behind them, as Hajime Kondo confessed, when it came to his own participation in gang rape.

Normally, he said, "rookies" were not "invited" by the other soldiers to take part in rape. The Japanese army — like Japanese society — was based on a rigid hierarchy, and the senior soldiers could use the junior ones as their packhorses. "We were treated so badly," said Kondo, "and the older soldiers were so mean to us that I could never think of women." But all that changed one day when he was in his third year in the army in China. His more senior comrades had caught a woman, and one by one they raped her. Then one of the fourth-year recruits — one year above him in the hierarchy — called out to him, "Kondo, you go and rape her."

Kondo's feeling as he heard this invitation was that "you couldn't turn it down". It was an indication that he was accepted by his seniors, a rite of passage into a new and perhaps better stage of his army career. The actual act of rape was scarcely sexual for him; it was a process of initiation. Between ten and 20 soldiers of his unit raped that unknown Chinese woman that day. And Kondo cannot remember what happened to her afterwards (though it was standard practise to kill the woman after gang rape). Indeed, he claims he cannot "remember anything about her".

Kondo did recall one incident when — unusually — a woman was not killed after she had been gang raped. Instead, naked apart from her shoes and clinging to her small baby, she was taken on a march to the next military objective. But the track was mountainous and the woman soon became tired and unable to keep up. So Kondo's comrades wanted to "get rid" of her. "Two or three metres away from me the soldiers were talking. Suddenly one of the soldiers stood up and grabbed her baby and threw it over a cliff which was thirty to forty metres high. Then instantly the mother of the baby followed, jumping off the cliff, and when I saw what was happening in front of me I thought what a horrible thing to do. I felt sorry for them for a while, but I had to carry on marching."

What was in that Japanese soldier's mind as he threw that woman's baby over a cliff? A desire to rid the unit of an encumbrance? A demonstration of power? A feeling of contempt for the Chinese? A similar sense of "curiosity" to the one Petras Zelionka felt (see page 14) as he shot a child? All of those, perhaps.

Kondo claimed he had committed only one rape himself — his "initiation". And I was inclined to believe him, because shortly afterwards his unit was shipped to Okinawa in a fruitless attempt to defend the island against Allied attack. On Okinawa he was captured by the Americans as he attempted to mount a banzai (suicide) charge against them, and his war was over.

Hajime Kondo was a thoughtful man. And he had clearly thought a great deal about the Japanese actions in China in general and the reasons for his own culpability in particular. This was his final attempt to explain why he had done what he had done: "Maybe if you're in the battlefield for a year, you can bear it. But we were there for two or three years and you go crazy. I mean your mind will be so sick that you do such embarrassing things. But that's the mentality created after a stay in the battlefield. In peacetime I can't imagine this, because in the battlefield it's so abnormal. In every battlefield the same kind of thing happens, but especially when human beings are thrown into an abnormal battlefield — then everyone becomes beasts. Unless you're highly educated, maybe a selected few can behave rationally, but I wasn't educated . . . it's very important that each individual has the power to think and behave as an individual. I'm only an uneducated, silly man, but this is my conclusion."

WOLFGANG HORN
AND SHOOTING RED ARMY SOLDIERS

On 22 June 1941, Wolfgang Horn, a 22-year-old non-commissioned officer in a Panzer artillery unit, watched as high-explosive shells pounded into Red Army positions during the first moments of the German invasion of the Soviet Union. The sight made him feel good: "I enjoyed the strength of our army, sending thousands of shells into the Russian border defences . . . it was partly a great feeling about power being unleashed against the dubious and despicable enemy." It was the beginning of five exhilarating months for Horn — five months that would culminate in the single most exciting day of his life.

Wolfgang Horn told me his story with laughs and smiles and chuckles. War for him had clearly not been a journey into a Heart of Darkness, more a romp into an adrenalin-filled big-game hunt.

Like a number of the German veterans I met, Horn claimed that he had not been a fanatical Nazi. He said he had joined the Hitler Youth in the 1930s because "it was the only possibility to stay in high school and advance normally . . . so I went to Hitler Youth once a week for evening classes and on Sundays for field exercises, preparing for a war — how to take cover and how to advance in groups and these kinds of things . . .

I didn't mind." Horn had even seen Adolf Hitler up close at a convention in Weimar — and been unimpressed: "He marched on the road with all his entourage of high-level Nazis and he was very pale and looked very insignificant; nothing special at all. I was disappointed. There was nothing to it . . . nothing special at all. And in his speeches he repeated things again and again. I found I knew all that stuff anyway."

But, significantly, his disinterest in Hitler and the Nazis did not prevent him thinking that the war against the Soviet Union was justified. As Horn's story illustrates, it was possible at the time not to support Hitler personally and yet still wholeheartedly believe that Communism had to be crushed. And even looking back from the perspective of the late 1990s when I interviewed him in London, he maintained that the German invasion of the Soviet Union "might have saved Europe from Communism".

As Wolfgang Horn saw it, the Germans were on a mission to protect Western civilization from Stalin's barbarism. And it was this belief that was one of the chief reasons he embarked on the campaign with a sense of righteousness. Another was that he felt he was fighting an inferior people: "We saw the difference in standard of living . . . The primitive Russian houses and the way they lived that was so much below our standards that we didn't take it so seriously to fire a Russian house or damage them . . . They were on a lower level . . . One divided Europe into three areas — Europe A, B and C — so Russia was Europe C, the lowest standard of all. England and Germany were

Europe A, Poland maybe Europe B and Russia was C." Wolfgang Horn delivered this judgement, as he did most of his testimony, with a faint smile on his face. He believed that there were a number of certainties about that brutal war against the Soviet Union — and high amongst those certainties was that the Russians were "on a lower level" than the Germans.

Later in the war, when he took part in the scorched-earth conflict against Soviet partisans who operated behind the German lines, he openly confessed that he burnt down a village suspected of housing partisans, throwing women and children out into the snow. When I suggested that many of these women and children might have died as a result, he replied, "I know, I know — it could have happened. But we know Russians are quite resourceful, coping with the cold." And when I asked him if, looking back on his actions in burning a village, he felt any sense of shame about what he had done, he answered with a slight laugh, "Not much — I was to some degree elated that we had succeeded in doing it."

It is important to understand that this mentality did not develop in Wolfgang Horn during the war as a result of his experiences. He possessed these views before he set foot in the Soviet Union; then from his first day in enemy territory he sought evidence that supported the conclusion he had previously reached. And this prejudice had, from the beginning, a surprising effect. It allowed Horn to feel *excited* about the war. Freed from any sense that he might be inflicting suffering on fellow human beings, he was able to revel in the experience of blowing them apart. This was a feeling that was magnified by the technological superiority the Germans possessed. Horn was part of the most sophisticated armoured attack that the world had yet seen. Up to this point, conventional military theory had insisted that armoured attack warfare be conducted in waves: first bombing, then artillery, then tanks and finally an infantry advance. But something very different was practised by the Germans in those early months of the war.

Pioneered in their invasion of Poland in the autumn of 1939, and further developed during their conquest of France and the Low Countries in the spring of 1940, the German blitzkrieg (lightning war) tactics were honed to technical perfection by the time of their attack on the Soviet Union. Here the idea was not to attack the enemy in waves. No, the feat the Germans managed was to focus every military effort on one small point — often one single road — with bombers, motorized infantry, tanks, motorcycles and artillery attacking simultaneously. The skill needed to coordinate this technique was one that no other nation possessed at the time. A few metres out in artillery calculations, a few seconds' delay, and the Germans would have destroyed their own forces. "We could all communicate all the time easily," Horn told me proudly. "It was one big advantage, naturally, that the attack was so coordinated."

The sense of exhilaration these soldiers felt as they shattered Soviet defences is almost impossible to exaggerate. And, initially, their overweening self-confidence seemed justified. There has never been so successful or swift an advance as the one the Germans achieved in the summer of 1941. By the autumn they had captured 3 million Red Army soldiers, often trapped in giant encirclement actions as the swift blitzkrieg punch through the Soviet line allowed whole armies to be swallowed. By the end of September the Germans had advanced some 650 kilometres into the Soviet Union. In just over three months they had captured most of the Ukraine, including the capital, Kiev, all of Belarus, including its capital, Minsk, and all of the Baltic states. And as if this weren't enough, they were also laying siege to Leningrad and were en route to Moscow.

It was at the peak of all this success, just as Hitler announced at the Sportpalast in Berlin that the Red Army would "never rise again", that Wolfgang Horn experienced his own moment of near ecstasy. In October 1941, inside the so-called "Vyazma pocket", 150 kilometres west of Moscow, five whole Soviet armies were surrounded by the 3rd and 4th German Panzer armies. Panic-stricken Red Army soldiers did whatever they could to try to break out of the encirclement, even running at the Germans without guns in their hands. Horn witnessed "waves and waves of advancing soldiers. And [when] the first row was mown down, then the second bent down and took the guns of the dead and continued to move forward until they were mown down also ... No German solider would have attacked without any weapon. Incredible for us, you see, but it seemed normal for them ... totally unfamiliar to us, but that's the way they fought."

One night, near the town of Vyazma, Horn and his unit came into close contact with fleeing Red Army soldiers. Horn had just been wounded by splinters from a Soviet hand grenade, which had made him "angry". Now he "just threw my hand grenades and shot at the Russians advancing towards me. You see, some came with fixed bayonet charging, so I shot them from the hip."

Horn and his comrades also attacked a truck full of Red Army soldiers as it tried to pass by: "The Russians were so cowardly that some of the crew of this truck hovered behind the vehicle, crouching on the ground and not moving at all." He felt contempt for these soldiers who, petrified, were pretending to be dead. After shouting in Russian, "Hands up!" and receiving no response, "we started shooting them — naturally. Under the impact of the bullets they wavered and shook a bit . . . When they didn't surrender we shot them . . . They are cowards — they didn't deserve any better anyhow." At this point in the story Horn laughed again, adding, "That was our feeling . . . I would never have done that. We would never have done that. You're crouching and doing nothing." He estimates he killed between 20 and 30 Red Army soldiers during what he describes as the most exciting night of his life.

Wolfgang Horn was an intelligent man — after the war he became an academic specializing in research into IQ tests — yet he gave the following answer when I asked him why this experience had been so thrilling: "[because] I could kill so many Russians with hand grenades and rifle shots," he said simply and with great feeling.

I had thought before meeting Wolfgang Horn that fighting in a war would be frightening, dangerous and perhaps exhilarating on occasion. Since meeting him I have understood that for certain individuals war can be all of that and something more besides. I learnt that, for some people, the bloodshed and violence of war can be enormous fun.

MASAYO ENOMOTO
AND RAPE, MURDER AND CANNIBALISM

The Ancient Romans were concerned that civilization would make them soft — that exposure to hot baths and comfortable beds would take the edge off their ability to destroy their enemies in battle. But my own concern over the last 20 years or so has been precisely the reverse — that prolonged exposure to countless stories of human distress and degradation would blunt my sensibilities and harden me to suffering. But in 2000 in Tokyo I met Masayo Enomoto and realized that I had not grown hard at all — because his story haunts me to this day.

Enomoto was a farmer's son from the provinces of Japan who joined the army at the age of 17 to seek his fortune. And after a brutal training that mirrors the experience of Hajime Kondo (see page 71) he found himself in the heart of enemy country in the north of China. Here he discovered that he could do anything he liked to the local villagers — people he had been taught were "lower than cockroaches".

The defining experience of his life happened in May 1945. He and his comrades were hungry and tired; they'd been away from base for many months inside enemy territory, and they sought distraction. So when Sergeant Major Enomoto heard that a Chinese woman from a nearby deserted village had returned, he went to investigate. He spotted her as soon as he entered the village. "She could speak Japanese," said Enomoto, "and she said that her parents had tried to persuade her to leave. But she said that the Japanese people aren't such bad people, so she'd decided to stay in the village."

She had made a mortal mistake, because the sight of this woman drew forth one basic response in Enomoto: "When I saw a woman in this enemy zone, the first thing that would come to my mind unconditionally would be to rape her. No hesitation." Enomoto looked around to check that no one was watching and then, behind a fence, he raped her: "She did resist. But such resistance didn't affect me whatsoever. I didn't listen to what she was saying." After he had raped her, he did what he always did to women he raped — he killed her: "I stabbed her with a sword — on television you see a lot of blood flow out, but that's not the reality . . . I've cut people with swords, but you're not covered with blood. Based on my experience you really don't experience such things. It doesn't splash you like you see in the movies. If you cut the neck, you do see just a bit of blood, but it's not like what you see in the films . . . So when I killed the woman I wasn't covered with blood."

And as he looked down at the body of the woman he had just raped and murdered, another thought came into his head. He and his comrades were hungry — it had been days since they had tasted meat. So why not eat her? Enomoto dragged the woman further behind the shadow of the fence and began to dismember her body. He cut chunks of flesh from her legs, arms and torso: "I just tried to choose those places where there was a lot of meat." Then he carried the pieces back to his unit and distributed them amongst his comrades. He did not tell the ordinary soldiers where the meat had come from, and they did not ask. But Enomoto felt he had to tell his commanding officer that they were eating human flesh. When he heard the news he made no comment.

Enomoto ate some of the meat himself and describes it as "nice and tender. I think it was tastier than pork — at least that's how I felt at the time." And he felt no sense of guilt about what he was doing: "Raping her, eating her, killing her — I didn't feel anything about it. And that went for everything I did [in China]. It was only afterwards that I really came to feel remorse."

Rape, of course, was officially a crime in the Japanese Imperial Army. But when asked why the officers did not object, Enomoto replied simply: "Because the officers were doing it as well . . . We felt we were doing everything for the emperor, so everything was all right so long as it was done in the emperor's name. Rapes, killings, burnings etc . . . Perhaps you shouldn't do all this, but the soldiers had to console themselves. They were fighting for the emperor, so this was a sort of consolation." In total, including the woman he ate, Enomoto said he raped eight women during his time in China. And he claimed that, at the time, because he was "young" rape felt "all right", and that whilst committing the crime he "also felt some satisfaction as a soldier".

By the time he said these words I had been listening to Masayo Enomoto for over an hour. Night was falling, and the lantern in the room in the traditional Japanese inn where we filmed the interview cast shadows on the ricepaper walls. Gradually I had a sense that the room itself was filling with the stories he had been telling — that the recitation of his wartime experiences had polluted the place. In all of the hundreds of interviews I had filmed with veterans from the war — many of whom had committed terrible atrocities — I had never felt anything like this. I don't believe in ghosts or spirits or any other form of supernatural visitation, so there was no sense in which I felt I experienced any kind of psychic vision. No, it was the kind of feeling you get when you visit a place and it just feels bad, or you meet a person for the first time and before they speak you know there is something badly wrong.

Seconds later we stopped filming to change tapes in the camera and I opened the door to let in the fresh night air. Suddenly the atmosphere in the room changed, and whatever had been in the room with us vanished. And I have never felt such a thing since.

After the war Enomoto was imprisoned by the Chinese. Along with around 1000 other Japanese prisoners he was held in a detention camp in Bujan in northern China. Given the terrible crimes he and his comrades had committed, one would have expected the Chinese response to be draconian. But it wasn't. "The

Chinese staff provided us with three meals with white rice a day, whilst they were only eating twice a day," said Enomoto. "And all the food, all the ingredients, were very good. And these were things that we couldn't eat in Japan. And this continued throughout the whole of my imprisonment."

The surprisingly lenient treatment he received at the hands of the Chinese made Enomoto reassess his actions during the war: "If I'd continued to think of things from my perspective I don't think I would have felt a sense of remorse. It was only because I came to appreciate things from a Chinese perspective that I started to feel remorse. That was the feeling I acquired when I was exposed to the generous attitude of the Chinese people. And not once did they beat or scold me."

Enomoto felt that his Chinese captors — the enemy he had been taught to despise — were treating him better than his superiors had done during his time in the Japanese Imperial Army. And so he came, of his own volition, to confess: "They [the Chinese] didn't tell me to do anything. I decided to confess on my own — because I recognized I had committed crimes. There were no instructions given by the Chinese. I asked for pencil and paper to write down all the things that I had committed . . . And based on this list the Chinese people went to the sites to check — it took them about a month. And everything that I wrote down was proven to be accurate. And they came to understand that what I was saying was the truth." The Chinese did not reward Enomoto for having confessed — nor did they punish him after learning the nature of his crimes. Instead, he said, "nothing changed — the Chinese treated me in exactly the same way."

It is significant that the Chinese authorities took such care to double-check the testimony of Japanese war criminals against other evidence, gathering corroborative statements from a variety of eye witnesses. Unlike many investigations conducted in non-democratic states, this one genuinely seems to have been seeking the truth.

Masayo Enomoto was the first Japanese prisoner in the camp to confess to committing rape. Until he spoke out all the other prisoners had talked of "stealing, looting but never talked of raping women. But because I confessed, everyone disclosed the fact that they had raped women."

In 1956, after all his crimes had been investigated, the Chinese authorities decided on an action that, at first sight, is the biggest shock of all — they allowed Enomoto to return, as a free man, to Japan. This policy of repatriating self-confessed war criminals was actually extremely enlightened. Because if the Chinese had simply shot Enomoto, what would the world know of his crimes? And since it was obvious in the years immediately after the war that the Japanese authorities were not pursuing the same policy as the Germans and openly acknowledging the offences committed during the conflict, it would have served Japanese interests if none of their war criminals had returned from China. But now, here were a number of veterans of the Imperial Army who were prepared to speak openly about the crimes they had committed in the name of the emperor — an emperor who was still, incidentally, permitted by the Allies to remain on the Japanese throne after the war. It is not surprising, given this background, that there was an attempt by some Japanese to dismiss the claims of these repatriated veterans as the product of "brainwashing" by the Chinese. But the fact that their stories tallied with the experiences of the few Japanese veterans who had previously spoken out, and with assessments by independent witnesses, made their claims impossible to ignore.

Before we interviewed Masayo Enomoto, we were also keen to substantiate, as far as we could, that what he was telling us was credible — in particular his tale of cannibalism. At first I thought such a story was simply outlandish, but the pioneering research of Professor Yuki Tanaka[1] demonstrates that "the practice of cannibalism [amongst the Japanese Imperial Army] was much more widely practised than previously thought". And though Professor Tanaka's work is based on the actions of the Japanese in New Guinea, there is no reason to suppose that Japanese soldiers in China did not possess a similar mentality. And it also seems that, in the 1950s, when the Chinese investigated Enomoto's confession, they too found it credible.

But it wasn't learning of the sophistication of the Chinese treatment of Japanese war criminals that made

---

[1] Yuki Tanaka, "Hidden Horrors", *Japanese War Crimes in World War Two* (Westview Press, 1998)

the biggest impression upon me. What I remember most from this section of Enomoto's interview was his apparently minor remark: "The Chinese praised me and said I always wrote the longest and most accurate confessions." I thought that comment was significant because Enomoto had previously revealed that he had been the keenest member of his army unit during the war. For example, he was always the first person to volunteer to bayonet live Chinese prisoners in training. He had done everything in his power to please his superiors in the Imperial Army, and once he was imprisoned he did everything in his power to please his captors. His belief system, such as it was, shifted 180 degrees without him suffering any internal doubt or conflict; all because the dominant feature of his character was the desire to please his boss and to fit into whatever system he happened to live in at the time. As I drove back after the interview through the neon-lit streets of Tokyo, I thought this revelation was almost as troubling as Masayo Enomoto's original story of rape, murder and cannibalism.

PART FOUR

PRISONERS

Not only were more people taken prisoner during World War II than in any previous conflict in history, the variety of experience endured by those who fell into enemy hands was also unlike anything seen before. The nine personal histories in this part of the book demonstrate these two points and also offer us a chance to learn how people coped in circumstances that were almost beyond imagining.

The diversity of the ways that captors treated their prisoners during the war also means that we have to widen our idea of what constitutes "imprisonment". Aleksandr Mikhailovski saw no prison walls during his first day in German captivity, but he was "imprisoned" just as much as Peter Lee, who endured several years as a prisoner of war behind the barbed wire of a Japanese camp.

In the face of this history we have to rethink our traditional narrow definition of the word "prisoner". Normally we think of "prisoners" as people whose liberty is withdrawn for a specified time and who receive similar treatment for similar "crimes". But many nations redrew that definition during the war — notably the Germans, who treated their prisoners according to Nazi ideological theory. For example,

Soviet prisoners of war were, as a general rule, treated much worse than British — more than 3 million Soviet prisoners died in German captivity. But to be Jewish and captured by the Germans was to endure a form of imprisonment unlike any other. Jews could be held in a ghetto — like Estera Frenkiel and Lucille Eichengreen, or sent to a camp such as Treblinka, like Samuel Willenberg. But what these places had in common was that they were "temporary" in the eyes of the Nazis. Jews were imprisoned for years in the case of the ghetto or minutes in the case of Treblinka, but ultimately the Nazis wanted the end to be the same — death for every single Jew. That is a form of "imprisonment" unique in history.

World War II also marks a revolution in penal history because of the mass imprisonment of millions and millions of civilians. Old people, mothers, children, small babies — all were liable to face captivity. As a result a wide range of people experienced the sudden catastrophe of imprisonment. And what I learnt from meeting a variety of former prisoners was that there was never just one way of coping with the trauma. What worked for Peter Lee — focusing only on the moment and not dreaming of the future — would not have worked for Tatiana Nanieva, who was sustained by imagining her liberators drawing ever nearer.

ALEKSANDR MIKHAILOVSKI
AND THE NAZIS' HUMAN MINE DETECTORS

Anyone who has spent time studying history knows that our view of the past is constantly shifting. Events are reinterpreted, argued over and disputed. Reputations wax and wane. And, crucially, our very access to the archives and witnesses that constitute the basic building blocks of historical record can either be granted or denied. Our knowledge and opinion about the history of the Soviet Union, for example, has altered as a result of the fall of the Berlin Wall and better access to the East. But there is a danger that we see this as a benefit once granted that cannot be taken away — something that is far from the truth. We must always remember that, whilst history offers us many warnings and possibly a number of lessons, there is only one immutable rule — things change.

And things have certainly changed since I was able to visit Belarus on a research and filming trip at the end of the 1990s. This landlocked country bordering Poland, the Ukraine, Russia, Latvia and Lithuania had been part of the Soviet Union since 1922. During World War II it was the scene of countless atrocities, as first, the German Army Group Centre fought through it on their way to Moscow and then a bloody internal war developed behind the lines between the Germans and

Stalin's partisans. Poland is traditionally thought to be the country that suffered proportionately most during the war, losing 6 million people — 18 per cent of its pre-war population — but that is only because Belarus, since it was a republic of the Soviet Union at the time, was not classed as an independent country. As a consequence few people realize that 2.2 million Belarusians died — a staggering 25 per cent of the pre-war population.

In 1991 Belarus declared itself independent and three years later Aleksandr Lukashenko became president. In 2006 his re-election was condemned as unfair by outside observers, and there have been a number of serious human-rights abuses in the country. Lukashenko is an eccentric, authoritarian ruler who treats Belarus as his personal fiefdom. He distrusts foreign journalists, and today it would be almost impossible to obtain a visa to make an investigative historical film in the country. But in 1998, during a temporary thaw in relations between the Belarusian authorities and the Western media, I was able to make a visit.

I was struck by how much I liked the place — not the regime, of course — but the geography and the people. Belarus is one of the least-populated countries in Europe, and for the most part is an extraordinarily silent place. The country has the same population as Portugal — about 10 million — and yet is more than twice the size. Minsk, the capital, is an attractive city with open boulevards and tree-lined streets. But, of course, it was the chance to meet people who had endured the maelstrom of the war in Belarus that drew me there in the first place. And during this interlude of openness about the country's history it was possible to challenge one of the strongest myths about World War II in Belarus — the partisan war. For behind the propaganda films about noble Red Army partisans and their virtuous partnership with the locals lay a darker truth. A number of villagers I met talked of the partisans as drunken murderers who had stolen their livestock and food. They revealed how the partisans would come from the forests at night, select locals whom they thought might have collaborated with the Germans — accusations that could be based on the merest suspicion — and kill them. One woman even told me that, compared to the Germans, the "partisans were worse". If she had said these words publicly before the fall of Communism she would have gone to jail.

However, remarkable as this collective memory about the actions of the Red Army partisans was, the single person I remember most from my filming trip to Belarus was subjected to a German, not a partisan, atrocity. His name was Aleksandr Mikhailovski and he lived in the tiny hamlet of Maksimoky, deep in the countryside. His story affected me most because of the sudden, nightmarish quality of the single day he described. On the night of 21 July 1943 he had gone to bed expecting tomorrow to be a normal day like any other. But he had been wrong: around four o'clock in the morning on the 22nd German soldiers smashed down his front door and burst into the house where he lived with his deaf-and-dumb brother. They shook both of the teenagers awake and then dragged them down to the road that led from Maksimoky to the next village. Here they were tied, hand to hand, to half a dozen other villagers and spread out in a line across the road. Then all eight of them were told to start walking, taking small, measured steps. The Germans followed, a safe distance behind.

Aleksandr Mikhailovski knew very well what he and the other villagers had become — they were human mine detectors: "There'd been times when people had been blown up — the partisans had planted mines. And they [the Germans] sent us out in front intentionally, so that we would get blown up." He also knew that he and the other villagers with him were in a situation where any action they took could lead to their deaths: "We knew that if we avoided one mine and a German blew up behind us, it meant that we would die all the same. Reckoning this, we walked without any hope, because we knew that if we didn't blow up then a German would, and that meant that the other Germans would shoot us — you'd perish one way or another."

Given, as they saw it, the certainty of their death that day, Aleksandr and the other villagers chose to keep away from areas of the road they thought might still be mined: "We walked along if possible on horse tracks — any suspicious places we tried somehow to avoid." Their logic was straightforward. If they missed a mine, there was a small chance that the Germans following behind might miss it as well. And even if a German blew himself up, their own consequent death by shooting was preferable to death by explosion.

Not surprisingly, Aleksandr Mikhailovski found it hard to articulate what his feelings had been that day. "From fear, your mouth dried up . . . because of the tears we couldn't see the road . . . Your heart turned to stone . . . You walked along, not knowing what, where, how and why . . . they brought us to a living death — that was what it was like."

He and the rest of the villagers were lucky — there were no mines planted on the route they walked. But it could easily have been otherwise. During the huge anti-partisan action called Operation Kottbus conducted by the Germans in eastern Belarus, the same technique of using human beings to clear minefields was implemented on an enormous scale. The SS commander recorded in his report that "approximately two to three thousand local people were blown up in the clearing of the minefields".[1]

But though Aleksandr and the rest of the villagers had completed their lengthy trek without injury, they were not out of danger. Once they reached the village of Beshchady the Germans separated four of the original eight, including Aleksandr and his brother, from the rest. The reason for selecting these particular four appears to have been the Germans' desire to target fit, healthy young men, since they were working on the basis that such people were most likely to be partisans. By this point in the war — the summer of 1943 — the Germans had lost control of much of the Belarusian

---

[1] Quoted in Timothy Patrick Mulligan, *The Politics of Illusion and Empire* (Praeger, 1988)

countryside, and roving bands of Red Army partisans exercised more power over the locals than they did. The German solution was to use terror in an attempt to traumatize the civilian population into acquiescence. Aleksandr, his brother and the two other young men selected that day were about to experience the practical application of that policy of terror: "They [the Germans] put us in a pit meant for potatoes and said, 'Come on and see, we're going to shoot bandits!' So they set up three machine guns near the pits."

By pure chance, some locals from the Mikhailovskis' home village saw what was happening, and three of them went to speak to the German officer commanding the unit. Again, through pure chance, that officer spoke Polish, as did the Belarusians, and so the locals could communicate with him. "They're orphans," the villagers said. "Their father and mother have died. They aren't bandits — they farm their land, they're not anything . . . that one's an invalid, deaf and dumb."

Aleksandr and the other three stood in the pit, looking up at the machine guns, and watched as the officer decided their fate. It was entirely up to that unknown German whether they lived or died. He deliberated for a moment, and then ordered all four to be pulled out of the pit. Who knows why he changed his mind? Perhaps it was the presence of Aleksandr's deaf-and-dumb brother that made the difference — maybe the German officer objected to killing someone who was disabled (though many other Germans had no qualms about doing just that). We shall never know.

The four of them were imprisoned overnight in a storeroom in the village, and then taken to Minsk where they joined a group of other Belarusians about to be sent to Germany as forced labour. Once the war was over, Aleksandr Mikhailovski and his brother returned to Maksimoky and carried on farming the land.

After a morning filming our interview with Aleksandr, we drove him the short distance back to his small wooden house and said goodbye. Then we started filming various shots of the countryside to illustrate his story. It was quiet and peaceful; the only sound the birds in the nearby forest. And it was then that I felt the full force of what he had told us that morning.

I experienced a strange feeling — something that I had not felt even at the site of the death camps of Treblinka or Auschwitz. It was absolute confirmation of the knowledge that nature — as represented by the serene, green countryside around me — was utterly indifferent to the suffering of Aleksandr Mikhailovski. The grass would have grown and the flowers would have bloomed whether he had been killed or not.

And the horrible words of that arch-Darwinist Adolf Hitler came into my mind: "The earth continues to go round — whether it's the man who kills the tiger or the tiger who eats the man."[1]

---

[1] *Hitler's Table Talk 1941–1944*, 23 September 1941, introduced and with a new preface by Hugh Trevor-Roper (Weidenfeld and Nicolson, 2000)

SAMUEL WILLENBERG
AND SURVIVING A DEATH CAMP

Hundreds of trains clattered across central Europe during 1942, taking more than a million people to their deaths. And on one of those trains, in the spring of 1942, was a 19-year-old Polish Jew called Samuel Willenberg. Along with others from the village of Opatow in southern Poland he had been caught in a round-up of Jews — one of the many that were taking place all across Nazi-occupied Poland.

Everyone crammed into the freight wagon with Samuel knew what was likely to happen to them when they arrived at their destination. Rumours about the existence of Nazi killing factories were rife, and as the train slowed to pass through a station they heard their fellow countrymen — Catholic Poles — shout: "Jews! You'll be turned into soap!" But still they hoped they would not die. Hope, many survivors say, is what endures almost until the last.

Samuel was travelling towards a place that perfectly encapsulates the logical consequence of Nazi hatred: a camp in the middle of a remote forest, east of Warsaw, called Treblinka. Unlike Auschwitz, the most infamous camp of all, which was a combination of concentration camp and killing factory, Treblinka had only one purpose — murder. It was the largest of what have become known as the Operation Reinhard camps, named by the Nazis in "honour" of Reinhard Heydrich, the senior SS man who was assassinated by Allied agents in Prague in May 1942. But it was still tiny — about 600 metres by 400 metres. Yet between them the Operation Reinhard camps killed around 1.6 million people; Treblinka alone around 800,000. So nearly as many people died in this one camp by the river Bug, a place whose perimeter fence you could walk around in 20 minutes, as the British and Americans — put together — lost in the whole of World War II.

But it is not just the sheer number murdered in the camp that makes Treblinka so appalling. It is the cold and careful way the killing was organized as a result of the Nazis' desire to keep themselves as distant as possible from the mechanics of the murder process. Heinrich Himmler, commander of the SS, had witnessed in the summer of 1941 how participating in the shooting of civilians caused psychological problems for many of his men. As a result he called for experiments to be conducted to find a "better" way of killing — better for the Nazis, of course, not for those they wished to murder. Places like Treblinka and its gas chambers were the result. Only a handful of Germans — about a few dozen or so — were needed to run the camp, along with just over 100 Ukrainian SS guards and around 1000 Jewish prisoners who were forced to assist in the killing process or else immediately lose their own lives.

And small as it was, Treblinka was divided into two: a lower camp where the Jews were prepared for the gas

105

chambers by having their heads shaved and where their belongings were sorted, and an upper camp, connected to the lower only by a path know as the "tube", where the gas chambers and open cremation grids were situated. In both upper and lower camps, just as at Auschwitz, most of the basic tasks were performed by Jewish prisoners — including the most gruesome task of all, emptying the gas chamber of bodies. These Jewish prisoners, the Sonderkommando, were themselves murdered every so often and replaced with fit new arrivals. But this happened only every few months. So it would take a statistical miracle for any individual to be selected on arrival at Treblinka to be a member of the Sonderkommando. The figures were stark: on arrival prisoners stood, on average, a 99 per cent chance of being dead within three hours.

But when Samuel Willenberg entered the gates of Treblinka a miracle did indeed occur. In the chaos, with the SS guards screaming and beating the disorientated Jews forward from the trains, he heard one of the Jewish Sonderkommando calling out to him and asking where he was from. Samuel told him, and then the man said, "Say you are a bricklayer." Samuel did as he was told, and as a result an SS guard pulled him from the line of people about to be sent immediately to the gas chambers. He was simply "lucky". That one day — unusually — the Nazis needed to select a few of the new arrivals as construction workers. That one day — coincidentally — one of the Jewish Sonderkommando already working in the camp recognized him and told him what to say to escape immediate death.

Once admitted to the camp, Samuel worked not just as a bricklayer but as one of the hundreds of Sonderkommando who sorted out the trousers, shirts, underclothes, suitcases, tinned food, papers, jewellery and other goods which belonged to the Jews who had been murdered. It was, he says, "like a Persian bazaar". In the sorting area Samuel worked under the direction of a sadistic SS lieutenant, Kurt Franz, nicknamed "Doll". Together with his giant St Bernard dog called Barry, Doll terrorized the prisoners. Barry had been trained to bite into a man's genitals — a punishment usually resulting in painful death. And Doll decided who was to suffer this treatment on a whim — it might be that he simply didn't like the way a prisoner looked at him.

The suffering endured by the Sonderkommando in Treblinka was not just physical. The mental agony of watching as thousands upon thousands of fellow Jews — including mothers clutching babies and small children — arrived at the camp, were stripped of their clothes, had their hair shaved and were then forced up the small passageway to the gas chambers, could be almost as bad. The lowest moment for Samuel Willenberg came when he found his own sister's coat amongst the clothes he was sorting: "I recognized it by the extended sleeves — Mother had extended the sleeves with green plush. And I saw that next to it lay my sister's skirt . . . It is hard to describe what I felt . . . suddenly I felt I wanted to scream. The pain, the

107

powerlessness . . . I screamed inside. At night I cried —
I never cried, but that night I did. Just as I told a boy
who had arrived here [in Treblinka] and was crying,
'One does not cry here. Here one only hates.' And that
is how it was. I cried too like a small boy. The pain
which is difficult to imagine . . . The dearest beings in
that bloody sand . . . Hatred, powerless fury."

As Samuel and the rest of the Sonderkommando
endured all this, Franz Stangl, the commandant of
Treblinka, oversaw a variety of "refinements" to the
killing process, all designed to lull new arrivals into
thinking they had arrived at a transit stop rather than a
murder factory. Fake timetables were placed on the
walls of the mock station on the arrival ramp, and
flowers planted by the entrance path. "Hurry up!" one
SS man was heard shouting to the new arrivals. "The
water in the showers is getting cold!"

Those who were too sick to walk to the undressing
rooms and down the "tube" to the gas chambers in the
upper camp were discreetly escorted away towards
the camp "hospital", where a Red Cross flag flew next
to a solid fence. Outside the fence was a bench where
the sick could wait until they were ready to be seen.
Each person was then called through individually for
"treatment". But as soon as they walked past the fence
they saw that the Treblinka hospital consisted of a pit
full of dead bodies — and standing by the pit was an SS
man with a pistol, waiting to shoot each "patient" in the
back of the neck and throw the corpse down amongst
the others. "Cynicism," said Samuel, "cynicism . . . the
like of which the world had not seen before . . . For

who would have thought that going to see the doctor, one would come in, undress and get shot in the head?"

Samuel and the other members of the Sonderkommando tried to understand how this crime without precedent could possibly be happening on the face of the earth. "There were discussions, quietly," said Samuel. "People asked each other, 'Why?' That question all the time — why? Why?" And, of course, it was a struggle to articulate any answers. But they still kept trying to find some rationale, some purpose behind these appalling events, arguing at night amongst themselves in their barracks. By acting in this way the Sonderkommando of Treblinka were behaving as human beings have done for thousands of years. Even a cursory glance at the history of civilization shows that a defining quality of the human species has been the search for meaning. Religion, obviously, provides one kind of answer; absolute commitment to a philosophy or an ideological creed provides another. But, according to Samuel Willenberg, for the majority of those struggling with the horrific and seemingly arbitrary horror of the death camps these traditional remedies were of little use. One of Samuel's former teachers, Professor Mering, was also in the Treblinka Sonderkommando. He found some comfort in placing the nightmare world they endured in the context of the past. "I look at it from the point of view of history," he told Samuel just before he died. But this approach was of little use to Samuel: "I looked at him as if he had gone mad."

It is difficult to isolate exactly how Samuel Willenberg himself managed to come through an experience that destroyed so many — how he found the will to survive many months in Treblinka before escaping during the successful Sonderkommando revolt in August 1943. Samuel had obvious strengths. At the time he was a young man, determined to live his life. He did not let his mind dwell on the past or dream of the future, but focused his thoughts entirely on the present. Above all, he was physically and mentally tough. Yet others in the Sonderkommando possessed similar qualities and did not survive. Samuel himself believed he was simply "lucky" to have remained alive: "I do not feel guilty and I do not feel like a hero. It was pure chance. It could have turned out differently in a thousand different ways. It did not matter what I said or did — I could have been burnt just as well. I would have ended up in the ash. It was all a question of luck ... and maybe a bit of hot-headedness."

He is right, of course. The most important quality needed to survive Treblinka was luck. But when I met Samuel Willenberg in the mid-1990s, at the site of the camp, this still formidable character gave another clue as to why he in particular had been able to cope with the daily horror of the camp. After the filmed interview was over, I remarked that he must have been tested in harsher ways than almost any other human being in history.

"Oh, no," he replied, "others suffered more. It wasn't like I was actually one of those forced to work in the gas chambers. They worked in terrible conditions. They had to drag the corpses out of the gas chambers as fast as they could."

So when he was in Treblinka he thought that, no matter how bad it was for him, it was worse for some of the other Sonderkommando. And that must have provided him with the smallest crumb of comfort. If these others could come through the day, then why couldn't he? It takes a man of rare qualities to suffer as Samuel Willenberg did and yet understand that there might be others suffering more — to find any positive thought of any kind that might be sustaining in Treblinka. But Samuel Willenberg managed to do just this, and it helped him survive.

PETER LEE
AND THE VIRTUES OF AN ENGLISHMAN IMPRISONED BY THE JAPANESE

One of the great challenges of trying to understand historical events is to imagine ourselves in the past. We have to picture not just a world that is physically very different from the one we live in today — no internet, no jet travel, no mobile phones — but one in which a whole series of personal values are very different as well. Take my parents' generation — the war generation — for example. They were the last generation to grow up with the knowledge that the British possessed the biggest empire the world had ever seen. Yes, the British Empire was built on the mistaken racial belief that the white man was superior to the black; yes, this was exploitation, and, yes, it was right that the Empire faded away. But, still, some of the values that characterized the British Empire — like the "stiff upper lip" — which today are perceived as old-fashioned, were in their own way admirable.

I thought about all of this when I met an impressive individual called Peter Lee. He came from a solid working-class background in the north of England, and the values he absorbed when he was growing up in the 1930s helped him face one of the worst experiences of World War II — imprisonment by the Japanese.

112

Peter Lee joined the RAF in 1939, just before the start of the war, and immediately after his training course was posted as a junior supply officer to the Far East, where in 1942 he fell into Japanese hands. He and his men endured imprisonment first in Java, then at the notorious Changi jail in Singapore, and next at a prison in Jesselton (as Kota Kinabalu in North Borneo was known at the time). At Jesselton, Peter Lee remembered that, "The quality of the food they [the Japanese] supplied to us was absolutely abysmal. For example, they were supplying us with sacks of rice that had congealed . . . In the six months we were there we lost over fifty men out of eight hundred. Now that's a very, very high percentage of people to lose."

In the spring of 1943 the Japanese moved the British from Jesselton to Sandakan at the northeastern tip of Borneo. What the prisoners did not know was that for the vast majority of them this would be the final destination of their lives. But, to begin with, Sandakan seemed better than Jesselton. The food improved a little, there was even a small amount of fish to supply protein, and there was more space. But still, according to Peter Lee, "many of our men died in the early days in Sandakan because they were really too far gone after the experiences in Jesselton to make a recovery. I can remember every day I used to go and see our men in the sick bays. And you'd find a young man that I'd known as a typical example of young British manhood — fit as a fiddle in Singapore — and you'd either find them horribly emaciated, ghosts of their former self, or incredibly bloated with beriberi, with enormous

113

distended stomachs, their private parts distended, and just lying back naked on the bench. And inevitably, of course, people who'd reached that degree of malnutrition and illness, they didn't recover."

The Japanese had moved the British to Sandakan because they wanted an airfield constructed just outside the town and the prisoners were to build it. The heat at the site was intense. When I filmed there in the 1990s the fierce sun and high humidity were scarcely bearable — and I was not malnourished and forced to carry heavy loads. "It was basically shifting earth," recalled Peter. "There were no machines to assist. It was all human labour." If the prisoners did not work as their captors wanted, they were beaten. Special Japanese soldiers — known as "the bashers" — smashed the British about: "Whether you were an officer or another rank, you had to obey the orders of the lowest-rank Japanese private. If you didn't obey it immediately, depending on the personality of that particular Japanese soldier you'd get a crack over the head or a crack over the backside with a stick. There was one occasion on which an officer [British] intervened when one of his men was being beaten up by some Japanese guards, and he was horribly beaten up by quite a number of them." All of which led Peter Lee to this conclusion: "My considered opinion, over the whole range of our experience, was that the Japanese treatment of prisoners of war was brutal, sadistic and uncivilized."

So, given all that, how did he manage to survive? "Well, the natural emotion is anger. That's the natural emotion of anyone, any reasonable person — if they're attacked it's to defend themselves. But as a prisoner of war of the Japanese you very quickly realized that was not on. If you attempted to defend yourself you were bashed senseless . . . And the law of survival comes in. You have to realize the situation you're in and order your actions according to that situation. In other words, in those situations you have to take it. In the old British phrase, you have to grin and bear it."

The man who sat in front of me as he said those words, looked like a well-turned-out schoolmaster, and it was hard to imagine him sweating and steaming in the heat of Sandakan camp in Borneo. But then I realized that whilst he would, of course, have sweated, he would never have steamed. Not for him the intense expression of personal emotions proselytized by the so-called "me" generation in the 1960s. No, by an exercise of phenomenal self-discipline, Peter Lee had banished hatred and even anger from his emotional make-up.

Not only that, but during his time at Sandakan he excised another "negative" force too: self-pity. He saw that it was a "positive disadvantage to have that frame of mind as a prisoner of war. The best thing you could do was to think of ways of assisting the community . . . in those sort of circumstances, keep your mind and body occupied as much as you can and don't mope about and never feel sorry for yourself."

Peter Lee believed it was vital to try to focus only on "living in the present — to take the situation as it was, not as I wished it to be . . . There was no point in reminiscing about the past — about your family, about your friends, because the past was the past and all you did if you reflected on the past, in relation to the horrible present, was to torture yourself." And so he took whatever he could from each moment — even finding aspects of living in the camp that were positive: "We were fortunate that many people had gone into prison camps with books and we passed them around. So if you had a spare moment you'd read a book." He even managed to find humour in the camp: "There were amusing incidents. I was summoned across by one Japanese guard, I remember, and I expected to get a beating for something or other. One had no idea what you were being beaten for. And he beckoned me over and when I got there he said to me, in very stilted English: 'Easto is easto, westo is westo — no bloody mixo!' He'd obviously been told that by one of the lads, to come over and say this to me."

I found it hard to reconcile Peter Lee's words, both with the other recollections of Sandakan I had read — stories of torture and abuse — and with the sights I had personally witnessed at the place. The camp is now a museum, in which I had seen a replica of the "punishment hut" where POWs were kept in restricted space without proper sustenance to be taken out only for regular beatings. It was not that Peter denied these realities; rather that he chose not to focus upon them. His strength of mind, his stoicism, his toughness, all of these qualities became his protection against self-pity and a spiral of physical and mental decline.

Then, in August 1943, came a surprise announcement: "We were suddenly informed that we had to be ready — all officers, with the exception of ten who were allowed to stay." No one knows exactly why the Japanese decided to move the officers to a different camp. One possible reason was that, after discovering a small resistance movement at Sandakan, the Japanese had concluded that the remaining NCOs and ordinary soldiers should be without leadership from above. Peter confessed that he would have "given my right arm to have stayed ... It's rather like being separated from your family." But as events turned out, to have remained at Sandakan would almost certainly have resulted in his death. Food rations were cut still further for the remaining 2500 POWs — 1800 Australian and 700 British — at Sandakan; then, in January 1945, those POWs who were thought fit enough were forced to march back through the jungle to Jesselton. Virtually no one survived that journey. By the time the war ended, of the 2500 POWs left at Sandakan in August 1943 only six Australians, who had managed to run off into the jungle during the trek, had survived. Every single one of the 700 British prisoners had died. "Absolute horror!" recalled Peter Lee of his reaction at learning the news: "Because nobody at the time had any idea that such a thing could possibly occur in what is called a civilized world."

With hindsight, of course, we can see that all the pre-conditions for this crime existed within the Japanese Imperial Army: the Japanese contempt for prisoners of war, their own belief that to surrender was

117

contemptible, the brutality that pervaded the administrative and leadership structure of the military and the Japanese desire to work the POWs like beasts of burden on starvation rations. Given all this, an atrocity like Sandakan was always possible.

Although Peter Lee believes, understandably, that what happened at Sandakan was a "major crime", he is wary of drawing general conclusions about human nature from his experience: "I think various races of people have different ways of thinking. They're brought up in a different way, they're brought up in different societies, they have different values. And it's rather useless trying to apply your own values, the values you've been taught as a child throughout your life — of civilized behaviour, for example."

After the war Peter Lee chose to join the Colonial Service, serving first in Africa and then in Hong Kong. But when I met him, at the end of the twentieth century, the world of the Empire had long disappeared. The "colonies" that Peter Lee had served so faithfully were now independent countries. But it was important, I thought as I said goodbye to him, that we all still recognize the worth of the "old-fashioned" values that helped him to survive the horror of Japanese imprisonment.

TATIANA NANIEVA
AND THE REVENGE OF STALIN

One moment can change a whole life — and the moment that changed Tatiana Nanieva's life occurred on the morning of 26 October 1942. It was a bright and sunny day in the Ukraine, and she was working as a nurse in a forward Soviet-military field hospital. Suddenly she heard a terrifying, metallic clanking noise in the distance, and when she looked up she saw tanks appear on the horizon. They were pitch-black against the sun, and she knew at once they were German.

Up until this moment her life had been filled with certainty. She was a devoted Communist who thought that "everything was wonderful in our country — that there could be no other kind of life which was better than ours . . . I was always in a good frame of mind; I was always an organizer, always full of initiative." When the Germans invaded in June 1941 she had "rushed like lightning to be drafted". Once in the army she had been accepted into the Communist party via the "fast-track acceptance scheme" and had received her full party-membership card on 11 September 1942 — just six weeks before the arrival of German tanks into her life.

Alhough she was only 22 years old, she had already experienced battle. The Germans frequently encircled

Soviet troops and created chaos — and on several previous occasions that year Tatiana and her medical unit had been caught in one of these "cauldrons": "People are very resourceful — using lanes and paths, crawling — they got out somehow and regrouped . . . It was like porridge out there . . . Who was shooting at whom?"

But this time was different. The Germans had appeared so suddenly and in such force that no escape was possible: "But you know I never thought about death. Rather, and it might be stupid to say this, I thought it was impossible to survive in a war like that. I was always ready for death, as long as it didn't find me in one bad place [i.e. the toilet]."

"The political officer said, 'Split up and run!'" she recalled but "there was nothing to run to, not one thing, nowhere." Bullets flew around and dive bombers joined the attack from above. "I got a flesh wound — not deep, it just glanced through . . . And that was my good fortune. This is where my luck, or bad luck you can say, began. If it had gone deeper and broken a bone then I would have been executed. I would not have been able to walk when later they [the Germans] rounded us up."

Then, suddenly, she remembered her party-membership card. This one document, which had been so precious to her just moments before, had now become her death warrant: "I pulled out my membership card and tried to bury it in the ground so they wouldn't get their hands on it. I couldn't bury it deep and I don't know where the place is now — but I buried it." Moments later the Germans were upon them: "We were herded off in a bunch to some house, or some kind of gathering point. In the morning, the Germans began combing the remnants. And who couldn't move was shot. So here I was in some small way lucky that I could move and I remained alive. After that life started spinning in large circles."

The certainties of Tatiana Nanieva's previous life were destroyed for ever. That one day, 26 October 1942, was the fulcrum on which her life turned. The moment was so memorable that, when I met her in the late 1990s, she said that when she closed her eyes she could still instantly "imagine the sky is bright — as bright as on 26 October and the planes are glistening as they fly on to Baku above". It was almost as if for her that one day marked a moment of enlightenment, of revelation as to the nature of her own life and the world she lived in. But it was to be a revelation of the worst kind imaginable as she was transported to a prison camp in Poland. Soviet prisoners like her were treated appallingly by the Germans. Tatiana was to beat the odds and survive, but only after suffering hugely: "When we got to Czestochowa [in southern Poland] we were washed and sent to the barracks ... What paralysed me with fear was when they began to choose pretty girls. There were a lot of us, but there were a dozen or so who were pretty ... And they'd be taken away to satisfy their needs. Then they'd be returned, so dishevelled. But I wasn't taken in such a group and I'm glad that they overlooked me."

As has been noted elsewhere in this book (see Hajime Kondo, page 74) whilst the Japanese Imperial Army and the Red Army committed many rapes during the war, there seem to have been fewer instances of German soldiers perpetrating the crime. None the less rapes did occur — there were even instances of rape in the most notorious camp of all, Auschwitz.[1] And Tatiana Nanieva bears witness to the fact that rape was committed in German labour camps as well. No matter which camp they were transferred to, the rapes continued: "We were already in barracks. And right in front — brutally — right in front of your eyes the Hun would take a girl and he'd lay her out, like a hound taking a bitch. Afterwards he might even spit at her. And the girl would get up, come back dishevelled and you'd feel so sorry for her. That happened a lot. That didn't happen to me, I say again, because of my face or my character.

"You know," she added. "We weren't people in their eyes. They had a completely different way of thinking. They were beings of a higher race and we were their subjects, slaves or underlings. We weren't people . . . They loved themselves very much."

But as the war continued, Tatiana Nanieva and the rest of the Soviet women held captive in the German camp were sustained by one hope — that the Red Army was approaching: "We knew our armies were in Warsaw. It's right close by to where we lived in the last camp . . .

---

[1] Laurence Rees, *Auschwitz: The Nazis and the "Final Solution"*, (BBC Books, 2005), pp. 190–192

We believed that victory was at hand and that we would be liberated and that a normal life would begin again . . . I was yearning for my motherland, for my family. And I really wanted to live so badly." And when the day finally came that the Red Army neared the camp, Tatiana heard them arrive with "pomp — singing songs . . . Do you know what kind of mood they were in? One of victory. They walked so proudly, with heads up, with a great sense of achievement." She was overjoyed when she saw her fellow countrymen. At last, she thought, she could put the ordeal of her imprisonment behind her. At last, she thought, she could return to the straight and certain path she had been travelling on before the arrival of the black German tanks into her life on that bright October day in 1942.

But she was wrong. "Two [Red Army] officers approached me. One was angry, all het up. 'So how did you live it up here?' he said, or something of that kind. 'You whores!' I was a whore in his eyes. He grabbed his pistol. The second [officer], maybe he was less drunk or something, he signalled me to beat it: 'Just run for it!' Later we found out that the one who had slighted us, who went for his gun, had suffered his own agony. The Germans had executed his sister. Therefore many of our soldiers acted coarsely towards those girls who had been deported to Germany only because their family had suffered. Plenty of them were really inflamed: 'The Germans shot his sister and you're [still] alive!' It meant that I was just a whore. Just a whore."

The "indescribable joy" that Tatiana Nanieva had felt at the arrival of the Red Army vanished in an instant.

Not only were individual soldiers angry with her and the other Soviet prisoners, they soon learnt that they also faced the wrath of another, even more powerful enemy — Josef Stalin. The Soviet leader had decreed that the Soviet Union had no citizens in German captivity — "only traitors". "Prisoners were not envisaged by our leadership," said Tatiana. "We weren't allowed to surrender. You have to commit suicide — not surrender."

Instead of immediate liberation and return to her homeland, she was sent to a Soviet "filtration" camp where she was interrogated for days. In essence the investigators only ever asked one question — over and over again. "What orders did the Germans give you? What orders did the Germans give you?"

"Even if you could tear yourself to pieces," she said, "you couldn't prove a thing . . . absolutely no one believed you. 'I'm innocent! I'm innocent!' I said. But there was no way I could prove my innocence." Eventually the interrogators told her that she was to be charged under Article 58 of the Soviet penal code. "I asked, 'What does that mean?' And they replied, 'Betrayal of the Motherland.' And that's when I cried. I never betrayed her. I loved her very much, but at that point I cried for the first time." After a 15-minute trial she was sentenced to six years in a Soviet labour camp with a further three years' exile and loss of rights: "Our treatment in the camps was felt more painfully [than treatment in German captivity]. We were at home." It wasn't until after Stalin's death in 1953 that she was able to return to the Ukraine. Then she got a job working on the river boats — but on reduced wages. She was punished throughout her career for the "crime" of being captured by the Germans in October 1942.

By the time I met her, in the late 1990s, she was so weakened from her time in the gulag that she confessed she was "breaking up completely . . . I've got broken vertebrae and a broken hip . . . Because of all the hunger my body deposits too little calcium in my bones." But despite all the horror in her personal history, it was fear of the future that obsessed her. As she sat in her freezing, rundown flat in the suburbs of Kiev, where she lived with her badly disabled husband, she revealed that "the most frightening thing is that we do not have anything to even bury ourselves. That's the most frightening thing." Again and again during the interview she repeated this concern — that she lacked enough money to pay for her own funeral. And looking around at the destitution in which she lived it was a wholly believable claim. By the end of the interview the combination of the terrible injustices in her past life and the practical horror of her current fears had deeply affected me and my camera crew. We asked how much a funeral in Kiev cost, and were told it was a few hundred dollars. So we pooled the money in our pockets and handed it to her. Tatiana Nanieva died a few weeks later.

We are taught in the West that 1945 marked the end of World War II. In that year the Allies destroyed Nazism and brought forth a new beginning. But for Tatiana Nanieva and millions like her in the Soviet

Union, 1945 marked not the end of their suffering but merely the beginning of a new phase. She did not cease suffering as a result of the war until the moment she drew her last breath in 1998.

ESTERA FRENKIEL
AND CHOICES IN THE GHETTO

To live through World War II often meant being faced with difficult — almost impossible — choices. Whether to pull the trigger, drop the bomb, hide your neighbour or save yourself; whether to die for your principles or live by expediency. But no one, I thought when I first heard of her dilemma, had wrestled with a potentially more impenetrable problem than Estera Frenkiel. The choice she had to make was stark — who should live and who should die.

In the spring of 1940 Estera Frenkiel and her parents were just three of the 160,000 Jews who were forced by the Nazis into a small area of the Polish city of Lodz. The German plan was to collect the Lodz Jews in this ghetto, prior to deportation to some other country. In the summer of 1940, believing the war was about to end, the Nazis even contemplated shipping the Jews to the island of Madagascar, off the coast of Africa, in a bizarre plan that would still have ultimately led to genocide — but not the Holocaust as we know it. But the war, of course, did not end in the summer of 1940 — which presented the Nazi administrators with a problem of their own making. What to do with the Jews they had imprisoned in the ghetto?

After a fractious internal debate, the Nazis decided to force the Lodz Jews to work in order to pay for food that would barely keep them alive. Hans Biebow, the Nazi ghetto manager, was the chief proponent of this scheme. He hadn't acted out of any desire to see the Jews survive; he merely wanted to advance his own career, help the German war effort and make money for himself on the side.

As with the other ghettos they established, the Nazis couldn't be bothered with the daily administration of the one in Lodz, so they made the Jews establish a council of elders to make day-to-day practical decisions. There was even a Jewish police force within the ghetto. Germans seldom entered its precincts, preferring to guard the Jews from watchtowers on the ghetto wall. This meant that the Jewish Council of Elders in Lodz, and especially its chairman, Mordechai Chaim Rumkowski, possessed considerable power over the lives of their fellow Jews. It also meant that those close to the centre of power around Rumkowski had the chance of living a better life than the majority of other Jews in the ghetto.

The teenage Estera Frenkiel was — in the context of the privations of the ghetto — one of these more "fortunate" ones since she was selected to work as a junior secretary in Rumkowski's office. Her new boss abused his position of power in a number of ways, not least by forcing some young women to satisfy his sexual desires.[1] But, for whatever reason, Estera was not chosen by Rumkowski as one of his sexual targets and she spent her time in his office unmolested by him.

She was still anxious, however, that she might be attacked not by Rumkowski but by the German ghetto manager. She knew what had happened to another Jewish girl of 16 or 17 who had taken Biebow some coffee in his office: "She gave him the coffee. He saw the pretty girl, and touched her up. In all her life the girl had not seen a German man. She had seen the Germans from afar but not close to. And she didn't want to do it. She was still a young girl. And she fought back. Thereupon he tore off her dress. It is highly likely that nothing happened because she ran away. And he shot her and hit her in her ear. She went back and lay down in her room. It was terrible."

From her privileged position in Rumkowski's office Estera Frenkiel learnt not only about the predatory sexual nature of the Nazi ghetto manager, but also about the true fate of Jews who were deported from the ghetto. One day in July 1942, Biebow's deputy handed her a letter for Rumkowski. It was part of her normal duties to open Rumkowski's mail, so she was able to read the contents of this special dispatch herself. The Nazi ghetto manager had written: "I request that you check immediately whether there is a

---

[1] Quoted in *Documents on the Holocaust*, edited by Yitzhak Arad, Israel Gutman and Abraham Margaliot (University of Nebraska Press and Yad Vashem, 1981), p.283

bone grinder in the ghetto. Either to be electrically or manually operated. The Sonderkommando at Kulmhof [Chelmno] is interested in such a grinder."

"One's heart misses a beat," said Estera. "The thoughts came flooding in — what for? Why? For what purpose? These questions came automatically." And immediately she posed these questions she knew the answer: "That these people [who had been deported] weren't alive any more and that they [the Nazis] didn't want the world to know what had taken place." She was now one of the few inhabitants of the ghetto who realized the truth — that the Nazis were murdering the Jews once they left the ghetto. And that knowledge makes what happened next all the more poignant.

In September 1942 the Nazis ordered the deportation from the ghetto of all those who could not work — the children, the sick and the elderly. And Rumkowski, believing that this was a necessary sacrifice, addressed his fellow Jews on the subject. "The ghetto has been struck a hard blow," he told them. "They demand what is most dear to it — children and old people . . . I never imagined that my own hands would be forced to make this sacrifice on the altar. In my old age I am forced to stretch out my hands and beg: 'Brothers and sisters, give them to me! Fathers and mothers, give me your children!' "[1]

---

[1] Entry for 14 September 1942, *The Chronicle of the Lodz Ghetto 1941–1944*, edited by Lucjan Dobroszycki (Yale University Press, 1984), p.252

"The children were taken away from their parents," recalled Estera Frenkiel, "and their screams reached the sky. Many mothers simply went with their children."

It is one of the most controversial moments of the Holocaust. Those who support Rumkowski point to the fact that the only hope of keeping the ghetto "productive" in the eyes of the Nazis was to cooperate with the removal of those who weren't working. Those who condemn him raise the issue not just of his hand-in-glove cooperation with the Nazis over this and other issues of governance in the ghetto, but also the disturbing fact that Rumkowski and those close to him enjoyed a better quality of life in the ghetto as a consequence.

It wasn't only that Rumkowski and these others received more food, it was that at the time of the September deportations they were given the opportunity to save their own offspring. "Biebow came to our office," said Estera Frenkiel, "and said, 'I shall give you ten release forms for the release of your children.' And quickly as I could, I typed them up on my machine so that he could sign them. Not only I got these forms, but my colleagues did as well." Estera now had the power of life and death. She had the chance to save ten lives — children, the sick or the elderly. Whom would she choose to escape the eventual attentions of the bone-grinder machine? How much would she agonize over this terrible choice?

The answer is: not at all. She didn't agonize for a second, but acted purely by instinct: "What could I do? I also had close family. I had an uncle who had to be saved. I had a cousin. To me, one's own family is always closer. I had to take care of them all. Out of these ten certificates I had first to consider my own relatives . . . in these cases tears are shed, but when there are so many tears, then one thinks only of one's own situation." And once she had saved her own relatives, she turned to those closest to her family: "I gave the neighbours two certificates and also gave the caretaker, who had a little girl, one as well, so that these three release forms were used up almost immediately . . . The children [of the neighbour] used to come to my home, to my flat. I knew them. They weren't my children, but they were children I had known, and once one knows someone it gets very difficult."

Estera Frenkiel wasn't about to pretend, long after the event, that she had been driven by anything other than a desire to protect those nearest to her. She did confess that "later on" in the ghetto she experienced a slight "guilty conscience" when she saw the despair of mothers whose children had been deported. Once or twice she felt that perhaps she should have taken more care over the destination of her ten release forms — maybe even using some of them to save people who might objectively have been of more use to the ghetto as a whole — but these feelings never lasted long. Ultimately, she was never shaken from the belief that she had done the right thing. In crisis, she believed, we all look after ourselves and those closest to us first. "When it came to the deportations, the [Jewish] ghetto police [who cooperated with the Germans in organizing the action] could keep their children." She paused after saying these words, before almost spitting out, "Do you understand now?"

The chronicle of the Lodz ghetto, written by Jews who were there at the time, confirms that, "To encourage the Jewish police and the firemen to conduct the operation conscientiously, promises that their closest relations would be spared had been made . . . there were some 1500 of these lucky ones who in spite of their age and infirmity were spared resettlement. Of course, these were not people who were making any contribution to society, not even people able to perform any especially valuable work in the ghetto but were, we repeat, people with connections." In the event, the certificates brought no more than a stay of execution for the children, the elderly and the sick. "Later," said Estera, "everyone was sent away whom one had previously rescued. That's how it is. That's the reality."

In the summer of 1944 the ghetto was liquidated and most of the surviving Jews were transported to Auschwitz where the majority — including Rumkowski and his family — were murdered. But some, Estera Frenkiel among them, were sent to the women's concentration camp at Ravensbrück: "That was hell. That was pure hell. The ghetto was a story in its own right. That was a tale of hunger. That was a battle for food, avoiding deportation. But there [in Ravensbrück] it was hell; neither day nor night." Ravensbrück reinforced the bleak view of human nature that she had formed in the ghetto: life is a Darwinian struggle in which everyone strives first and foremost to look after themselves and their family: "You had to keep the shoes you wore under your head or on your chest," she said, talking of life in Ravensbrück. "And even then they were stolen during the night. I was beside myself."

Fortunately for Estera Frenkiel, after only a few weeks in Ravensbrück she survived a "selection" and was transported to a Nazi labour camp where she managed to work until liberation. After the war she settled in Israel, but agreed to return to Lodz in 1996 for her filmed interview. My last memory of this remarkable woman is of her standing defiantly dry-eyed in Lodz cemetery after the filming was over. As she stood by the cemetery wall, I remarked to her that she was one of the toughest and most decisive people I had ever met.

"If I wasn't tough and decisive," she replied, "I wouldn't be standing here today."

MARIA PLATONOW
AND BETRAYAL BY THE BRITISH

In January 1991 a film called *A British Betrayal*, which I had written, produced and directed, transmitted on BBC2 — and it got me into a lot of trouble. Lord Aldington, a senior figure in the Conservative party, took great exception to it, complained to the chairman of the BBC and then made a formal complaint, which was considered independently by the BBC's internal complaints unit. Only after lengthy consideration did the complaints unit dismiss the charges against the film. Obviously not satisfied, Lord Aldington took his grievance to an appeal committee of the BBC's governors, which — again after very lengthy deliberation — decided not to uphold his complaint. Rumours that he would mount a legal attack on me and the film then circulated for many years.

Why did Lord Aldington, and a number of other senior figures in British society who supported him, respond to the film in this way? After all, at no stage in any of the exhaustive analysis undertaken by the various authorities was any factual error discovered in it. My own belief is that the reason so many people loathed the film and disliked me for making it was that it told an awkward truth: in the immediate aftermath of the conflict the British had betrayed the very principles

135

that many people believed they had fought the war to uphold.

World War II is looked on by many today as a uniquely moral war — a conflict in which the good guys behaved well and the bad guys behaved badly. Indeed, in Britain it is almost the period by which we define ourselves: our values, our beliefs and our sense of self can all be traced in large measure back to those years. All of which makes it inconvenient that there exist moments in this history when the good guys did not behave well — moments, in fact, when the good guys behaved very badly indeed. And the circumstances surrounding the handover by the British to the Soviets in 1945 of around 42,000 Cossacks make for particularly disturbing reading.

What is ironic about this story of suffering is that it occurred immediately after the war in Europe was over, at a time when many thought the worst was behind them. Soldiers of British V Corps arrived in the province of Carinthia in southern Austria on 8 May 1945, the day after the armistice had been signed. They thought, as they surveyed this beautiful land of high mountains and lush valleys, that they had reached a paradise of peace. But they were wrong, because this part of Europe was now awash with hundreds of thousands of refugees, many of whom had been driven west before the advancing Red Army. Mixed in with them were thousands of enemy troops — often with their families — who had fought against Stalin and who now wished to surrender to the British. Prominent amongst them were the Cossacks, who had fought for the Germans in a brutal war in Yugoslavia against Marshal Tito's partisans — a war in which atrocities had been committed on both sides.

In May 1945 the teenage Maria Platonow arrived with her mother and the rest of her family at a camp at Peggetz, near the town of Lienz. It held about 5000 people, and was one of a number of camps set up by the British along the valley of the Drau in order to hold the Cossacks. Maria had relatives in the Cossack Cavalry Corps and they were all overjoyed that they had managed to surrender to the British: "I thought these British are such nice, nice people . . . I loved the British people because I was brought up on the British literature, and my mother and myself, we had all the books of Dickens and Shakespeare." More than that, in common with others in the camp, Maria believed in the sanctity of British "justice". Now that they were in British hands they were certain they would be treated according to the rule of law. When I met Maria Platonow at her home in Canada in 1990 she was still, 55 years after the event, visibly moved by her recollection of the happiness she had felt when the British had taken responsibility for her and her family. Technically, of course, the Cossacks were prisoners of the British, but she and her family believed they were in British care.

Initially, British troops were for the most part friendly and approachable. But all this bonhomie was shortly to change. For the British government had agreed with Stalin that all Soviet citizens encountered in their area of control would be handed over to the

Red Army for repatriation — whether they wished to go back or not.

Many of the Cossacks were citizens of the Soviet Union. But equally, an unidentified number were not: they held other passports or were simply displaced people with no settled allegiance. What was needed was a filtering and selection process that would divide the Cossacks into two groups — the Soviet citizens who had to be returned to the Soviet Union, and the non-Soviet ones who most definitely should not be handed over. The stakes could scarcely have been higher. The future British prime minister, Harold Macmillan, who was British political adviser for the area, wrote in his diary at the time that he was aware that to hand over the Cossacks to Stalin's men "is condemning them to slavery, torture and probably death".[1] Nonetheless, British V Corps did not instigate any systematic screening in order to save those Cossacks who were not Soviet citizens, and who therefore should never have been deported.

The commander of V Corps was Lieutenant-General Charles Keightley, and his chief of staff was a bright young brigadier called Toby Low (later Lord Aldington). On 21 May 1945, four days before his thirty-first birthday, Brigadier Low decreed that whole formations of Cossacks, en bloc, were eligible for repatriation — whether they were Soviet citizens or not. He later

---

[1] Harold Macmillan, *War Diaries: Politics and War in the Mediterranean, January 1943–May 1945* (London 1984) pp. 757–8

138

maintained that his ruling could have permitted some screening to take place since the document contained the clause: "Individual cases will <u>NOT</u> be considered unless particularly pressed." (He said the words "particularly pressed" implied some kind of selection — although, of course, the words "Individual cases will <u>NOT</u> be considered" meant the opposite.) But later orders issued by other officers in V Corps, after Brigadier Low had left Austria on the 22nd, made it apparent that every Cossack — regardless of citizenship — was to be handed over to the Red Army.

The unjust, but convenient, decision not to instigate the necessary screening brought an additional benefit for the British. It meant that they could take the Cossack officers away from their families with the minimum of fuss — as long as they lied to them. On 28 May Cossack officers at Peggetz camp were told that they were needed at an important meeting to discuss what was to happen to them. British officers gave their word of honour that the Cossacks would be safely returned to their families that evening. The Cossacks then spent time cleaning their best uniforms and polishing their medals before climbing on board the waiting trucks.

Maria Platonow's uncle dropped in on her and her mother before leaving: "And I said, 'Where are you going?' He said, 'Well, Mary, I come to say goodbye because we are now going to the conference.' He smiled and said, 'Oh, Mary, don't you worry because you know we have the word of British officer[s] and they told us there is just a conference and at supper time I will come back and tell you all about it.' So we say goodbye and he climbed on to an open truck and waved to me and he was gone. I never saw him again."

There was no conference: no meeting to discuss the Cossacks' fate — because their fate had already been decided. Around 1500 of the Cossack officers were driven along the valley of the Drau to a secure barracks at Spittal, where they were to stay overnight before being handed to the Soviets the next morning. When the Cossack officers learnt of this deception they became desperate, and at least three of them committed suicide during the night.

Back up the valley at Peggetz camp, the families of the Cossack officers spent a night of despair, realizing that they had been deceived and that their husbands, fathers, brothers and uncles would not be returning. Then, on the morning of 1 June, a unit of the Argyll and Sutherland Highlanders arrived to clear the camp and transport everyone to the Soviet lines for repatriation. No systematic screening of any sort was planned to separate the non-Soviet citizens who should not have been handed over.

Major "Rusty" Davies was one of the officers with the Argyll and Sutherland Highlanders that day. He witnessed horrific scenes at the camp: "Soldiers were trying to drag the odd child, the odd woman, the odd man — and literally throw them on to the trucks. And by this time there were mothers who'd lost their children. Children lost their mothers . . . There were people trying to throw themselves on the bayonets. There were people trying to shoot themselves. And one chap did rush forward, pressed the trigger of one rifle and blew the head off a chap standing alongside him."

Maria Platonow watched as an old man fell to his knees in front of British troops: "He was terrified. He was kissing the boots [of the soldiers] and he said, 'Please don't send me back. Don't send me back.' And they were hitting him on the head methodically, without any expression on their faces. I just looked at them. I was so stunned. I say, 'Is that truly happening?' And they hit him and they hit him and the blood was streaming off his face and then finally he lost consciousness and they threw him on the truck."

The exact number of fatalities on this black day for the honour of the British army is unknown — estimates vary from a handful to a hundred. Major Davies, disgusted by the scenes he had witnessed, instigated on his own initiative a rough screening of some of the remaining people in the camp. Maria and her family — who held Yugoslav passports — subsequently escaped deportation, but not before an unknown number of other non-Soviet citizens at Peggetz and other Cossack camps had already been "repatriated".

It is significant that many of the survivors, like Maria, focus their anger not just on the injustice of the forced repatriation, but also on the manner in which the British carried out the action. Some of the Cossack officers, tricked into thinking that they were only leaving the camp for a few hours, never said a proper goodbye to their loved ones. The anguish of that one denied farewell, of the words unsaid, of the embrace that never occurred, torments their relatives to this day.

Lord Aldington played an important part in the chain of causation that led to this tragedy. He issued the ruling that in its key opening paragraphs categorized whole Cossack formations as "Soviet" and therefore eligible for repatriation. And though he refused to be interviewed on camera for my film, I did meet him twice whilst researching the subject. He was clearly bruised by the infamous libel trial he had just brought — and won — against the historian Nikolai Tolstoy, who in a pamphlet full of hyperbole had accused him of being a war criminal whose offences could be compared to the "worst butchers of Nazi Germany".

I wanted to know, not surprisingly, why Lord Aldington had decided to categorize the Cossacks en masse as Soviets. But what was interesting was that he claimed not to remember the reasons behind the wording of his ruling — other than to claim, implausibly I thought, that sections of it could be interpreted as allowing screening. He accepted no blame for what had happened; if other people had subsequently read his ruling in a certain way, that was their responsibility.

Some historians, like Nikolai Tolstoy (whose pioneering research into this subject, it has to be said, made my film possible), have constructed elaborate conspiracy theories around the decision to send all the Cossacks back. But having met Lord Aldington and studied the relevant documents, I didn't agree. I thought the most likely reason for Aldington's action was the all too prosaic one that senior British officers wanted to be "rid" of the problem of the Cossacks as quickly as possible. They had many other calls on their time — not least dealing with Tito's bandit partisans — and they had little or no sympathy for the plight of the Cossacks.

An insight into the mentality of some senior British officers at the time is given by the contents of a cable that Alexander Kirk, the American political adviser for the area, sent to the State Department on 14 May 1945. Kirk had questioned decisions General Robertson, the British chief army administration officer based at Field Marshal Alexander's headquarters, was taking regarding both the Cossacks and the surrendered Yugoslav forces: "CAO [Robertson] expressed disappointment that we did not seem to agree with him on this point but added that he was faced with a grave administrative problem, with hundreds of thousands of German POWs on his hands and could not bother at this time about who might or might not be turned over to the Russians and the [Yugoslav] partisans to be shot."[1]

The words "could not bother at this time" seem to capture the mood of these British officers precisely. They didn't care that, against Allied policy, they were handing over a number of people "to slavery, torture and probably death". After all, hadn't all the Cossacks — even the non-Soviet ones — been the enemy? A number of British officers acted callously — and unjustly — at a time when they were under a variety of

---

[1] US National Archives 740.00119 Control (Italy)/5 – 1945

different pressures, and then more or less forgot about it.

These two encounters, with Lord Aldington and with Maria Platonow, were, I felt, a reminder of a reality that we sometimes forget. Just because a decision has a catastrophic impact on thousands of people, it doesn't necessarily need to have had any real effect on the handful of people who made it.

TOIVI BLATT
AND THE PHILOSOPHY OF SOBIBOR

I learnt a huge amount from Toivi Blatt; not just, as I had expected, from his specific personal experiences — first as a Polish Jew under Nazi occupation, and then from his ordeal at Sobibor death camp — but also generally about the behaviour of human beings under the most extreme conditions imaginable. More than almost anyone else I met, his views ought, I believe, to influence how we think about the mentality of people in crisis.

He was born in the small town of Izbica in eastern Poland in 1927. Before the war around 3600 Jews lived in the town and rubbed along with the majority Catholic population without too many difficulties. Toivi in particular escaped suffering from much direct anti-Semitism: "I was in a privileged situation because my father was a legionnaire [a veteran of the Polish army] ... He was wounded, he was invalided, and because of it he was very well known as a Polish patriot. So I was protected."

All that changed with the arrival of the Nazis. And whilst their anti-Semitism was obvious, what was surprising to Toivi was the sudden change in the attitude of many of the Polish Catholics: "The [Catholic] population noticed that the Jews are [now] second-class. You could do with them whatever you want without problems . . . a lot of them [the Jews] were beaten up now . . . In the end I was more afraid of my neighbours, Christian people, Catholics, than of the Germans because the Germans didn't recognize me — my neighbours did."

In April 1943, the Germans decided to clear Izbica of all Jews. There had been periodic raids for the past year, but a number of Jews still remained — particularly the skilled leather workers in the local tannery. Many of these Jews thought they were of more use to the Nazis alive than dead. They were wrong.

"About four o'clock in the morning a rifle shot woke me up," said Toivi Blatt. "I ran to the window to look down and I saw the whole tannery surrounded by Nazis . . . I was apprehended, taken outside by a Nazi and pushed into a group of people . . . surrounded by guards . . . I realized that this was the end. What could I do?"

Then, suddenly, Toivi saw an opportunity to escape. One of the guards turned slightly away to light a cigarette: "Seeing this I took the chance and thought I must run now if I want to live. And I simply walked out."

But as he mingled with the rest of the villagers who had come to watch the deportations he felt immensely vulnerable: "I realized that I wouldn't be free for too long. At that time you know your best friend would be the person who pretends he doesn't know you at all. Anyway, looking around I saw my friend Janek. We were

146

very friendly. He was a guy who slept sometimes at my place."

He approached Janek, saying, "Please help me!" Janek replied, "Of course!" and told Toivi to run out of the village and up to a barn, not far from Janek's own house, and that he would meet him there in a few minutes. Toivi did as he was asked, but when he got to the barn he found it was padlocked.

As he waited for Janek a Polish Catholic woman saw him and shouted: "Toivi, run! Toivi, run!"

"What's happening?" asked Toivi.

"Janek is coming! Janek is coming!"

Toivi was bemused. Why should he run if Janek were coming? Then he turned to see Janek approaching with a German soldier, rifle at the ready.

"Janek!" exclaimed Toivi. "Tell me you are joking!"

"He's a Jew!" said Janek to the soldier.

And as the German began to take Toivi away, Janek said farewell in a way that still haunts him today.

"Goodbye, Toivi," said Janek. "I will see you [next] on a shelf in a soap store." (There had been rumours that the Nazis were killing Jews and turning the fat from their bodies into soap.)

Although Toivi finds this incident "difficult even now" to talk about, he was not completely surprised by Janek's action since "it wasn't the first time" that he had seen such "betrayal".

Toivi was taken back down to the marketplace where he found that his mother, father and brother had all been captured and were awaiting deportation: "I was scared. I don't even remember how I felt. I was scared that this is the last day of my life, and when you are young and you are fifteen years old . . . you see the trees, you see the flowers — you want to live."

The Jews of Izbica were then shoved on to freight wagons. And just as on the train taking Samuel Willenberg and his fellow Jews to Treblinka (see page 104), the people on board didn't want to believe that the Nazis planned to murder them: "Leather is very important for the German army," Toivi heard people say. "They won't kill us. They will take us to a concentration camp."

But after several hours the train arrived at Sobibor, a death camp that functioned in a similar way to Treblinka (see pages 104–108). What struck Toivi was how "nice" the place looked. He had been expecting a "kind of hell" but instead he saw flowers and a freshly painted fence. The station had been decorated to look like a normal train stop, with timetables and signs. Toivi was certain it was a trick, designed to fool transports of Jews arriving from outside Poland — people who had not heard the rumours about what went on here. But still, even though by now most of the other Jews from Izbica must have realized that the rumours were true, and that they were about to be murdered, they didn't resist as they were ordered to split up into two groups — women and children on one side, men on the other — and then moved further into the camp.

Many people today are surprised that prisoners arriving on transports at death camps who knew, or strongly suspected, that they were about to die didn't somehow fight back. For the most part the Jews went to their deaths without causing the Nazis many difficulties. It's something that some Jews today — particularly in Israel, in my experience — are almost ashamed of. "I'm not one of those Polish, submissive-type Jews," I remember one Israeli telling me, when he found out the subject of the film I was making, "I'm an Old Testament, blood-and-thunder Jew! I wouldn't have gone so quietly!"

Having met many survivors of the camps, and also a number of the perpetrators involved in the killing process, I find this charge of implicit "cowardice" at best ill-informed and at worst an insult to the memory of those who were murdered. For it was virtually impossible to resist. In the first place, the new arrivals were harassed by tough and vicious guards armed with whips and batons from the moment they got off the railway wagons. Furthermore, they disembarked only once they were already in the camp behind wire fences, above which were watchtowers containing guards with machine guns.

Even if the arriving Jews could somehow have negotiated those defences, another problem would have confronted them. Where could they run to? They knew that many of the local non-Jewish population were willing to help the Nazis persecute the Jews. Even the Jewish Sonderkommando who had worked at Sobibor for weeks knew the difficulties that lay beyond the wire fence: "Where will you go when you escape finally into the forest?" says Toivi Blatt. "I have seen practically every day [once he became a member of the Sonderkommando] farmers who lived near by coming with Jews they caught hiding some place in the field. And [they] said we'll throw them over the fence for five pounds of sugar and a bottle of vodka. So where could we escape?"

And there was a further difficulty. Many of the Jews were old, or sick, or mothers with young children. It was a problem graphically brought home to me by the testimony of a woman I met in Lithuania, who was one of the rare cases of a Jew who had successfully managed to escape from the Nazis. As a young woman in her late teens in 1941 she was ordered out of her village, along with the rest of the Jewish population, and forced to march towards a forest where they all knew they would be shot. But since there weren't that many guards around them, she resolved to try to escape through the fields. She asked the woman next to her to come with her. "But how can I?" she responded, gesturing down at her two little children. "How can I leave them?"

The presence of children was clearly a decisive factor for many mothers caught up in the maelstrom of the Holocaust. Even at Auschwitz, where a full selection process was held to divide those who could work from those who were to be killed immediately, the commandant, Rudolf Hoess, remarked that virtually no mother chose to prolong her own life by opting for work when it meant that her children would have to face the gas chambers on their own.

Then, of course, no doubt some of the arriving Jews still wanted desperately to believe that the rumours about Sobibor were untrue. Perhaps this was, as the

Nazis insisted, merely a hygiene stop and perhaps they were genuinely going to have a shower?

But Toivi Blatt did not believe that Sobibor was as innocent as the Nazis claimed. And when the guards asked if anyone amongst the new arrivals were a carpenter, he was one of a number of people who put up their hands. He wasn't a carpenter — he simply "wanted to live". And as he waited, he "prayed to this German, please take me! And I believe that my strong will some way reached [him] . . . because I believe there's some communication besides vocal communication between people. So I think that my strong will reached this German whilst he was pacing back and forward in front of the group, and I felt he looked at me and I said to myself, 'God help me!' and he said, 'Come out, you little one.' "

And so Toivi was included amongst the tiny group of people who were sent to join the Sonderkommando and so spared from immediate death. But he watched as his mother, father and younger brother were all taken away to the gas chambers. And he was surprised at his own reaction to this tragic sight: "To be honest, I didn't feel anything . . . You see, if one of my parents had died two days earlier it would have been a terrible tragedy. I would cry day and night. And now in the same hour and the same minute I lost my father, my brother, my mother . . . and I didn't cry — I didn't even think about this . . . and after the war when I met survivors and I asked them did you cry, 'No, I didn't' [they said]. It's like nature protects us . . . If I show any sign [that] I weep [then] I would be killed."

151

Once he became a member of the Sonderkommando, Toivi found that his desire for self-preservation was so strong that he was able to perform the most potentially heart-rending tasks without apparent emotional damage to himself. He cut the hair of women and girls who were just about to be murdered and watched as they were sent, naked to the gas chambers. Still he did not cry.

Once he was ordered by one of the German administration officers to take two naked girls down from a truck that had just arrived at the camp. The girls had been hiding in the countryside and had been captured by local farmers. Toivi was told to escort the girls over in the direction of the gas chambers whilst the German officer followed at a distance. One of the girls, who was about 17 or 18, started pleading with Toivi, begging him to save her. Toivi, of course, could do nothing and left her with the guards at the entrance to the gas chambers. Moments later he heard rifle shots — the Nazis couldn't be bothered to start up a gas chamber to murder just two individuals.

Toivi believes that the SS man ordered him to take the girls over to the gas chambers so that he himself would be spared their inevitable pleading. That was, after all, what the Sonderkommando were there for as far as the Germans were concerned — to take as much of the emotional stress away from the perpetrators as possible.

It took the arrival of a group of Jewish Red Army prisoners in September 1943 to act as the catalyst for change in the attitude of many of the Sonderkommando.

These Soviet soldiers had been trained as a fighting force and had retained their internal discipline under the charismatic leadership of a Red Army lieutenant called Alexander Pechersky. Over the next few weeks they planned a revolt. And on 14 October, having lured a number of the guards into the Sobibor workshops and killed them, many of the Sonderkommando rushed and then breached the barbed-wire fence. Amongst them was Toivi Blatt: "I was running to the forest. I fell down about two or three times — each time I thought I'm hit but I got up, nothing happened to me, and I ran to the forest, a hundred metres, fifty metres, finally the forest."

Around 300 of the 600 Sobibor Sonderkommando managed to escape that day. But, significantly, the majority of those who escaped did not survive the war. Many were handed back to the Germans by non-Jewish Poles. Toivi, however, was one of the minority who did make it — and whilst he found that some non-Jewish Poles did try to betray him during the war, equally a number helped him to survive.

After this searing life experience, Toivi is clear what lesson we should take from his personal history. "People asked me," he said, " 'What did you learn?' And I think I'm only sure of one thing — nobody knows themselves. The nice person on the street, you ask him, "Where is North Street?" and he goes with you half a block and shows you, and is nice and kind. That same person in a different situation could be the worst sadist. Nobody knows themselves. All of us could be good people or bad people in these [different] situations. Sometimes when somebody is really nice to me I find myself thinking, How will he be in Sobibor?"

CONNIE SULLY
AND RAPE BY THE JAPANESE

I had wanted to meet Connie Sully very much. She had suffered at the hands of the Japanese in the early days of their invasion of Hong Kong in December 1941, and had never before spoken publicly about what had happened to her. She was therefore able to offer new first-hand testimony about an atrocity that had become infamous in the history of the former colony.

Connie had moved to South Africa after the war and now lived in the suburbs of Durban. But the South Africa to which Connie had emigrated to in the 1950s was nothing like the place I encountered in the year 2000. The injustice of apartheid had been removed, that's true, but the South Africa I saw was a rough and violent place. Just before I arrived, a guest at my hotel had been murdered as he'd taken a walk along the nearby beach at dusk, and the Indian lady who drove me in a cab to visit Connie told me that only the previous month her husband had been shot and killed in a car-jacking in central Durban.

Connie Sully lived with her sick husband in a kind of last white enclave on a hill above the city. She told me that when she had decided to emigrate the choice lay between Rhodesia (or Zimbabwe as it is known today),

Canada, South Africa and Australia. "Could've been worse," she said, "I could've picked Zimbabwe!"

There was a sad atmosphere in the house. Much of it was caused by the fact that both she and her husband were depressed that "the blacks" (as they put it) had gained power and that the two of them were now simply waiting out the end of their lives alone, in a place radically different from the one they'd originally bought into — one that, we must remember, had been based on the racist fantasy of white supremacy.

As we set up to film the interview, Connie sent her husband into another room to "look after the dogs". We all felt that "looking after the dogs" was something of a euphemism. It was clear that Connie didn't want her husband to hear what she had to tell us.

She began by saying that before the Japanese arrived she remembered a life of fun and pleasure in Hong Kong. Her parents had moved to the British colony when she was just three years old, so it had always been her "home". She'd left school at 16 and got a job working as a secretary at the Hong Kong and Shanghai Bank, but she found plenty of time for "swimming, hockey and tennis" and enjoying herself on the "many beautiful beaches". And though she lived in the heart of Asia she still felt "100 per cent" British.

The pleasurable tranquillity of her life in Hong Kong was smashed apart by the warplanes of the Japanese on 7 December 1941. They began bombing Hong Kong just five hours after the attack on the US naval base at Pearl Harbor in Hawaii.

Connie volunteered to act as a nurse and reported for duty at the makeshift hospital at Happy Valley racecourse on Hong Kong Island. She was on the roof of the building when Japanese planes swooped down overhead. "We saw planes coming down the valley," she said. "First of all we thought they were Americans, and then of course we saw the great sun on them. Then we realized . . . I'd never seen it before — bullets were coming out of the wings." What made Connie all the more shocked was that there were three red crosses on the Jockey Club roof, clearly signalling that this was a hospital: "So they could see that. But they never worried about that. Didn't mean anything to them."

Rather like Peter Lee (see page 112), Connie faced adversity with a "stiff upper lip". She revealed that, though she felt nervous and scared at the arrival of the Japanese planes, "When you've got a crowd of you, you mustn't show that. You mustn't show that you're afraid."

It was obvious from the first that the British defenders of Hong Kong stood no chance of holding out. The few outdated RAF planes that constituted the colony's entire air force had been destroyed on the ground at Kai Tak airfield moments into the initial Japanese attack. And Winston Churchill had already admitted to the War Cabinet in London that "there is not the slightest chance of holding Hong Kong or relieving it". The gigantic presence of the Japanese Imperial Army just across the hills in mainland China made the colony's swift capitulation inevitable.

Just two and a half weeks after the initial bombing, Connie Sully and the rest of the nurses at Happy Valley were confronted by 50 Japanese soldiers. They arrived at the hospital at seven o'clock on the morning of Christmas Day. "We felt a bit scared," she says, "but we'd all been told just to sit down and do things. We made dressings, we rolled bandages, unrolled them, rolled them. And one of the Japanese didn't like tin hats, and this one fellow, I think he'd been drinking . . . He came down to us, you see, and he had a revolver in his hand . . . I was pretty scared. I think I just froze. I was afraid to move, even bat an eyelid . . . But he only wanted this woman to take her [tin] hat off. But of course nobody at the time knew it, we were so scared . . . So they said, 'Take her hat off.' A few polite words were thrown in. And when she took it off and threw it away, he just nodded and walked off."

After the initial incident with the tin hat, the nurses weren't much bothered by the Japanese during the daytime. But one night soon after they had arrived, four Japanese soldiers came into the room where the nurses were sleeping, shone their torches around and selected four of the youngest women. They included Connie, the only non-Chinese girl taken.

All the women were forced upstairs to "a big open area. They'd taken everything out of it. It was just a shell. We were all in the same room. But I think we realized that to put up a fight was useless. They were armed. We weren't . . . They never said a word. Well, they couldn't speak [English] . . . And, unfortunately for us, we were all raped. Wasn't very nice. But if you tried to do anything you'd have got a bullet . . . it was either a bullet or you gave in. So I think I valued my life too much to take a bullet. And I thought, "Well, I can recover from the other, but I can't recover if I go." And then when they finished they just marched us back downstairs. I couldn't tell you what they looked like. I have no idea."

Like most well-brought-up Englishwomen of her generation, Connie had expected to remain a virgin until her wedding night, so the rape was her first experience of sex. "It was degrading. I think they must have thought it would be degrading. But you didn't give in. You just kept going. I mean, you felt it. For a long time afterwards I couldn't stand to look at them. But you get used to it. They say, 'Love your enemies.' Don't believe it."

She also felt that the Japanese had been motivated to commit the rapes for another reason: "Well, I mean [rape] that's their entertainment. They didn't have any radios or TVs or anything else. I know the British tommies used to sing and have concerts, but I never heard of the Japanese ever doing that."

The next day Connie and the other nurses who had been raped returned to their normal duties in the hospital. "The best thing to do was to get back down to it and work," she said. "People who sat down in camp died. People who just sat around and complained of what they'd lost, they were put in the cemetery. A lot of them died. You had to do things. You had to keep going. I mean, people did things they'd never thought of doing before."

But it was impossible for her simply to pretend that this crime had never happened. And she was helped in the immediate aftermath of the rape by a friend of her sister's who was in the same group of nurses: "She was quite a bit older than I was, and fortunately I had the camp bed next to her and she was very good. She gave me a lot of strength. Talking, just talking, was the only thing you could do. Couldn't do anything else."

Though she had to endure the hardship of the Japanese occupation until the end of the war, there was no repetition of the events of that night at the Happy Valley racecourse. And once the war was over, she tried to resume "normal" life. But it proved impossible to return her personality to the moment before the rape — not least because she still felt deep and unresolved revulsion for the Japanese: "When I was at work, when we started doing business with them, and they came, the first time I had to take one [Japanese businessman] into my boss, I said, 'I had to put some lead in my foot' because I wanted to lift it [and kick him]. It just made me sick that I had to bow and scrape to him, even though he was a businessman. But fortunately we never had much to do with them."

After she emigrated to South Africa she finally married, at the age of 45. But still the memory of the rape meant that "something was locked away in your own being". And it's a remembrance that could be triggered by watching the television: "I see these Japanese films, you know, the war films, and I sit absolutely mesmerized. And he [my husband] gets so angry because he knows I had a bad night. But

160

something gets you ... in my inside I'm fighting, knowing what they will do and what they can do. And it doesn't matter now — it's so many years later, but they're still the same."

Her post-war feelings of antipathy for the Japanese were partly focused around the refusal, as she saw it, of the Japanese government to accept full responsibility for the terrible crimes that had been committed by the Imperial Army: "The Japanese don't pay anything. They're not paying for any of the humiliating things that they did. I mean, they went into our flat and they went to the wardrobes and they just took the bayonets and slashed through your clothes. What good was that? We had a picture of my father in First World War uniform. They took it off the wall and they just put bayonets through it."

A few months after we filmed the interview, Connie's husband finally succumbed to the cancer from which he had been suffering. Connie herself died a few years later. She never revealed why she had allowed us to film an interview with her. But everyone who met her that day and listened to her speak knew the chief reason. It was as obvious as the sun in the clear blue South African sky above us. Connie had spoken out at the end of her days because she wanted the world to know how much she still hated the Japanese; for what they had done to her body, her mind and her whole life.

LUCILLE EICHENGREEN
AND ABUSE IN THE GHETTO

Lucille Eichengreen was forced to endure one of the most terrible physical and emotional journeys of the twentieth century. It was made all the worse by the fact that she was a child when she began it, and just 20 years old when the war ended. And on her journey she learnt first hand the reality that during the war violent prejudice was not confined to the Nazis, nor was the capacity to take abusive advantage of the young and vulnerable.

I listened to her tell her story in Krakow, where she had agreed to come to be filmed while on a trip to Poland. She was a small, handsome, immaculately groomed woman who spoke English perfectly.

"I was born 1 February 1925, in Hamburg, Germany," she began. "My father had a business of wine import and export, and from what I gathered after the war it was rather successful." She lived with her father, mother and younger sister in a solid, middle-class quarter of the city, in "a rather large apartment — it had about six or seven rooms. It had a room in the back for the maid.

"Until 1933 [the start of Nazi rule] it was very easy — it was very careless, carefree. We travelled a great deal — we were in Denmark, we were in Poland frequently. It was a very nice, comfortable life. We had tennis lessons, we had riding lessons and private English lessons."

Both her parents were originally Jews from Poland, and though everyone in the family spoke fluent German, Lucille was aware of her origins: "I thought of myself as Polish because I was told very early on that I had a Polish passport . . . When my parents didn't want us to understand something they spoke Polish or French." Her Polish background wasn't something that she thought at the time was of particular importance — though it came to be of considerable significance later on.

What she did notice was that when Adolf Hitler became chancellor of Germany on 30 January 1933, just two days before her eighth birthday, the effect on her and her younger sister was almost immediate: "The children that lived in the same building . . . no longer spoke to us. They wore the Hitler Youth uniform. They threw stones at us, they called us names . . . And we couldn't understand what we had done to deserve this. So the question always was why? And when we asked at home the answer pretty much was, 'Oh, it's a passing phase. It won't matter. It will normalize.'"

Lucille's and her sister's normal, happy childhood had been extinguished. They were told by their parents that they shouldn't draw attention to themselves on the street or in a bus. They should "stand in the back, don't talk loudly and don't laugh — just sort of disappear."

Their 45-minute walk to school became an ordeal. Other children shouted and spat at them while "the adults were looking away". Like other Jewish children she became afraid that anything she did or any question she asked "would be taken the wrong way and there would be a punishment". So she became suddenly "careful — and for a child that's very unusual. It is something that is acquired, not taught. You are not born with this feeling. It was acquired due to the circumstances . . . It's a feeling of, of a wasted life . . . I could have had fun, I could have had friends. All that was eliminated, and it really is not fair to treat a child in this manner."

Over the next few years a whole raft of anti-Semitic measures were imposed by the Nazis. Jewish children could no longer attend ordinary schools, or play sport with other non-Jewish children. Then, when the Nazis started investigating the citizenship of Jews living in Germany, it was revealed that Lucille was technically "Polish". Now she was bullied even by other Jewish children. "Remarks were made to a ten, twelve year old kid [like]: 'Well, Polish Jews are stupid. They are dirty, they don't have money and we really don't like them.' So for a while nobody wanted to play with me . . . I was more or less ignored, I just didn't exist for a while, or remarks were made. And remarks to a child are very, very hurtful."

The Polish origins of her family were to have still worse repercussions for her father. He was arrested on the day the Nazis invaded Poland — 1 September 1939 — because he was classed as a foreign alien. A short while afterwards he was sent to Dachau concentration camp near Munich. Then, 18 months later, in February

1941, two members of the Gestapo arrived at Lucille's house: "They threw a cigar box on the kitchen table and all they said was, 'Here are the ashes of Benjamin Landau [her father's name].' Whether these are the ashes of my father or just a handful of ashes from the crematorium at Dachau we will never know . . . We took the death of my father very hard, all of us, especially my mother and my younger sister, who was very much traumatized by it. She was somewhat quieter than she used to be, and just the fact that we would never see him again was very difficult to accept."

Lucille was 16 years old when she heard that her father had died in a Nazi concentration camp. And her emotions were ones of "Hate, pure hate. I hate each and every one of them [the people who killed her father]. That they were able to murder without a court, without due process, without justice, without justification, without reason. Because I had learnt the Bible and one of the commandments is 'Thou shalt not kill' and I just couldn't understand. I was naive enough to believe what I had learnt. I did not realize that life was quite different."

Eight months after she learnt of the death of her father, Lucille, her sister and her mother were deported from Germany to the Lodz ghetto in Poland. The Nazis had decided that Germany must be made "Jew-free". And whilst the systematic destruction of all the Jews of Europe had not yet been sanctioned, all Jews were to be forcibly removed from the Reich.

As Lucille was marched with the other Jews to Hamburg station she observed the response of the non-Jewish citizens: "No reaction, no words, no nothing — it was either an ugly word or they looked away. There was no . . . I wouldn't even say compassion . . . there was no recognition of what was happening, nothing. They were just stony-faced, and didn't react." Lucille remembered their attitude for a long time: "[And] sometimes in my private mind I would say, 'Some day I will get you.' You know, like a child says, 'I'll get even.' The day never came, but you think that way."

After several days crammed into a train carriage they arrived in Lodz, and were shocked at what they found: "We saw people within the ghetto — they looked ragged, they looked tired, they looked drawn and they paid us no attention . . . We saw the streets partly unpaved, partly dirty. We saw the sewage run along the gutters. We saw old, dilapidated houses. We saw an area that resembled a slum, except none of us had ever seen a slum but we assumed this was it. We couldn't understand why they looked the way they did — not decently dressed. We didn't know what kind of a place this was."

The German Jews had to find shelter in the ghetto wherever they could — Lucille and her family camped out on the floor of a schoolroom before managing to find one small, shared room. They had neither adequate food nor adequate accommodation: "The food was not enough to sustain life. And it wasn't balanced. There was no milk, there was no meat, there was no fruit, there was nothing."

Having had problems in Germany because she was perceived as Polish, Lucille now had difficulties because the Poles didn't accept her either: "In the beginning I did not get along at all. I sat in between two chairs. To the Germans I was a Polish Jew and to the Polish Jews I was a German Jew because of the language."

The German Jews were not welcome in the ghetto. "The very first transport [from Germany] were very critical of the way things were done in the ghetto, or rather in Poland. And there were remarks made in the beginning, that this is not official, this is not correct, we will teach them. Well, you can't walk into somebody else's house and rearrange the furniture, and this is what they were trying to do . . . And it backfired — it did not work."

One of the first deportation lists, drawn up at the Nazis' behest by the Lodz ghetto Jewish authorities, contained predominantly German names. Lucille, her sister and her mother were on the list, so she ran from office to office within the ghetto showing their Polish passports, trying to get permission for them to remain. Even though Lucille had no knowledge that everyone on this transport would be sent to a death camp to be murdered (by now it was 1942 and the policy of exterminating all the Jews had been authorized by Hitler), she realized that they were still safer in the ghetto rather than leaving for some unknown destination. Eventually — because, she believes, she could demonstrate that they were of Polish origin — the three of them escaped the first deportation.

But it was all too much for her mother: "We stayed in the ghetto and my mother really lost all interest. She didn't do much any more — she was blown up from hunger, which meant all the water accumulated. She couldn't walk properly and she died on 13 July 1942. The ghetto had a little black wagon with a grey horse that came through every morning and picked up the dead, and they picked up my mother ... And more than a week passed, which is not Jewish custom because you bury the next day, and my sister and I walked out and found a vacant spot and we dug a grave and we carried her out. There were no coffins; there were just two boards and a string around them. And we had to find them in a big house adjacent to the cemetery that had nothing [in it] but dead bodies, unburied bodies.

"We didn't feel anything. We didn't say a prayer. We didn't cry [because] we were numb — there was no feeling left. We went back to the room, to that furnished room with the other occupants, and my sister essentially just stopped talking — she didn't talk any more. She was very bright, she was tall, she was very pretty, but there was nothing left to say. She was totally deserted and my mother had made me promise that I would take care of her, and I couldn't do anything. I tried [but] I couldn't."

Her sister was five years younger than Lucille, and so was especially vulnerable. Lucille trudged through the ghetto trying to get her a job: "You had to have connections to accomplish anything, to change a job or to get a better job or to get employment. When I first tried to get my sister into the hat factory it was almost impossible, because the answers I got from the directors of those factories was, 'What will I get in return?' In the ghetto everything was paid for one way or another, and payment was high — it was not cheap. But that was ghetto life. This is what life had done to human beings. Whether they were the same before the war I doubt it very much. I was seventeen and I was absolutely shocked."

At last, and after showing the same kind of persistence that had managed to get her family removed from the first deportation list, Lucille obtained a job for her sister in the hat factory and for herself in the ghetto administration. But the atmosphere remained dangerous: "You really couldn't trust anybody, because if I would tell a co-worker something she would use it for her advantage. You had to be very careful. There was a lot of back-stabbing and you can understand why — it was a matter of life or death."

In September 1942 Lucille heard Mordechai Chaim Rumkowski, the Jewish leader of the ghetto, give his infamous speech in which he called for the Jews to give up their children for deportation (see page 130): " 'Hand me over your children so the rest of us may live.' I was seventeen when I heard that speech. I could not comprehend how somebody could ask parents for their children. I still can't comprehend that.

"They [The Germans] came into the ghetto with uniforms, with guns, with horse-drawn wagons and with trucks. And they went from house to house, from street to street, and we had to assemble in the

169

courtyard and they picked people at random — not just the old and not just the very young, but whomever they deemed too old to work.

"I put some make-up on my sister [to make her look older and healthier] and we stood in the courtyard. And they took my sister. They were not supposed to. She was twelve and the cut-off was eleven. And I tried to go up on the truck with her and the end of a gun hit my arms and I couldn't go on the truck, and those people disappeared." She never saw her sister again. Most likely she died just days later in the gas vans at the Nazi death installation of Chelmno.

Lucille was now alone, with no family to comfort or support her. And at this moment of absolute vulnerability, Rumkowski, who was in his sixties, began to take an interest in her. He personally selected Lucille to work in the administration of a ghetto restaurant and kitchen. Her job was to sit in an office and calculate what quantity of raw ingredients were needed for each meal.

Rumkowski took to visiting her daily: "He would come into the office and you could hear his uneven steps, sort of a slight limp in the hallway. And I was alone in the office and he would pull up a chair and we had a couple of conversations. He talked, I would listen and he molested me . . . he took my hand and he placed it on his penis and he said, 'Make it work!' I had no idea what he meant by it and nothing happened, and he got very angry. But then later on, many years later, I found out that the man was impotent so nothing would have happened or could have happened. But what crossed my mind was a pregnancy, because I had no idea ... until one of my friends told me, 'You're ridiculous, it doesn't work that way!' I felt angry and I felt abused, although I didn't really know the true sense of abuse, and I couldn't understand why anyone would want to do that.

"To me it was shocking. He wanted me to move into a private apartment to which only he would have access, and I started to cry, I did not want to move." Lucille refused to become Rumkowski's mistress and live in a special flat where, he said, he "could see her naked". But she could do nothing to prevent being abused at work. "If I would have run away he would have had me deported. I mean that was very clear — there were rumours of other instances: I think your life was at stake if you had run away. Why a man by the name of Rumkowski, the head of the ghetto, would sink so low ... but sex in the ghetto was a very valuable commodity. It was traded like you would trade anything else."

One day the kitchen was suddenly closed, and all the workers were sent to a leather factory within the ghetto to sew belts and other related items for the German army. Lucille never saw Rumkowski again.

In 1944 the Germans liquidated the whole ghetto, and most of the remaining Jews were sent to Auschwitz. Rumkowski and his family died there, but Lucille was selected to work and transported to a labour camp. She survived the war, eventually settling on the West Coast of America.

At the end of the interview this immensely impressive woman tried to put into words what she had taken from her experience, both in Nazi captivity and during her pre-war years living in Hamburg. "I have learnt that if you do not believe in a cause, be it a war or any other reason, you have to speak up. It is not always popular to speak up, but if you want to change things you have to take chances. You have to speak and you have to vote. To be silent doesn't help."

PART FIVE

SOLDIERS OF BELIEF

Unlike the epic conflicts of the past, such as the Crusades or the Muslim conquest of North Africa, religious belief played little part in either the origin or conduct of World War II. Even the most infamous crime of the war — the extermination of the Jews — had as its central background the Nazis' so-called "biological" hatred of the Jews, rather than the more traditional religious-based anti-Semitism of the past. Moreover its chief architect, Adolf Hitler, despised all "traditional" religions.

But whilst religious belief played only a small part in the motivation of most soldiers — including the five veterans whose personal histories are gathered here — this was still a war dominated by faith and conviction. Jacques Leroy, for example, was on a "crusade" against the Soviet Union — though not a Christian one. He subscribed to the Nazi view that he was fighting an inferior people in the East, and his passionate belief that Communism had to be eradicated filled him with a sense of quasi-religious rapture.

For the true believer, Nazi ideology wasn't just a substitute for religion — it was superior to religion. "Those who see in National Socialism nothing more than a political movement," said Adolf Hitler, "know scarcely anything of it ... It is more even than a religion: it is the will to create mankind anew."

The three former Soviet soldiers included in this section were also motivated by firmly held convictions. But, unlike Jacques Leroy, their motivation was not primarily ideological. They took their lead from Stalin, who on 3 July 1941, in his first public speech after the German invasion, addressed the Soviet people not just with the ideologically correct "Comrades" but also with the pre-Revolutionary "Brothers and Sisters". To many Soviet citizens at the time this was a clear sign that their leader wanted to appeal to their sense of nationalism as much as their Communist beliefs.

As is apparent from their testimony, these three Soviet veterans were driven by a feeling that was both non-religious and non-ideological — a feeling that came almost to overwhelm them: hatred. Never has there been a greater example in history of what the Buddha called "karmatic consequence": the idea that, if you do something bad to someone, something bad will happen to you in return. The Germans had invaded their country and murdered their families and friends; now these Soviet soldiers were going to fight back and take revenge.

Of the three former Soviets in this section, it is Zinaida Pytkina who most dramatically demonstrates the enormous power of hatred as a motivating factor. Once the Germans had unleashed Zinaida's darkest emotions, there was no return. She was a terrifying figure to meet, even 55 years after the end of the war.

As for Hiroo Onoda, a veteran of the Japanese Imperial Army, the depth of his commitment meant that he carried on fighting World War II on an island in the Philippines for 29 years after it was officially over. His sense of honour was something that perhaps only a medieval knight would have fully understood.

Obviously, as we look at the world today, we see many examples of crimes committed out of intense religious belief. But the testimony in this section reminds us that you don't need religion to create belief systems of immense power.

VLADIMIR OGRYZKO
AND THE PANIC IN MOSCOW

If I were asked to choose the single most decisive day in the history of World War II, I would not pick one of the obvious landmark moments — like 3 September 1939 and the British declaration of war, or 7 December 1941 and the Japanese attack on Pearl Harbor, or even 22 June 1941 and the German invasion of the Soviet Union. These dates — important as they are — mark only the implementation of previous decisions. No, I would plump for a moment of genuine and intense choice, when I believe one man decided the course of the entire conflict. I would choose Thursday, 16 October 1941, and a decision taken at the most crucial moment in the war between Hitler and Stalin.

It is popularly believed that Hitler's decision to invade the Soviet Union was the act of a madman — that no one could conquer that vast space, and that it was an act of pure hubris even to think the Nazis could win. But that is the judgement of hindsight and not what many — on all sides — believed at the time. Both the British and the Americans feared that the Soviet Union would collapse in 1941 under the Nazi blitzkrieg. President Roosevelt was told by his Secretary of the Navy, the day after the German invasion, that, "The best opinion I can get is that it will take anywhere from six weeks to two months for Hitler to clean up on Russia." And the BBC was notified by the British War Office not to give anyone the impression that Soviet resistance would last longer than six weeks.[1]

By the autumn of 1941 it looked as though that pessimism was justified. In October, in the aftermath of their victory at Vyazma, the Germans were less than 150 kilometres from Moscow and the capital was under direct threat, defended by fewer than 90,000 combat troops. Documents only available since the fall of Communism reveal that Stalin himself was considering abandoning the capital at this most vital time and fleeing further east — some 650 kilometres away, to the safety of Kuibyshev on the Volga. A secret document, number 34 of the State Defence Committee, dated 15 October 1941, records that it had been decided "to evacuate the Presidium of the Supreme Soviet and the top levels of government (Comrade Stalin will leave tomorrow or later, depending on the situation)."

The next day, an armoured train waited at Moscow's central station to evacuate Stalin. Communications equipment was taken from the Kremlin and loaded on board. And on the night of 16 October members of Stalin's personal staff, including his telegraphist, Nikolay Ponomariov, boarded the train. Stalin now had to make a vital decision. Should he get on the train himself, or should he stay and risk becoming trapped in Moscow? This moment assumed such importance

[1] Alan Bullock, *Hitler and Stalin: Parallel Lives* (HarperCollins, 1991)

because the war in the East was poised to move decisively one way or the other. And if Stalin had boarded that train and left Moscow, then I believe the war would have ended shortly afterwards in an ignominious defeat and humiliating peace for the Soviet Union.

There was, after all, a precedent for such an action. By the terms of the Treaty of Brest-Litovsk, agreed between the fledgling Soviet Communist government and the Germans in March 1918, the embryo Soviet Union gave up its claim on the Ukraine, Poland, Belarus, the Baltic states and a number of territories in the south captured by the Russians from the Turks. If Lenin had been prepared to bargain his way out of World War I by giving up large chunks of land to the Germans, why couldn't Stalin act the same way now? And since more than 90 per cent of the German war effort was directed against the Soviet Union, an end to the war in the East would have meant a very different war in the West. If the full might of the German army could have been positioned in France and Italy it is hard to see how a successful invasion of western Europe by the Allies could have been possible before the advent of nuclear weapons.

Of course, we know that Stalin did not board the train. Equipment was unpacked from the carriages and installed once again in the Kremlin. His personal staff went back to work. Stalin had decided that Moscow must not fall and that his presence in the capital was essential. But he knew that he alone could not save the

180

city; he relied on tens of thousands of other people to support him — like Vladimir Ogryzko.

When I met Ogryzko in his central Moscow flat in the late 1990s he was more than 80 years old. But he was like no old man I had previously encountered. He had muscles like a night-club bouncer and his back was as straight as a bar of iron. Back in 1941 he had commanded a unit of NKVD troops — forerunner of the KGB — in Moscow: "On 14 October, the enemy had already reached the nearest approach [to Moscow] and a section of tanks had reached the border with the Khimki reservoir. When you could see the enemy through binoculars, then Moscow began to feel a bit shaken because people were afraid . . . Food rationing was of course very tough and people were already panicking. Panic was spread by diversionary groups and spies who had broken through Moscow's defences . . . there were robberies, everything you can imagine happened, because as usual the people lost their head. The scum of the earth did show its face. It seeped through."

Stalin and the Soviet authorities instigated a "State of Siege" that October in an attempt to quell the panic, and Vladimir Ogryzko and his unit were amongst those charged with enforcing the new order: "There was panic on the roads. The people who fled Moscow, thinking that they would be saved and would survive — they were so primitive. And these people blocked the roads . . . It's very simple. If someone was in the way, that was it. Russian men are strong. You shoved him in the ditch, that was it. And then the next lot would get

181

the picture . . . Absolute powers. I still admire the fact that my company refused to let anyone pass who showed himself to be an enemy, a marauder. We didn't touch the ones who were confused, and there were a few of them — we simply brought them back in line. Those who resisted were executed. These severe measures, these beautiful measures, are the essence and content of war. You cannot say that they go against human rights — they are neither cruel nor mad. It was right to execute the people who didn't understand their position at a time which had become even more cruel for their country."

Ogryzko was certain that he had done the right thing back in October 1941 — even to the extent of killing anyone who stood against him: "It isn't peacetime. You're not going to say, 'Stop or I'll shoot!' a thousand times before you shoot, nor are you going to shoot in the air. Of course not. You shoot them on the spot. It was a tough command. Anybody who resisted and didn't obey orders on demand — especially if they also moved away or opened their mouths — was eliminated on the spot, without further ado. And that was considered to be a truly heroic act — you were killing the enemy. It was the way to dampen down the panic."

These special NKVD units didn't just play their part in brutally subduing the panic in Moscow, they also operated behind the front line as "rearguard detachments". Their job was simple — to prevent any Soviet soldier running away. The first four months of the war had been characterized by the mass retreat of the Red Army, and Stalin had decided that a line would now be drawn west of Moscow to mark the last point of withdrawal. At whatever cost, the Red Army was now ordered to stay where it was. "These rearguard detachments played, I would say, a psychological, morale-supporting role," said Ogryzko. "They induced a sense of responsibility in our soldiers and officers to maintain the front line . . . Once you're in battle, then it's no longer desertion, it's treason. The order went out: 'Moscow is behind us, there's no falling back!'"

When Red Army troops attempted to retreat they were physically confronted by Ogryzko and his men: "When you look at a soldier in that situation, whether or not he's an officer, when he's struck by panic he loses control of himself. So you have to stop him in time, you have to give him a shake or even punch him. And you see then he becomes a soldier again. It's very heavy, psychologically . . . you have to see it to believe it . . . you had to stop him, tell him to turn around, drop to the ground and keep fighting. And that brings him round. His stress leaves him. If he resists or something or runs away, we eliminate [him]. We shot them, that's all. They weren't fighters."

It struck me that threatening traumatized soldiers to return to the front line on pain of immediate death was a strange kind of "stress relief". And Vladimir Ogryzko was the most unlikely stress counsellor you would ever be likely to meet.

It was clear from his words and attitude that he felt entirely comfortable with his role of judge, jury and executioner. This was his response, for example, when questioned about the morality of summarily shooting his own fellow countrymen: "Pphhoo ... every country, not just ours, everywhere, has its traitors, the faint-hearted — many are traitors. They're given a chance, when you say, 'Stop or I'll shoot!'. And if they don't stop again, then they're shot. There are a certain number of rules in life, especially in the army, and even more so in war. There can't be demagogues — they are traitors. They are simply traitors. And traitors are treated as traitors. It should be considered a rule of life, it should be considered as part of people's education ... a traitor should get his come-uppance."

Vladimir Ogryzko's granite certainty dominated the room. But it was clear that during the war he thought he had served under someone considerably harder than he was: "Stalin did well. For all his deep-seated shortcomings ... Stalin will be very positively remembered in history. A strong man was required. They used fear to crush fear. If it was right or wrong, so what? It was a time of war, and there had to be certainty."

But, of course, the certainty that Ogryzko craved was only possible because Stalin had demonstrated his own bravery and had stayed in Moscow. There was, I felt, a clear case of cause and effect here. Stalin had remained in Moscow and men like Vladimir Ogryzko had been inspired to fight alongside him. And had it not been for the decision Stalin took on 16 October 1941, it could have easily been otherwise.

SUREN MIRZOYAN
AND HAND-TO-HAND COMBAT IN STALINGRAD

Most people who are even remotely interested in the history of World War II have heard of Stalingrad. They know that this Soviet victory more than any other helped turn the course of the war for the Red Army. But what is not as generally known is the extent to which Stalingrad became symbolic of the different approaches to modern warfare as practised by the Germans and the Soviets — something that for me was personified in a Russian called Suren Mirzoyan. I met him in Volgograd (as Stalingrad is now called) in the late 1990s. It was a typical autumn Volgograd day — grey, damp, with low cloud that seemed almost toxic — and the decrepit blocks of flats snaking along the bank of the river Volga exuded depression.

To the west of the city lay hundreds and hundreds of kilometres of flat steppe — land that had been ideal territory for the mechanized units of the German army. In Operation Blue in the summer of 1942 Hitler's tanks had scythed their way through this countryside, covering some 650 kilometres in two months, and in the last week of August 1942 they had reached the Volga and Stalingrad. For many German veterans I met, the sight of the Volga was an almost mystical one; it was a sign that they had "reached their goal" and the border of their new empire. Their only remaining task, they felt, was to clear the Red Army out of Stalingrad on the west bank of the river.

The Germans anticipated this would be easy. They first bombed the city, and then mounted a massive infantry attack. But Soviet resistance, which had proved so inadequate on the steppes, was now intense. In the rubble and bombed-out buildings the Germans' superiority in military technology counted for little — and soldiers like Suren Mirzoyan were determined to hold out: "Every part of the land that we had given up to the enemy was a big trauma for each of us. Now we thought that we would never surrender the city. We were holding our land with our teeth because we didn't want to surrender it."

Gradually the soldiers of the Red Army began to believe that they might stand a chance. It was a realization that first came to Suren Mirzoyan in August 1942 when he and one of his comrades had been ordered to "snatch" a German from the front line for interrogation: "There was a local road and by that road there was a bush. We waited there for an hour or so for the Germans to pass. We wanted to capture someone. So I said, 'Let's cut a wire and tie it to the tree and pull it across the road.' This is what we did. We tied it to the tree and we pulled it across the road and we hid on the other side. The wire hit somebody and then we attacked."

They had captured a major from the German Tank Corps: "He said he had two children at home and that his father had fought against us in the First World War.

He was very big and strong . . . He asked us to spare him. He gave us all the information [he had]." Instead of standing firm and refusing to give away intelligence to the Red Army that would surely damage his comrades, this German major couldn't wait to volunteer everything he knew. And so Suren Mirzoyan, 19 years old in 1942, came to the conclusion "that the Germans were not heroes. They were cowards. They were not convinced of victory."

What Mirzoyan believed he had discovered was the Germans' one area of weakness — close physical combat. It was all very well for the Germans to hide inside their tanks and speed through the countryside, destroying people and buildings from a distance. But the war in Stalingrad was a different kind of war, one much more suited to the strengths of the Red Army. "We knew that when you deliver the first blow on the Germans they immediately begin to retreat," said Mirzoyan. "Everyone knows there are few soldiers like the Russians."

The commander of Soviet forces in Stalingrad was Vasily Chuikov — a man of immense courage and ruthlessness who used to beat up his own senior commanders with a heavy stick if they displeased him. Chuikov gave orders that the Red Army in Stalingrad must stay as close as possible to the Germans. In some places the distance between the two front lines was a matter of only a few metres. This meant that the Germans couldn't use their superiority in aerial bombardment for fear of killing their own troops.

Stalingrad was fought over house by house, almost brick by brick. And inside the bombed-out buildings, Suren Mirzoyan took part in some of the most terrifying physical encounters of the war: "Suddenly one German jumped on my friend and he reacted and hit the German with his knee. And then a second German jumped on him and I lashed out against him — we had knives. Do you know when you press a ripe tomato, juice comes out? I stabbed him with a knife . . . I felt only one thing — kill, kill, a beast. And another German jumped on me and he was shouting and then he fell. If you were not strong enough physically, the Germans would have swallowed you. Each metre of Stalingrad meant possible death. Death was in our pockets."

These encounters were a world away from the mechanized warfare of the open steppes — indeed, such was the primeval nature of the struggle that Mirzoyan chose not to use sophisticated weapons: "I had a knife or a spade — a very sharp spade. It's better than a machine gun sometimes. I also used the spade in the front lines. You dig with your spade and then you can use it in man-to-man fighting. A machine gun takes a long time — you have to load it. But with a spade you simply lift it and you strike. It makes sense. These spades were very crucial in fighting."

Like all those who fought in the confined ruins of Stalingrad, Suren Mirzoyan endured the most terrible of battlefield conditions: "You can't imagine the horrible smell of dead bodies — the worst thing is a decomposing body. It can drive you mad. I can still remember. A body gets swollen and makes the sound *Pssss* as if there is air inside. I saw a lot of dead bodies that had been half burnt. Children and women, men. A lot of dead bodies of civilians. I remember also swollen dead cows. We couldn't fight because of that horrible smell . . . I've retained it in my memory for ever. When you kill you can see a man's blood. I sometimes see it in my dreams. It was atrocious on their part and on our part. Fascism and Hitler were to blame for all this. I saw such beautiful German boys who had been killed, and I felt very sorry for them. Why did it have to happen? I remember my intelligent and handsome friends who were also killed. They're alive, and then two or three minutes later they are dead. It's a horrible thing. War is the worst thing."

Mirzoyan believed he was presented with a simple choice in the ruins of Stalingrad — fight or die. He wasn't motivated by Communist ideals or Stalinist rhetoric. His belief system was as basic as the weapons he wielded: either he perished or the enemy perished.

For the Germans who had reached the Volga in August, their hearts lifted by the belief that the advance was over and they had at last secured their objective, the hideous reality of the fighting in the ruined city was devastating to the spirit. "As a tank unit we were used to driving tanks and trying to bring the enemy down with tanks," said one German veteran who fought in Stalingrad. "But that was all forgotten in the past, a long time ago."

And while Suren Mirzoyan and his comrades were grappling hand to hand with the Germans amongst the rubble, the Soviet High Command were preparing one of their most ambitious attacks of the war — Operation Uranus. This action, launched on 19 November 1942, finally demonstrated how much the Red Army theoreticians — in particular marshals Zhukov and Vasilevski — had learnt from earlier Soviet mistakes. Instead of a direct frontal assault on the Germans, they had planned a pincer attack on the supply lines into Stalingrad, cutting off the entire 6th Army of 250,000. Now it was the turn of the Germans to be encircled.

Hermann Goering, head of the Luftwaffe, boasted to Hitler that he could supply the 6th Army in Stalingrad from the air, but it was impossible. Field Marshal von Manstein tried to stage a rescue operation, but that too came to nothing. Finally Field Marshal von Paulus surrendered the 6th Army to the Soviets inside Stalingrad on 31 January 1943. He had taken a controversial decision because German field marshals were never supposed to surrender — if they faced capture, they were expected to kill themselves. Von Paulus's choice both infuriated and bemused Hitler. "What hurts me so much," Hitler said the day after the surrender, "is that the heroism of so many soldiers is cancelled out by one single characterless weakling . . . What is 'life'? The individual must die anyway. It is the nation which lives on after the individual. But how can anyone be afraid of this moment which sets him free from this vale of misery, unless the call of duty keeps him in this vale of tears!"[1]

For Suren Mirzoyan the effect of the battle of Stalingrad was, naturally, entirely different. He was confirmed in the belief that, despite their technical superiority in weaponry, "the Germans were not heroes" and nor were they "convinced of victory". More than that, his experience in the maelstrom of house-to-house fighting marked an emotional turning point for him. "I drank a toast," he revealed, "and said that after Stalingrad I am no longer afraid."

---

[1] Quoted in General Walter Warlimont, *Inside Hitler's Headquarters 1935–1945* (Presido Press, 1964), pp.305–5

JACQUES LEROY
AND THE MENTALITY OF A SS FANATIC

In popular culture — Hollywood films, the tabloid press and comic books — the link between Germany and Nazism is explicit. Consequently, not everyone realizes that Nazism appealed to a huge number of non-Germans. Indeed, the most fanatical member of the SS I ever met wasn't German at all — he was Belgian.

His name was Jacques Leroy and I filmed an interview with him in 1996. Meeting him was a strange business from the beginning. He lived in a futuristic-looking split-level house in the countryside of southern Bavaria — not for him the solid villa, stuffed with comfortable sofas and knick-knacks, of the other veterans I had met on that trip. I remember him standing on the doorstep: a small man in his seventies with only one arm and one eye, still exuding a combative, aggressive spirit. He had been tough in the war, and he was still tough today.

He was born in the town of Bache in Wallonia, the French-speaking area of Belgium. His father, the local mayor, was a rich man who owned a brewery and nearly a dozen restaurants. "I'm telling you this to place him," said Jaques Leroy, "to say that I had no financial need to do what I did ... it places me and the problem." As he grew up in small-town Wallonia he became "fascinated and influenced" by the political career of Léon Degrelle, leader of the Rexists — a Fascist party that was adapted to the predilections of the Belgians. "Léon Degrelle attacked the politicians of the day," said Leroy with passionate admiration, "the politicians who were, I have to say, corrupt . . . When I was eleven or twelve years old I would go to Léon Degrelle's meetings. I would listen to him, and I was attracted and fascinated by his politics." Just as Hitler's Nazi party appealed to many young Germans with its motto "Deutschland Erwache!" (Germany Awake!) and the pledge of a kind of spiritual renewal, so Degrelle's Rexist party promised radical change and a new beginning for all Belgians. And throughout their existence, a central plank of both Nazism and Rexism was fundamental opposition to Communism: "These days perhaps one doesn't attach great importance to these ideologies, but you have to place me back there, transport me to those times, because now it maybe doesn't mean anything any more, but in those days it was important. The whole of Europe was motivated, the whole of Europe was attracted by these anti-Communist and anti-Bolshevik movements."

But Leroy's youthful infatuation with the Rexists didn't mean that he considered himself a Nazi, or anything like. In fact, influenced by his parents' fears, he was terrified when the Germans invaded Belgium on 10 May 1940. Not yet 16 years old, Leroy "cried" on the day the Nazis arrived: "We were frightened because we had always been told that the Germans were

193

barbarians, that the Germans cut off the hands of small children . . . That's what we had been told at school, but I realized later on that it wasn't true, that we had been lied to."

In the wake of the German invasion the Leroy family fled to the south of France, but after a few days they decided to return home. And it was on the journey back to Belgium that Leroy and his family encountered Germans who were very different from the "barbarians" they had been expecting: "We had a breakdown in France on our way home — the Germans helped us, gave us petrol and repaired the truck. They gave us food. The Germans behaved correctly."

Leroy and his family, of course, were treated this way because they were not Jews or Communists. In fact, since he was a member of a Fascist party, it's scarcely surprising that they were helped. But from this one specific experience Leroy came to the general conclusion that the Germans "were perfectly well behaved, perfect with the local people." (A statement that is ludicrous given the subsequent deportation of the Belgian Jews.)

Leroy added that the Jews were "a matter of indifference" to him: "I worried about the Jews about as much as I worried about the year 40 BC." But whilst reluctant to be drawn into a discussion of the anti-Semitism that by now ran like a spine through the ideology of the Rexists he so admired, Leroy was happy to admit that he was a confirmed "racist". "The white race," he said, "the white race is important."

He explained the SS view of the world — one to which he subscribed: "The difference between the people whom you call *Übermenschen* [superior race] and the ones whom you call *Untermenschen* [inferior race] is that the *Übermenschen* are the white race . . . the white race. That's why at the moment there are so many foreigners who come to the white-race countries. It's deliberate — deliberately done by the politicians in order to try and marginalize this idea of racism. To create ethnic multi-pluralism . . . In those days we were proud to belong to the white race." Racist and deeply anti-Communist as he was, it is perhaps not surprising that as soon as he was old enough Jacques Leroy volunteered to join the German army to fight Stalin. What is more intriguing was the unit he joined — a special Walloon division within the SS, in which his hero, Léon Degrelle, was a senior officer.

The terrible losses suffered by SS units on the Eastern Front had meant that by 1943 Heinrich Himmler had relaxed his policy of accepting only recruits from so-called "Germanic" countries. In fact, by the end of the war more than 50 per cent of the fighting strength of the SS was provided by foreigners — a mix of recruits from France, Croatia, Norway, Denmark, Latvia, Ukraine, Hungary, Estonia, Albania, Italy, Slovenia, Serbia and Belgium.

"The ideological aim of the Waffen SS was to train men — elite men," said Leroy. "I know that this word is no longer very much appreciated nowadays, particularly in our multi-pluralist society . . . but it was to train elite men — men who could take over a command and serve their country." And the purpose of this "elite" force was clear. "It was the war against Russia, against Communist and Bolshevik Russia, that's it . . . because that was the motive for everything."

To many people, Jacques Leroy, by fighting in the uniform of the SS, was a traitor to his own country. "Yes," he said, "that's exactly what they would say, and what people still say now." During our interview he grew angry at this accusation, the words tumbling out of his mouth: "What is a traitor? What is a traitor, sir? Can you be a traitor at the age of sixteen? I didn't wear a Belgium uniform . . . You are a traitor when you fight ideas which are not those of Europe, which are not popular. When you take on ideas from abroad, you are a traitor. The word 'traitor' never once came into my mind!"

Leroy and the rest of the volunteers in the Walloon division (or the 5th SS Volunteer Sturmbrigade Wallonien, as it was formally known) were transferred to the Eastern Front. And Leroy soon proved himself a fierce, brave fighter: "One fought with weapons, one hid behind trees, one fought hand to hand." He even won a special medal for courage in hand-to-hand fighting. But in the snow of the forest of Teklino in western Ukraine in 1943, Leroy and his comrades faced a Red Army force that massively outnumbered them — with disastrous consequences: "These fights were truly terrible. We lost sixty per cent of our men. Two or three Panzer tanks were there to protect us, but they couldn't get into the forest." As he remembered these events, Leroy became even more animated. It was almost as if he were back in the forest fighting the Red Army once again: "We fought truly like lions! We attacked and we took position after position!"

But then Leroy's luck finally evaporated: "I was kneeling behind a birch tree — it's quite a slim tree — and then suddenly I felt something like an electric shock. I dropped my weapon . . . I dropped it and at that moment I saw blood, blood dripping into the snow. It was my eye which had been hit by a bullet, which burned it. And [I had] three bullets in my shoulder." Leroy collapsed on to the snow, where he lay bleeding until two of his comrades helped him to the edge of the wood and then carried him to a field hospital. Surgeons operated on his eye and his arm — and failed to save either.

And now we come to the truly extraordinary part of Jacques Leroy's story. For, badly disabled as he was, he still successfully petitioned to rejoin his unit. Which prompted the straightforward, but important, question: why?

"So as not to fall into mediocrity and to stay with my comrades," Leroy answered. "Of course I had lost an arm and an eye, but when you're very young one isn't affected by troubles in the same way that an older person might be. And, above all, so as not to fall into mediocrity. I don't like mediocrity. I don't like doing nothing, being idle and not having any aim in life . . . Sometimes you have to be a symbol in life. Otherwise what is your life for? Life is not about watching television all the time! You have to think, you must have a goal."

Leroy spoke these words passionately, his contempt for "mediocrity" made absolutely clear by the way he repeatedly spat out the French word *médiocrité*. But, as was often the case in these encounters, I felt his words had more significance than was at first apparent. The clue was in his remark: "Life is not about watching television all the time!" Because Leroy's house contained one of the biggest television sets I had ever seen, on which he could receive a huge number of satellite channels. And it was clear from other remarks he made in the interview, talking about how "I search, and every day I find films, biased films in which the Germans are badly treated, manipulated and considered as barbarians", that a huge proportion of Leroy's life was spent doing the one thing he thought life was "not only about" — watching television.

I had the picture of this angry old man, with one arm and one eye, sitting for hour after hour, railing at the television set. And so it was easy to believe that those years in the SS, fighting the Red Army, weren't just the happiest of Jacques Leroy's life but the only ones in which he felt he had experienced life to the full. It was as if those days had been in Technicolor, and the rest merely black and white.

But it's hard to feel sorry for Jacques Leroy; not only because he would have revolted against the very idea that anyone thought him deserving of pity, but because, as our interview neared the end, it was clear that he was one of the most loathsome of individuals — a Holocaust denier. Leroy emphatically denied having seen any atrocities committed against the Jews: "Never,

never, never, never! I have never seen a scene like that — that's why I don't believe it, I don't believe it! You know, the answers that I'm giving you, it could be serious for me, it could be serious, because you have to feel sympathy towards them these days." After the filmed interview — when Leroy clearly felt he could express his views about the Holocaust more forcefully — I pointed out to him that there was photographic evidence of dead bodies at Nazi concentration camps. To this he replied, "And you really believe these pictures are true?"

Leroy died shortly after we filmed our interview with him. And I am sure that he went to his grave consistent to the last: a fanatical former member of the SS, denying the reality of the Holocaust, and shouting at his TV set whenever it told him the truth.

ZINAIDA PYTKINA
AND SMERSH

One dark evening in Volgograd, in the winter of 1998, I walked up an icy path towards a house that resembled a cowshed. The night was bitter, the cold penetrating my thick coat, and the freezing wind made my cheeks raw. Above me the trees swung wildly and bits of branches cracked and fell. A fitting evening, I thought, to visit a ruthless killer.

Zinaida Pytkina was in her late seventies when I met her. At first glance, as she sat huddled in her rickety little house, she looked like a typical granny. But her directness of stare was at odds with her age. This was still a woman who unemotionally appraised everyone she met — and appeared to find most of them wanting. An attitude that was not surprising, if you knew her background.

In 1943, after the battle of Stalingrad, Zinaida Pytkina had received notification that an organization called SMERSH wanted to talk to her. (SMERSH was not, contrary to popular belief, dreamt up by the creator of James Bond — it really did exist, and the Russian acronym means "Death to Spies".) Zinaida Pytkina was frightened. She was just a 22-year-old nurse working with the 88th Tank Brigade — what did SMERSH want with her? Initially she feared that she might have been accused of some crime. But the SMERSH officers revealed that they merely wanted to see if she were a fit person to join them. SMERSH preferred to recruit by targeting suitable people themselves, and someone had suggested they take a look at Zinaida Pytkina. And they clearly liked what they saw, since she was subsequently commissioned as a junior officer that autumn.

I knew this was going to be an interview out of the ordinary when early on Zinaida Pytkina was asked to describe her job in SMERSH.

"My mission," she replied, "was to fulfil all the orders of my commanders."

"What did you do?"

"Whatever we were told."

Despite Zinaida Pytkina's initial reluctance to expand on the exact nature of her role, it soon became clear that her tasks — mirroring the objectives of the organization as a whole — were essentially twofold. The first was to ensure there was a "healthy spirit" amongst Soviet soldiers; the second to gather intelligence about the enemy — largely through the interrogation of captured German prisoners.

In pursuit of their goal of enforcing a "healthy spirit", SMERSH used informers to infiltrate suspected groups of Red Army soldiers. These informers watched to make sure "there is no chatting about defecting, no conversations about raping a woman and other things . . . There were occasions when soldiers, about five or six of them, agreed between themselves to defect to the German side and sometimes we were warned about

201

this." If a soldier were found to be planning to desert or acting in a way that lowered the morale of his comrades he was punished severely — most likely by being sent to a penal battalion or summarily executed. Zinaida Pytkina revealed that "It could also happen that our people defected to the German side and then returned having been given a mission by the Germans. We had to interrogate them . . . this work was hard, tricky and interesting."

Even more interesting to Zinaida Pytkina, and something that she unreservedly enjoyed, was gathering intelligence from captured German prisoners. Red Army soldiers would form raiding parties and snatch a German from the front line in order to take him back for interrogation by SMERSH. These captured Germans, claimed Zinaida Pytkina, were not ordinary "prisoners of war" since they had been captured by special Soviet squads. As a result, SMERSH operatives felt they could treat them as they liked. German soldiers were ordered to reveal their units, their mission, battle plans, the names of their commanders — a whole host of details. And if they didn't cooperate to the satisfaction of their captors, said Zinaida Pytkina, they were treated "gently". "Gently", it turned out, was her way of describing torture, because if the Germans didn't talk a "specialist" was brought in to "give them a wash" (the SMERSH euphemism for a beating) in order to make them "sing". After all, said Zinaida Pytkina, "No one wants to die."

Even 55 years after the event, Zinaida Pytkina was proud of the actions of SMERSH. She thinks it was right to treat German prisoners "the same way they treated us. What should we do — worship him? He kills our soldiers — what should I do?"

Zinaida Pytkina didn't just witness German soldiers being interrogated and tortured, she personally participated in the final stage of their involvement with SMERSH — their murder. One day her superior officer told her to go and "sort out" a young German major after his interrogation. She knew exactly what "sort out" meant in SMERSH vernacular — she was being asked to kill him: "When they brought prisoners after the interrogation, it was a normal thing to do . . . If they had brought a dozen of them my hand wouldn't have trembled to shoot them all . . . He had to be destroyed — the same way they treated us; we had to treat them the same way . . . Now I wouldn't do it whether he was an enemy or not, because I have got over it and I would leave it to others to sort things out. But at that time if they had lined up all those Germans I would have shot them all down, because so many Russian soldiers lost their lives at the age of eighteen, nineteen or twenty who hadn't lived, who had to go and fight against the Germans just because they wanted more land. What would you have felt?"

Zinaida Pytkina was full of loathing at the sight of the young officer she had been told to shoot: "What did I feel? As a member of the Communist party, in front of me I saw a man who could have killed my relatives. I would have cut him up if I had been asked . . . I hated seeing him. Not only me, all of us hated looking at them because so many Soviet people lost their lives —

young people. What for? Because the Germans wanted to get richer."

Amidst the shadows of her small wooden house, with the wind still blowing a storm outside, I almost felt I could picture the young German major being led out from the interrogation room, already badly beaten, to his death. What would have been in his mind? The knowledge, for sure, that he was about to die. There was a grave already dug for him and Zinaida Pytkina positioned him so that he would fall backwards into it when she pulled the trigger. Did he in those last moments regret his Führer's decision to invade the Soviet Union and arouse all this hatred? Or did he go to his death certain that the "crusade" against Bolshevism was right and that he died a martyr to the cause of National Socialism?

My own experience of meeting a variety of German soldiers who took part in Operation Blue, the great advance across the Soviet Union in the summer of 1942, and then faced the bitter retreat of 1943, made me feel that this young major who stood in front of Zinaida Pytkina would have been concerned not just about his own imminent death, but about the lives of those dear to him back home. He would have known that the German army had, by its own actions, unleashed a storm of vengeance that would destroy millions in the Fatherland. And so his last thoughts would surely have been ones of despair for himself and anguish for the fate of his loved ones.

Zinaida Pytkina's feelings, as she raised her pistol to shoot the officer, were very different: "I felt joy . . . My hand didn't tremble when I killed him ... The Germans didn't ask us to spare them. They knew they were guilty, and I was angry. I was seeing an enemy, and my father and uncles, mothers and brothers died because of them." She didn't look down as his body tumbled into the pit, but turned and went back inside: "I was pleased. I had fulfilled my task. I went into the office and had a drink ...

"I understand the interest in how a woman can kill a man," she said towards the end of the interview. "I wouldn't do it now. Well, I would do it only if there was a war and if I saw once more what I had seen during that war, then I would probably do it again ... One person less, I thought. Ask him how many people *he* killed — did he not think about this? I wanted to go on a reconnaissance mission, to crawl to the enemy's side and to capture a prisoner, perhaps kill him. I could have been killed too ... that was my mood ... and now if an enemy attacks I will do the same."

That night, after I had said farewell to Zinaida Pytkina and travelled back to my hotel and gone to sleep, something unusual happened. I dreamt about the story I had just heard. I saw the body of the major decaying in the pit and Zinaida Pytkina and her friends partying near by. Perhaps she had inspired me to have a nightmare because of the last words she spoke in her interview: "People like him [the young major she shot] had killed many Russian soldiers," she said. "Should I have kissed him for that?"

HIROO ONODA
AND THE REFUSAL TO SURRENDER

In 1974, a 52-year-old man flew into Tokyo's Narita airport to the kind of reception normally given to rock stars. As he emerged blinking into the light, his fans screamed and the photographers' flash bulbs lit up the sky. It was an ecstatic welcome home for Hiroo Onoda, a lieutenant in the Japanese Imperial Army who had spent the previous 29 years still fighting World War II on the remote Philippine Island of Lubang.

When I met him in Tokyo, 26 years later, Hiroo Onoda was still something of a celebrity. His refusal to surrender, his immense stubbornness, his overwhelming obstinacy had clearly touched a fundamental element of the Japanese psyche. He had never given a detailed interview to anyone from the Western media before, but now he had decided to answer our many questions and to tell his story.

He was born, the fifth child, in 1922 into a poor Japanese family. He remembers that his parents "were always scolding" him, angry that he was not content with simple things. He had a particularly fraught relationship with his mother, who appears to have been every bit as stubborn and tough as her son. When he was six he got into a fight with another boy and started wielding a knife. His mother immediately took him to a

Shinto shrine and told him he should kill himself and that someone this violent should just disappear. Even today, Hiroo Onoda wonders why he wasn't able — at the age of six, remember — to cut open his belly and commit suicide when he was accused in such a way by his own mother.

When he was 17 he resolved to leave home and seek his fortune: "I wanted to become a businessman and I wanted to make money. Because when I was a child Japan was so poor. And of course my parents always scolded me because we were so poor, and I felt poverty was so terrible, so hard, that I wanted to make money so that I could build a family where the children can't complain."

But his determination to become a wealthy entrepreneur took a knock almost from the beginning as he was called up to serve in the Imperial Army. He went unquestioningly since, as far as he was concerned, this was the army of the emperor: "The emperor was at the very top of the hierarchy . . . some old people used to say, they [the royal family] are above the clouds. And ordinary people live under the clouds, so we are living in two different levels . . . In those days the war was imminent and there was an atmosphere that we are going to war.

"Even though I wasn't too enthusiastic about joining the army, once I joined, and I was drafted, I had to do my best, because if I can't do it then it will be a shame. So I had to do my best, because I didn't want to be a loser. Maybe that's my personal characteristic . . .

Another thing was that I was quite a healthy, strong person. I was a self-assertive person."

When Hiroo Onoda joined the Imperial Army he was subjected to a brutal regime of systematic bullying designed to mould him into a soldier who would obey orders without question. It was a familiar tale — something I had already heard from a number of Japanese veterans — but Hiroo Onoda told the story with a new twist. Far from thinking the treatment he was receiving was unjust, he actually approved of it: "Well, actual war, in fighting conditions, is worse than that. Unless you can go through that severe training you can't really go through the actual fighting condition . . . So you really have to simulate what you have to go through [in battle] during the training, and then people can upgrade their level of endurance . . . Otherwise during the wartime in the actual situation they will be too startled and they can't do anything."

And so, with his level of endurance "upgraded" by one of the most violent training regimes in recent military history, and with the farewell words of his mother echoing in his mind — "Kill yourself if you have to become a prisoner of war" — Hiroo Onoda went off to fight the Americans.

At the end of December 1944, with the Americans advancing steadily through the Pacific, Hiroo Onoda was sent to command guerrilla activities on Lubang, an island in the Philippines. He had to turn about 250 relatively untrained soldiers into a fighting force capable of resisting the American Marines. And in pursuit of this goal, Onoda organized a series of supply dumps in the mountains and dispersed his army into the jungle to wait for the enemy.

The US Marines arrived in Lubang in superior numbers and with superior equipment. Onoda's army was little match for the Americans and many of them died: "They didn't really think that they were dying for the emperor or for the country. I don't think they thought so. They were just forced to place themselves in this situation, because they cannot just get away. Some soldiers died by screaming, 'Mother!' but nobody died or was killed shouting, 'Father!', and no soldier died shouting the emperor's name I ever heard."

Onoda was all too well aware of the overwhelming strength of the enemy he faced: "I knew we would never win. We knew we would lose, but if the situation would continue, we would be killed anyway, so we thought we should just stand up and fight. There was hope, if the US gets tired of the war and stops fighting, then we can stop the war. Of course later on the US waged a war in Vietnam, and the US was defeated . . . So even a rich country, an affluent country, will eventually have to stop a war because of problems."

This idea that the only way to stop the Americans was by making them "tired" of the fight was to be a crucial factor in making Onoda refuse to quit. He personified the policy of the Japanese military by this stage in the war. The Americans might have better weapons and a better economy to support the war, so the theory went, but, ultimately, the Japanese had better will power.

"The stake was whether your nation will survive or not," said Onoda. "You are not just fighting to get a medal or decoration or a pay raise — it's not that. Your country's now engaged in war, and you are forced to wage a war . . . The survival of Japan as a nation was at stake. Japan might actually disappear, become extinct."

Onoda's force knew nothing of the atomic bombs dropped on Hiroshima or Nagasaki or the subsequent Japanese surrender on 14 August 1945. They continued to hide out in the mountains, only venturing down into the valleys to steal food from the locals. It wasn't until October 1945 that one of his men found a leaflet that stated that the war was over and called on them to give up. Onoda immediately dismissed the document as a crude American trick and his unit — now just over 40 strong — carried on as before.

But other leaflets followed — some dropped from American bombers — and eventually the vast majority of his guerrilla army decided to give themselves up; many after a Japanese officer had called out to them by shouting through a loud hailer that the war was indeed over. And so, by April 1946 only Onoda and three other men were left carrying on the fight.

Onoda rationalized all efforts to get him to surrender as a simple attempt to make him betray his country in her hour of need. Even when some of the men he used to command came back up into the mountains yelling that the Japanese army had surrendered, he dismissed their entreaties as the product of American coercion. And even when newspaper articles were left for him — with some articles announcing events connected with

210

the imperial family — he found a way of explaining the information away: "I read the article on the royal wedding. I thought that Japan was totally occupied, and I thought that some kind of a new Japanese government was formed with American support. So I thought I was not under the control of this new government of Japan. I thought I was in a situation [like that] of General de Gaulle of France during World War II [who carried on the fight against Germany from London when the Pétain government had been established in France under German control]. I thought the Japanese establishment had left and taken refuge in some other place, and some kind of new government had been formed in Japan, but I thought the Japanese military and other forces were on the continent [and had escaped]."

There was a kind of logic to Hiroo Onoda's position. And it raised the bigger issue of the legitimacy of government. If the Nazis had invaded Britain and imposed a new regime compliant to their wishes, perhaps run by Oswald Mosley, and the Royal Family had fled to Canada (without Winston Churchill, who had vowed to die fighting the Nazis in the streets of London), then was it possible that some British servicemen would have felt the same as Mr Onoda? Would they have carried on fighting even though there was a new British government in London that called on them to surrender? And how long would they have persisted in the struggle if the new government — the Nazi-imposed one — had eventually been recognized

211

by the international community after some kind of compromise peace had been agreed?

And this kind of thinking allowed Hiroo Onoda to make sense of the narrow and distorted view of the world he received in the jungle of Lubang — especially when he saw bombers far away in the sky, which had taken off from Clark airbase in Manila: "I thought Japan was about to strike back, but afterwards it turned out to be [planes on the way to] the Korean war instead."

Years later, when there was more activity in the sky in connection with the Vietnam war: "I thought that the Japanese forces were still fighting there, coming to the south. It just continued . . . so I got mixed up . . . So those were some of the incidents that just led me to believe that war was still going on. So I was guessing like that for thirty years . . .

"It's destiny," he said. "Your own destiny. You were born to that life, and you have to live your own life. Can you die virtuously, or can you live virtuously? So it was like a grand experiment, I thought, because I didn't want to die easily. I didn't want to be defeated by the enemy so easily."

As he saw it, "Survival was [now] my mission. That was the mission given to me, to survive." And in pursuit of this mission he and his comrades took what they needed from the locals of Lubang — by force if need be: "I had a gun, so I could do it. I had the capability. And I could take things away from the residents, like cattle . . . On the island we were quite violent, doing whatever we wanted . . . Some villagers escorted the police to attack us, and then I would eliminate such a villager ... the police officers were not wearing uniform, so sometimes we can't distinguish. Within the jungle we have to shoot in 50-metre distance. You really have to shoot first ... I shot many times. The residents claim I killed fifty, but I don't think so — I don't remember killing fifty villagers ... Any crime occurring on the island, they always blamed on me."

One of the three other soldiers who initially stayed with him — a hatmaker called Akatsu — came down from the mountains and surrendered in 1949. He later implied that part of the reason Onoda didn't surrender was because he feared the locals might have exacted revenge upon him. This is a charge Onoda emphatically denied, and having met him I was inclined to believe him. He did not seem to be a man who would have felt such an emotion. There was too much other evidence that he had constructed his whole life around his own code of personal honour. And if Onoda's group had been so frightened of the revenge of the locals, then why did Akatsu feel it was safe to give himself up? No, it seemed much more likely, I thought, that Akatsu found he had some explaining to do himself when he returned to Japan and found this the most convenient way out.

Akatsu's departure left Onoda with only two followers, and one of them, Shimada, was killed by the Philippine security services in a fire-fight in the mid-1950s. That reduced Onoda's army to just two. Himself and his most loyal follower, Kozuka.

As the years went by and Onoda thought of the future, he realized that there would come a time when he would have to give up — his body simply wouldn't be able to function effectively in this harsh tropical environment: "I thought I'd continue until I became sixty. I was living a life like a beast or animal. So that was the limit of how long I could endure. When I shot cattle, the meat weighed forty, forty-five kilograms. It was heavy meat and I carried it on my back and I brought it up to the mountains, five hours' walking. After I get to sixty [I knew] I could no longer manage it. Of course, ammunition should be kept, and I set the limit: I should only use a maximum of sixty bullets per annum. [When I was sixty] I would have used up all the ammunition, and they would probably shoot me. So I knew the final destination."

But this was not to be Onoda's "final destination". Kozuka was shot dead by the Philippine police in the jungle in 1972 and the killing had a dramatic effect on Onoda, the last surviving member of the Japanese force on the island: "It was just terrible. Twenty-six years he was with me, and he was killed. I wanted to pay back what they did to him, sort of revenge. That was how I felt. Your feeling of revenge got stronger . . . I had to be more offensive, otherwise I thought I would be defeated when I was left all by myself. So I got sort of wilder and more offensive after I became all by myself, because you could no longer talk to your friend."

In the wake of Kozuka's death a last attempt was made to get Onoda to give himself up. After an initial contact had been made, a senior Japanese officer came

214

up into the jungle and personally read to Onoda an order that, he felt, compelled him to surrender at last.

Only this personal approach from the Japanese officer, and the death of his friend and comrade Kozuka, made him quit the mountains of Lubang: "I know myself very well. I never wanted to lose. I had a fighting spirit, ever since I was a child. I never even apologized to my parents, I never said sorry to them, even though I was a little child. I always was kind of stubborn, always assertive . . . My personal uniqueness is that I'm stubborn, I'm assertive, I never want to lose. I hated to be a loser."

And, in a way, when he returned to Japan in 1974, having received a personal pardon from President Marcos of the Philippines for any crimes he may have committed on Lubang, he wasn't perceived by many Japanese as a loser at all. He was someone who had kept the faith. The fact that the faith he had kept was in a dictatorial regime that had caused the destruction of millions seemed to have been forgotten in the joy of the moment.

But Onoda, in a last irony, found that he didn't really like living in the new Japan. He believed post-war Japan was corrupt and ill disciplined and — just as he had feared when living in the jungle — still occupied by the Americans. So he made a new home for himself on a ranch in Brazil, returning to Japan occasionally and bemoaning its fate.

PART SIX

SERVANTS OF THE REGIME

This section, featuring eight personal histories, represents the experience of the majority of people during World War II. Each of these eight interviewees embraced, to varying degrees, the regime they happened to find themselves living under. Some claim to have acquiesced under pressure, and some admit they supported their leaders wholeheartedly. But all of them ultimately went along with what was required of them by the state.

Of these eight histories, seven belong to people who lived in countries where democracy and freedom of speech had been crushed — four Germans (and one Swede) who supported Nazism, and one supporter each from the regimes in the Soviet Union and Japan. The eighth contribution is from someone from a very different background — an Englishman, Nigel Nicolson. I included his testimony because, like many of the other people featured in this section, he had to choose whether or not to act against his instinct for what was morally correct — whether to follow orders or "do the right thing".

All eight people share something else — having to deal with a past that now seems so alien. And they each deal with this feeling in different ways. Fritz Hippler, for example, practises simple denial, whilst Manfred Freiherr von Schroeder admits his own cowardice. Ken Yuasa almost creates another "him" who functioned in the past, and Erna Krantz clings to the notion that somehow cultured, intelligent Nazis were at some point corrupted.

Every one of these people wanted to fit into the world they inhabited. It must surely be one of the most common of human traits, and it's a sentiment that's at the heart of this sad report, written in 1936 by a member of the SPD, a German political party outlawed by the Nazis: "The average [German] worker is primarily interested in work and not in democracy. People who previously enthusiastically supported democracy show no interest at all in politics. One must be clear about the fact that in the first instance men are fathers of families and have jobs and that for them politics take second place and even then only when they expect to get something out of it."[1]

Of course every human being has a choice how to behave, and of course there are some brave people in every society who refuse to follow orders that they think are immoral, but we have to recognize in the face of this testimony that the human desire both to conform and to act out of self-interest is often more powerful than we might like to think.

---

[1] Quoted in *Nazism 1919–1945*, Vol. 2: State, Economy and Society 1933–1939, edited by Jeremy Noakes and Geoffrey Pridham (University of Exeter Press, 1984), p.591

ERNA KRANTZ
AND LIVING AN ORDINARY LIFE UNDER THE NAZIS

I had not anticipated meeting a particularly valuable witness to Nazism when I arrived at Erna Krantz's comfortable villa on the outskirts of Munich. Once inside her house I saw nothing unusual. Her sitting room resembled many I had already seen: the porcelain figures of dogs and shepherdesses, the over-stuffed sofa, the thick carpet and the china tea service. She herself was welcoming and hospitable — a contented old lady enjoying her retirement. There was nothing about her or her situation that prepared me for the fact that she would prove to be one of the most forthright people I would meet on my travels.

Erna Krantz was born into the German middle class, and all she had ever wanted was to enjoy a happy, normal life, secure within the enveloping arms of the bourgeoisie. Her house today was a precise reflection of that desire. Her surroundings shouted out: this is the world I want — these are the standards to which I aspire. But it was a life that was shaken by the effects of the economic chaos of the late 1920s and early 1930s: "There was great poverty here in Germany," she said. "There was almost no so-called middle class left . . . It was very hard for us, let's say we had to make things stretch. I went to the English Ladies' School in Pasing, and the English Ladies' was a private school. We had to pay for everything: every book, every pencil, the school fees and so on."

She was still a schoolgirl when Hitler became chancellor in January 1933, but she felt his arrival was a "glimmer of hope — a glimmer of hope for everyone. Not just for the unemployed, but for . . . well, for everybody, because we all knew that we were downtrodden." And whilst there remains dispute as to how much (or whether at all) the German people as a whole became economically richer under Nazi rule in the 1930s, Erna Kranz is in no doubt as to the way life changed for herself, her family and their friends: "Lots of things got better. Salaries became more stable. Everything was improving a little . . . I only know about that time from our personal situation as a household — it got better. You saw the unemployed disappearing from the streets. That was already a big plus . . . They started the construction of the motorways, and all that provided work and took people off the streets."

As she entered her teenage years, Erna completely embraced the Nazi view of culture. "Degenerate" art — modern paintings, sculptures and music — was banned, to be replaced by works of art that experts today deem kitsch in the extreme. But they appealed to the young Erna Krantz and millions like her. "We saw a flourishing of culture," she said. "I personally felt that the exhibitions in the Haus der Kunst [Munich's art gallery] were very beautiful. I liked all this, this aesthetic, in the sculpture, in the paintings. For me it was beautiful . . .

"I can only speak for myself," she continued. "I thought it was a good time. I liked it. We weren't living in affluence like today, but there was order and discipline. And there were also a great many people who were role models. That was encouraged. Good writers, they were being emphasized, philosophers too were emphasized. They were our heroes; we emulated them in our youth because young people need role models. Today, they are lacking. And it was, I thought, a better time. To say this is, of course, taking a risk. But I'll say it anyway."

Erna Kranz was no fool. She knew that it was deeply politically incorrect to voice the view that living under the Nazis had been "better" for her than living in post-war democratic Germany. But she was determined to speak her mind. She recalled that she absorbed an atmosphere in which "people had the conceit to say that a German is special, that the German people should become a thoroughbred people . . . should stand above the others . . . An elite race was being promoted . . . Well, I have to say it was somewhat contagious. You used to say that if you tell a young person every day, 'You are something special', then in the end they will believe you."

What is particularly significant about Erna Kranz is that she did not wholeheartedly embrace the Nazi regime by joining the Bund Deutscher Mädel (BDM — the Hitler Youth for girls). No, she was an altogether more intriguing character — someone who swept through these times in the mainstream, choosing the bits of Nazi culture that appealed to her.

And the event that best symbolized her enjoyment of those Nazi days was the Nacht der Amazonen (Night of the Amazons), a festival held just before the war in Nymphenburg Park in Munich. This gala night was the brainchild of Christian Leber, the corrupt (even by Nazi standards) leader of Munich City Council. It had as its centrepiece a parade of beautiful women representing historical and mythological figures. What particularly appealed to the audience — which contained a number of Nazi leaders in town for the horse races — was that many of the young women wore hardly any clothes.

"The girls were there the way God had created them," said Erna. "It was a celebration, and they wanted to re-create hunting scenes from the old legends, from the Greek myths, with the goddess Diana and the Amazons. It was a feast for the eye — it was a beautiful show, an aesthetic show, which many people saw as something naughty, something ambitious, which was for the bigwigs . . . They wanted to have a faithful representation, like you have in the church, of the old paintings by Tiepolo or Rubens . . . they are true to life as well. The Sistine Chapel — they're naked too, all naked, aren't they?" Colour-film footage of one these parades survives, and reveals an extraordinary collection of tableaux on carnival floats. There is Diana, the hunting goddess, standing naked apart from a G-string and her bow, a collection of topless girls with silver helmets holding spears, and even a girl covered in gold paint suddenly springing out of a multi-coloured box. It's a triumph of glitz and soft porn.

But Erna Kranz did not have to take her clothes off to take part. Also required were girls who could ride, to represent — somewhat bizarrely, but then the whole concept was bizarre — a troupe of Madame de Pompadours. Erna Kranz, a devoted member of her local riding club, wore a dress with a "very low-cut, plunging neckline" and rode side-saddle on a chestnut horse down the side of Nymphenburg Park. The whole evening ended in a mass firework display, and she was "so excited" after this "great experience" that she could "hardly hold" her horse. But, betraying her ultra-sensible middle-class upbringing, she left the festivities as soon as she could to catch the last train home, and was careful to put on the coat she had brought with her because "with the low-cut neckline I was slightly worried I might catch a cold".

These were happy times for Erna Kranz. And she revealed that she remained "pleased" with her life right up until the war started to go badly for the Germans. Her sense of pride was bolstered by the victories of 1939 and 1940; these triumphs merely confirmed what she and her generation had been told — that Germans were "special". And she believed that what kept her and her fellow countrymen going after the defeat at Stalingrad, and through the news of the relentless advance of the Red Army towards the West, was the sense of "German-ness" that had been "drilled and strengthened" in the pre-war years: "A German does not do this, a German does not betray, do you understand?"

But, of course, there was another side to life under the Nazis. Right from the beginning of Hitler's chancellorship in 1933 there was persecution of those who did not fit this "special" German ideal — most infamously the German Jews, but also Communists, gypsies, homosexuals and the mentally and physically disabled. Erna Kranz's philosophy during this period was, well, not to have a philosophy: "You were born into this time and you didn't think so much about it. You know, when you are in the middle of something, you don't really ask yourself, well, why, what is the reason for it? If you were to ask yourself all day long: how is this possible? Why do we have this brutality? Why is it like this? Then you couldn't live. And that's how it was at the time too."

She freely admits that life was "terrible" for the German Jews, and recalled how "sorry" she was when, in 1941, a rich Jewish lady who lived in a nearby street and who was very "nice" had to wear the yellow star. "But really, just like today," she said, "you can't help everywhere. It was the same then. You said: 'What can we do?' We were forced to do nothing and accept that a single person who was not at fault could be persecuted . . . Well, this is something the German people will feel for a long time, but it's not the first time and it was not only the Germans. The Jews have been persecuted the whole world over since they have been in existence . . . But I felt sorry when I saw that woman, every time . . . You see, at first you let yourself be carried along by a wave of hope, because we had it better, we had order in the country . . . and then you really started to think."

Nonetheless, the sight of Jewish persecution did not make Erna Kranz consider becoming an opponent of the regime. "No, no, no, no!" she exclaimed at the very suggestion. "When the masses were shouting, '*Heil!*' what could the individual person do? You went along. We went along. We were the supporters."

As our interview neared its end, Erna Kranz admitted that it had spoilt her happy and positive memories of this period "a bit" when she eventually heard what had happened to the Jews. "Well," she said, "you have a certain sense of shame. You do, it can't be denied. If you think about it, that a highly civilized people, as the Nazis saw themselves, that an elite group could lower themselves to do something like that — that is something which in retrospect we cannot understand, isn't it?"

What she had done, of course, was to concentrate on the best elements of the Nazi regime as she saw it — the parades, the sense of belonging, the discipline, the wonderful news that she was "special"; whilst feeling powerless in the face of the worst — the racism, the persecution and the mass murder of innocent civilians. She still fondly remembered the former and acted as if the latter were an unfortunate optional extra, a kind of add-on of horrific policies that happened when the "elite" Nazis inexplicably "lowered" themselves.

Erna Kranz was a remarkable woman to meet. She had no pretence and I admired her straightforwardness. But her very sincerity revealed a fundamental flaw in her attempt to make sense of the past. She still didn't realize that the two sides she had seen in Nazism — the "good" and the "bad" — were actually inextricably linked. Germans like her couldn't be told they were "special" without also defining the groups who were not "special". You can't be told you "stand above others" without thinking that those you "stand above" are inferior people.

MARK LAZAREVICH GALLAY
AND THE MIND OF JOSEF STALIN

"Stalin is probably sick in the brain," Adolf Hitler said in the late 1930s, "otherwise you can't explain his bloody regime."[1] Even to the Nazis — no respecters of personal freedoms themselves — Stalin seemed extreme. Not because he repressed his internal enemies: that was something the Nazis with their concentration camps understood. No, it was the seemingly arbitrary quality of Stalin's purges that left the Nazis bemused. And many other people since who have studied the Soviet dictator have been driven to agree with Hitler's "sick in the brain" thesis. But having met Mark Lazarevich Gallay in the late 1990s, and then examined the actions of the Soviet leadership in the early days of the Hitler–Stalin war, I came to an altogether different conclusion.

Born in 1914, by the mid-1930s Gallay was a young Soviet test pilot. Part of him looked back on this period with joy: "I was mastering new machines, flying new missions, and I felt I was growing professionally. I was courting my future wife and I was young. That's why in the morning I very willingly went to work and I enjoyed

---

[1] Recorded in *Goebbel's Diaries*, Vol. 3: Entry for 10 July 1937, edited by Ralph Reuth (Munich, 1990), p.198

learning new things." But then there was the other side to his life as the mass purges, instigated by Stalin, began to affect him in 1937: "Two or three times a week we would assemble for a meeting and in those meetings we had to discuss 'enemies of the people'. And all of a sudden it would be one of our people who was asked to speak about his connections with enemies of the people or with foreign spies."

The vast majority of people whom he saw selected as "enemies of the people" at these local Communist party meetings were innocent of all the accusations. But everyone present knew that if they did not select someone, the whole group was liable to be accused of concealing a traitor and then they would all be punished.

The purges were often conducted by quota. Each section of the armed forces, each party organization, had to deliver up a certain predetermined number of "enemies of the people". Ambitious party leaders knew that to make an impression on the bosses back in Moscow it was necessary to exceed the number requested. Thus in the late 1930s in the Soviet Union you proved your loyalty to Stalin by exposing more non-existent traitors than you had been asked to.

The crime of "enemy of the people" was carefully judged. Lavrenti Beria, head of the secret police, the NKVD, appears to have believed that merely "doubting the party line" was a sufficient offence to merit the charge. Thus you became an "enemy of the people" by questioning whether the buses were running on time or wondering whether your canteen lunch could be improved. It was a catch-all charge that destroyed completely any idea that the Soviet Union was controlled by the rule of law, rather than the personal whim and paranoia of the leadership in general and the supreme leader in particular. (This idea that some laws in Russia are deliberately vague in order to allow the elite greater control has not, I believe, been eradicated from Russian culture even today. On various filming trips there I have enquired of different officials whether something we proposed was permitted or not, only to receive the answer, "Well, it's kind of legal.")

And back in the 1930s, as Mark Gallay witnessed, there was no shortage of people willing to attack the selected scapegoat: "There are always people who like to push the other one who is already falling . . . Fortunately at that time I wasn't a [full] party member, I was a candidate party member. And I didn't have to take part in the voting. I knew that each of the people voting knew that a vote against [the charge] was like putting your head on the rails before the passing train. And, of course, all that contributed to the oppressive atmosphere. A lot of important people disappeared. Later we learnt that some of them simply perished in the gulag or were shot by firing squad without any trial."

Ever since Mark Gallay described these meetings to me I have had a mental image of that group of party officials, eyeing each other up, knowing that someone had to be sacrificed in order to save the group. Was it worth denouncing someone quickly, either in the room or an acquaintance elsewhere, in order to be spared denunciation oneself? Or would that only attract attention and create more risk for oneself at the next meeting?

The effect of this "oppressive atmosphere" was not only to punish innocent people, but also to harm the Soviet state. Take what happened to Andrei Tupolev, one of the most brilliant aircraft designers of his generation: "I remember how Tupolev was arrested," said Gallay. "It was a dreary, cold day. We came to work and saw how the painters were very quickly painting the tails of the planes that had the abbreviation for Tupolev's name on them."

The Soviet authorities had arrested someone who was of enormous help to their war effort and was innocent of the nonsensical charge against him — that he was trying to form a "Fascist" party in the Soviet Union. So having created an unnecessary problem, they solved it with an illogical solution — let Tupolev carry on working, but in prison. He was transferred to a special camp within the gulag system where he was provided with all the technical support he needed to continue designing planes. He was not released until 1944, seven years after his arrest, and not completely "rehabilitated" until after Stalin's death in 1953. There is surely no more telling image of the bizarre injustice of the Soviet regime than the picture of Tupolev, supposedly an "enemy of the people", carrying on helping his country from behind barbed wire. And it is astonishing that the obvious irrationality of this answer to their self-created problem did not occur to the Soviet authorities — because if Tupolev were truly an "enemy of the people", then why was he allowed to carry on designing planes for the Soviet air force?

And, as Mark Gallay observed, there was another damaging consequence of the purges: "During tests, planes from time to time crashed. That's unavoidable and it happens everywhere, in every country. What happened in the Soviet Union was that every crash was followed by an investigation . . . Usually the secondary people were arrested — some of the engineers who prepared the test. This chaos has no logic. If a plane crashed as a result of some sabotage, some neglect, some failure to perform duties, then it's natural to blame the people who made the mistakes. But sometimes it can be just small faults that lead to the crash. For example, when we were testing one plane the pilot got killed because, at the time, scientists just didn't know how the plane behaved at high speeds, and you can't blame scientists for this failure." The consequence of this culture of constant blame was, of course, to reduce the amount of risks that anyone was prepared to take. "When it comes to making crucial decisions about introducing changes into the design," said Gallay, "of course the atmosphere of repression affected people . . . If the atmosphere in the family is gloomy, this will not do good to a person's productivity and creativity. Whatever is oppressive binds a person's initiative."

The consequences for the Soviet air force of this loss of initiative and innovation were catastrophic. In the early 1930s some of the most innovative planes in the world had been designed by Soviet engineers, and

233

yet by 1941 and the outbreak of the Hitler–Stalin war the Soviet air force lagged disastrously behind that of the Germans. Stalin's purges had turned one of the jewels in the Soviet system — famous for record-breaking flights across the North Pole — into a second-rate force that proved little threat to the advancing Germans.

The destruction of the leadership corps of the armed forces during the purges also meant that, as Mark Gallay pointed out, "Eventually, regiments were commanded by young lieutenants. And in the years before the beginning of the war, the young commanders were unable to gain experience. People were afraid to show initiative because initiative may lead to mistakes. When it came to commanding the troops, commanders were frightened to go too far, and as a result very inexperienced people were in charge. Stalin thought that in aviation the most important thing [for a commander] was for the pilot to have had practical combat experience. But this is not the only thing a pilot needs. A pilot also needs a good education and good experience of command. You cannot promote yesterday's lieutenants into generals in charge of whole military districts. In the Western Military District, which was the first to be hit by the Germans, the majority of the planes were immediately destroyed because they were stupidly concentrated on the airfields [at the front line]. And eventually one young commander — a brilliant fighter pilot but an inexperienced commander — when he saw that in the first hours of the war he'd lost all these planes he was without any [internal] resources and was so desperate he committed suicide."

As Gallay saw it, even at 60 years' distance, there was simply no sane reason behind Stalin's actions: "It's really like killing the hen that lays golden eggs. There was no logic in Stalin's policy and his policy did a lot of harm to the country's economy for many years ahead. It's illogical to arrest a designer who can work well. You can't explain why it should be done . . . Stalin would be a more appropriate ruler for the Middle Ages — not for the twentieth century."

And at one level, of course, Gallay was right. Stalin's purges did enormous damage to Soviet society in general and Soviet military capability in particular. The purges were self-evidently unjust and patently cruel. But that does not mean that they were not the product of rational thought. The core of Stalin's motivation throughout his life was an immense desire for self-preservation. Unlike Hitler, who knew that without him there was no Nazi party to speak of, Stalin was well aware that he was simply a follower of Lenin — and that there were other followers of Lenin who could easily succeed him. This knowledge presented Stalin with a problem. Just how could he retain power?

His answer to this most vital question was simple: fear. Stalin knew very well the enormous power of fear as a controlling factor. And fear of arbitrary punishment in particular is one of the most debilitating emotions of all. Who would dare plot against Stalin when they witnessed even innocent people tortured and punished for imaginary conspiracies? The truth is that the purges *were* logical — at least from Stalin's point of view. Yes, they destroyed initiative and, yes, they

235

damaged the armed forces, but as far as Stalin was concerned that was nothing alongside the biggest prize of all: the purges helped him stay securely in power.

At the moment of greatest crisis in Stalin's leadership it is likely that the memory of the purges prevented him losing his job — and probably his life. On 29 June 1941, just seven days after the German invasion, Stalin attended a disastrous meeting at the Commissariat of Defence on Frunze Street in Moscow. He was told that the Red Army was in headlong retreat and that the city of Minsk was about to fall. He left the meeting shocked, remarking, "Lenin founded our state and now we've fucked it up." Then he retreated to his country dacha and stayed there.

Stalin's senior colleagues, including Molotov, Mikoyan and Beria, faced a dilemma. Stalin didn't seem able to cope with the crisis, so should they join forces and replace him? But the purges had destroyed any confidence they might previously have possessed that they could act together and trust each other to present a united front against their leader. They knew Stalin would never lose the capacity for revenge — especially unjust revenge: revenge based on the merest paranoid suspicion. And so a delegation from the Politburo scurried round to Stalin's dacha and pleaded with him to lead the Soviet Union to victory. It must have been obvious to all of them that Stalin was the man responsible for getting them into this perilous situation, but none of them came forward to propose the suggestion that the creator of the purges should be — justifiably — purged himself.

Thus the price that Stalin was all too willing to pay to keep himself in power was the torture, imprisonment and murder of thousands upon thousands of his fellow citizens who had committed no crime. And to achieve this goal there were countless meetings held throughout the Soviet Union, similar to those that Mark Gallay attended, which condemned the innocent. In the process all who participated were tainted, as Stalinism corroded the human spirit.

MANFRED FREIHERR VON SCHROEDER
AND WORKING WITH HITLER

One of the most troubling aspects of Nazism is that it appealed not just to ignorant thugs but also to members of the German elite. And so, not surprisingly, I wanted to find out more about how the rhetoric of an unappetizing former corporal called Adolf Hitler touched this upper stratum of German society. Which is why I was so pleased that I could question Manfred Freiherr von Schroeder in 1996.

He was about as high up the German upper stratum as you could possibly get. He lived in a grand house in the smartest area of Hamburg and was a man of great personal charm. His manners and his English were perfect. The only reason he would not have fitted into my own family was that he so clearly came from what my granny used to call a "better class". Like, I guess, many people in Britain, whilst my parents could be described as middle class, my grandparents and all my other ancestors were resolutely working class. In contrast, my impression of Manfred Freiherr von Schroeder was that the only link anyone in his family had managed to have with the working class over the last few hundred years was to ask one of them when breakfast was being served.

238

He was born in 1914, just before the outbreak of World War I, and was brought up partly in England. His family had strong financial links with London — in fact they owned a bank, founded in 1846 in Hamburg. His elder brother went into the family business, but Manfred wanted to do something else. His first ambition was to become a naval officer, but he had weak eyesight and so that dream had to be abandoned. Then he decided to become a diplomat.

He had no problem in serving the Nazi regime — in fact he became a member of the Nazi party himself. "At that time the young people were enthusiastic and optimistic," he told me, "and believed in Hitler, and thought it was a wonderful task to overcome the consequences of the First World War and especially the Treaty of Versailles. So we were all in high mood."

During the early years of the Nazi regime he never believed that the Führer was a dangerous expansionist. Even though Hitler had written in the second part of *Mein Kampf* ("My Struggle"), published in 1926, that Germany should one day conquer the East — by which he explicitly meant the Soviet Union — Manfred (and many others at the time) dismissed the idea: "Nobody believed that *Mein Kampf* was of any importance, you know. That a young man has written a book — what would politicians think today of what they had written twenty years ago! So nobody took it really seriously. I have read it probably as a student once and didn't think it was very interesting and then never opened the book again. One should have but we didn't."

But Manfred did realize that Adolf Hitler was no ordinary politician. And he revealed that one of the key reasons a large number of sophisticated Germans like him embraced the leadership of this ill-educated son of a minor bureaucrat was that they believed the "shame" of Germany's defeat in World War I, and the "unfairness" of the subsequent peace treaty, demanded radical solutions — and with radical solutions went a radical, out-of-the-ordinary leader: Adolf Hitler.

"In 1933 [when Hitler came to power], you thought it was the beginning of a new Germany," he said. "Everything was now in order again and clean . . . So there was a feeling of national liberation, a new start . . . 1933 really saw a true enthusiastic movement in the people . . . So one knew of these concentration camps and said, 'So what? The Communists would have done the same thing, and this is a revolution, huh!'"

The idea that Hitler becoming chancellor marked the beginning of a "revolution" was an important one for men like Manfred Freiherr von Schroeder. It meant that the crimes committed by Nazi stormtroopers had to be seen in the historical context of previous revolutions. "You have never had anything of that kind since Cromwell in England," he told me. "Closest is the French Revolution, no? To be a French nobleman in the Bastille was not so agreeable, either. So people said, 'Well, this is a revolution. It is an astonishing, peaceful revolution, but partly it is a revolution.' So, you know, people couldn't look ahead. Impossible for somebody in '33 to look ahead to '45. You can't. It was only twelve years, but it seems too much."

240

Bolstered by the notion that he was participating in an "astonishing, peaceful revolution", Manfred passed his exams and joined the German Foreign Office. His first day at work in 1938 coincided with the immediate aftermath of one of the "high points" of Hitler's pre-war rule — the German union with Austria, known as the Anschluss. "It was the summit of Hitler's popularity," he said. "It was a sort of national dream — German unity ... The Holy Empire of the German nation ... That included Austria — and everybody thought that it was a mistake of history that in the Bismarck time they both had been separated ... I don't think I met anybody in Germany, at that time, who wasn't proud of the Anschluss. [It] might be for the Jews and some opposition in Austria [that] it was very different."

I thought Manfred Freiherr von Schroeder's almost throwaway remark at the end of that answer was significant. He was obviously still in awe at Hitler's achievement of the German unification with Austria, and then as he finished speaking enthusiastically about it to me felt it necessary to acknowledge that pursuing this "national dream" had brought the persecution of the Austrian Jews and opposition parties in its wake. But his tone and general attitude in this and subsequent answers demonstrated that he did not really care about the persecution of a minority of Austrians in 1938. He was, as he had already said, participating in a revolution, and in revolutions — even "astonishing, peaceful" ones — people get hurt. It was not, for a man like Manfred Freiherr von Schroeder, a matter of justice or injustice; it was simply a reality of history. He happily continued to serve in the German Foreign Office, and in the autumn of 1938 even attended the Munich conference when Neville Chamberlain agreed to let Hitler move the German army into the largely German-speaking Sudetenland, part of Czechoslovakia. And subsequently Manfred witnessed first hand one of the seminal moments of Hitler's "diplomacy" — the seizure of the whole Czechoslovak state.

The German occupation of the Sudetenland had deprived the Czechs of their extensive concrete fortifications on the old border and they were now uniquely vulnerable to Nazi aggression. Hitler now pressed the Slovak leaders to declare independence from Czechoslovakia, threatening that if they refused he would claim their territory as his own. And on 14 March 1939, reading from a text prepared for them by the Nazi foreign minister, Joachim von Ribbentrop, the Slovaks duly did as they were asked.

The elderly President Hacha of Czechoslovakia was forced to travel to Berlin to discuss matters personally with the Führer. He and his delegation arrived on the evening of 14 March, and Manfred Freiherr von Schroeder was assigned the task of "looking after" them in the grand new Reich Chancellery: "That's a normal politeness at international conferences of that kind, so that the Czech delegation had somebody to ask where they could find paper or something to drink or have a telephone connection with Prague and to arrange all these things for them."

But Hitler was not about to behave with "normal politeness" to Hacha. He made the Czech leader wait for hours, while he ate a meal and watched one of Goebbels's latest comedy films. During the long wait Manfred had "nothing to do" and neither, so it would appear, did one of the most senior Nazis of them all: "Suddenly Hermann Goering came into the room and asked whether he could have a beer. We didn't talk about much. He just wanted to have a rest."

Hitler eventually saw Hacha at one o'clock in the morning and brusquely informed him that at six o'clock German troops would invade his country. Goering, no doubt refreshed by his beer, described with glee the damage his Luftwaffe bombers would wreak upon Prague unless the Czech President agreed to "invite" the Nazis into his country. It was all too much for Hacha, who collapsed. "We needed a doctor," said Manfred, "and that was my task." So he called for Hitler's own doctor, Theodor Morell, to attend to their guest. Morell came at once and gave Hacha an injection. The bullied and browbeaten President then recovered sufficiently to sign away the freedom of the Czech people, just two hours before the German troops were due to invade.

Hitler was now master of all the Czech lands. There was a jubilant atmosphere at the Reich Chancellery, and Manfred Freiherr von Schroeder and the other Nazis present attended a "sort of victory party" in Hitler's office: "And then I got a very close impression of that man. It was amazing to see how he behaved when he was amongst friends alone and hadn't to behave like a statesman for the public." He then demonstrated how Hitler sat, with his legs dangling over the side of an armchair, the top button of his shirt undone. "He was talking the whole time, dictating to two secretaries — one proclamation to the Czechoslovakian people and a letter to Benito Mussolini. I thought he was behaving like a genius, but that was wrong, of course. When I look back today and I have the clear picture of him standing up and then sitting down again I think he was absolutely behaving like a maniac."

Manfred Freiherr von Schroeder followed Hitler — the man who at the time he thought was a "genius" — to war in 1939. Committed Nazi as he was, he joined the German army and fought on the Eastern Front. "Once there's a war going on," he said, "of course, the national feeling is so strong that you say: 'Right or wrong my country!' Then every thinking stops . . . Human life is cheap in a war. If you hear that somewhere near by some Russian prisoners or partisans or even Jews have been shot, then the feeling was — when the same day five of your comrades were shot — you think, And, so what? There were thousands dying every day . . . so you thought, How do you try to be alive yourself? And everything else doesn't interest you very much, you know."

As his answer above demonstrates, Manfred Freiherr von Schroeder freely admitted that his reaction to atrocities on the Eastern Front was to say "so what?" But when he learnt about the realities of Auschwitz, some months before the end of the war, he believed that this crime demanded a different response:

"Terrified. Terrified," he said when I asked what he had first thought when he heard about Auschwitz. "What can you think . . . you didn't believe really that it could happen, and [you] suppressed it. That is a big shame, and the responsibility of the Germans. They looked away, you know, because they couldn't — they couldn't do anything. I couldn't avoid Auschwitz, I couldn't do anything against it, so better not to know. It's too terrible, you don't want to know it if it's too terrible . . . there was only the question: either you wanted to be a martyr or look away, otherwise you couldn't do anything else."

He paused for a moment before adding the words that he knew were the most important. "I wasn't brave enough to be a martyr."

KEN YUASA
AND HUMAN EXPERIMENTS IN WAR

As I progressed through my work, meeting more and more veterans from different countries, I came to realize the importance of understanding that the twentieth century — for much of the time — was the era of the immoral state. To live in Germany, Japan or the Soviet Union, during the years when democracy was suppressed, was to exist in a society where the basic institutions that surrounded you were corrupt.

The nightmare of that reality was brought home to me most tellingly by a Jewish man who told me how on Kristallnacht, the Night of Broken Glass in 1938 when synagogues were burned and Jews attacked, he had rung the German police for help — only to realize that his local police were actually encouraging the violence.

Swiftly, and with enthusiasm, whole professions embraced the immoral order. The German legal system was corrupted in a matter of months, as a parallel world of concentration camps controlled only by the "Führer's discretion" was established and accepted. In the Soviet Union (as discussed on pages 229–231) a catch-all "crime" of "enemy of the people" was created, which meant that anyone could be arrested for anything — and the judicial system adopted it with gusto. In

Japan the authorities legalized slavery and rape in the "comfort stations" — and the military approved.

But what should perhaps concern us most of all is the eagerness with which the medical profession in these three states cast aside its Hippocratic principles and ran full pelt towards immorality and crime. In Germany doctors embraced the "euthanasia" programme and murdered first disabled children and then disabled adults by lethal injection. Medical professionals were also central to the selection process at Auschwitz, deciding who should be murdered immediately and who should be granted a temporary stay of execution. Whilst in the Soviet Union doctors habitually declared "mad" perfectly sane political prisoners who were then tortured in special psychiatric hospitals, notably the infamous Serbski Institute on Kropotkin Lane in Moscow. Meanwhile in Japan the medical profession seized all of the opportunities the war in China offered them to conduct human experiments.

Ken Yuasa was one of the Japanese doctors who helped commit these crimes. When I met him in 1999 in Tokyo he appeared at first sight to be nothing more than a dignified former medical practitioner. His father had been a doctor, and Ken Yuasa had idealized him: "My father wanted to contribute to the community and to help under-privileged people. I remember from my childhood that he used to go and visit patients even during the night." So Ken Yuasa entered medical school with the intention of becoming a doctor every bit as dedicated to the public good as his father had been. But after he qualified in 1941 at the age of 25 he

247

realized that he ought to "volunteer" to join the
Imperial Army as a doctor or else he would shortly be
drafted in as an ordinary soldier. And so in October
that year he was commissioned as an officer and sent to
China.

He arrived on mainland China possessing the same
prejudices about the indigenous population as the rest
of the army — "We felt they were like waste. Garbage."
— and was posted to Roan military hospital in Shansi
Province. After about six weeks the general manager of
the hospital told him that there was to be an "operation
exercise" that evening, and he was ordered to attend at
seven o'clock. "That really shook me," said Ken Yuasa,
"It hit me. I thought, Now the time has come. And I
felt very uneasy, but of course I couldn't say anything."
The young Dr Yuasa was "uneasy" because he had
heard that operations were being conducted on healthy
Chinese in order to train Japanese doctors to become
surgeons. But he felt that "in the military system orders
are absolute" and feared that if he disobeyed his whole
family would suffer: "The authorities would say I'd
committed the crime of 'disobedience', and then my
parents at home would be in a difficult situation. I
would become a source of shame for them."

So he did as he was ordered and went along to the
operating theatre that evening. Once inside he saw two
operating tables side by side. Standing next to them
were two Chinese men. One was tall and well-built,
about 30 years old, whilst the other, who was crying,
was between 40 and 50. When the younger man was
ordered forward he climbed up on to the operating

248

table nearest to him, but the older man would not cooperate. Dr Yuasa had never hit anyone in his life, never used physical violence of any kind, but as he saw the older Chinese man resist he decided to act: "I held my feet strongly on the ground and pushed, and then the farmer got up and went forward." Dr Yuasa felt that, "We had to demonstrate our greatness in front of the Korean soldiers." [The Koreans, who were acting as guards in the operating theatre, were perceived by the Japanese as "inferior" members of the Imperial Army.]

Because of Dr Yuasa's actions the older Chinese man clambered on to the second operating table. And as he saw what he had "achieved", Dr Yuasa felt "very proud". Looking back from the perspective of the late 1990s he could scarcely believe he had acted as he did. "That's really terrifying," he said, speaking of his feeling of "pride" at forcing the Chinese man to cooperate, "a terrifying mental situation."

As he shook his head with wonder at the recollection of how he had behaved, Dr Yuasa appeared to be looking back at a different person. It was as if the mismatch between his behaviour in the past and his behaviour in the present had caused his mind to distance itself from previous wrong-doing by creating a picture of the younger "him" that wasn't the same person he was today. This person in the past was a kind of errant younger brother — someone he was close to, someone whose mind he understood perfectly, but not someone he could be held responsible for today.

Dr Yuasa went on to describe in a half-bewildered way how he had witnessed operations on the two

Chinese men. Neither of the procedures was necessary for the health of the patient — quite the reverse, in fact: "The first operation [on the elder of the two Chinese] was removing an appendix because there were many appendix cases amongst Japanese soldiers — we didn't have any antibiotics, and there were quite a few cases of soldiers dying as a result of that operation. The medical officer doing this operation was not very experienced and a healthy appendix is quite slippery so I think he had to make the incision three times. After that the intestine was removed, then his arms were amputated and then the doctor practised injecting him in the heart." Incredibly, the Chinese farmer survived all this mutilation, but he did not survive what happened next. Dr Yuasa and another Japanese officer held his neck, partly suffocating him, while he was injected with the drugs that finally killed him.

Then the younger Chinese man was "operated" on in a similar way. No one survived these "operations" — no one was supposed to. During his time in China Dr Yuasa participated in 14 operations on healthy Chinese — and every one of them died as a result. He also witnessed an even more barbarous "experiment" in a prison near another hospital. Here, in front of a group of Japanese doctors, two Chinese prisoners were shot in the stomach and then Japanese medics attempted to take out the bullets under "field conditions" without any anaesthetic. "I think they died of great suffering during the operation," said Dr Yuasa. "And in front of these others I didn't want to be criticized, so I tried to be very courageous and gallant."

The Japanese didn't stop there, they also organized a whole series of chemical and biological attacks. And as part of their research into the most effective way to kill people, members of the notorious Unit 731 experimented on innocent Chinese civilians by subjecting them to infectious diseases like typhus, smallpox and meningitis. Japanese doctors were central to this litany of crime. Many of them initiated human experiments that they hoped would help them understand how to carry out their "normal" work better. German doctors behaved the same way. Dr Mengele, at Auschwitz, believed his experiments on twins would benefit medical science. In the process, if children died at his hands then, since they were Jewish, they were, as he saw it, "expendable." And because the Chinese were believed to be "garbage", Japanese doctors murdered them with the same justification.

Amongst the hundreds of thousands of doctors in Germany, Japan and the Soviet Union there were, of course, some who did not go along with all of this. But they tended simply to move to the side and ignore what was happening. It is a telling fact that there were no great protest movements organized by the medical profession in any of these states. On the contrary, some doctors saw the ability to experiment on healthy humans as a wonderful opportunity to further their own research and thus their own careers.

We like to think that doctors are somehow different from the rest of us; that they are selflessly devoted to our care; that the Hippocratic oath they swore "not to harm anyone" actually means something. But what the history of doctors like Ken Yuasa demonstrates is how easily large numbers of them in Germany, Japan and the Soviet Union were corrupted.

After the war Dr Yuasa was imprisoned by the Chinese until 1956. On his return to Japan he resumed his career as a doctor — only this time attempting, like his father before him, to "contribute to the community".

FRITZ HIPPLER
AND "THE ETERNAL JEW"

After the war was over, many Germans hurried to rewrite their CVs. Yes, they might have been Nazis, but they had only joined "in order to try and change the party from within". Yes, they had attended Hitler Youth events, but they only went along as they "liked camping". Yes, they might have committed atrocities against women and children in the occupied territories of the Soviet Union, but it was only because "everyone who was targeted was a partisan".

I have heard these and many other attempts to minimize or even deny involvement in the Third Reich. But the most unexpected effort to diminish responsibility that I ever encountered was mounted by Fritz Hippler. He was credited as "director" on probably the single most disgusting piece of film propaganda ever made — Der ewige Jude ("The Eternal Jew"). This Nazi "documentary" purported to show the insidious way in which Jews try to burrow themselves into the "honourable" societies of the world. Its most infamous scene intercuts film of rats with pictures of Jews, with the aim of illustrating how the Nazis believed that Jews spread racial poison.

When I met Fritz Hippler at his home in Berchtesgaden in Bavaria in 1991 he was at pains to

253

point out that, despite his prominent credit as "director" on the film, it had been his boss, the Nazi propaganda minister Dr Joseph Goebbels, who had really deserved that title. All that he, Hippler, had been was a mere technician. It was a claim that, however unlikely on first hearing, needed to be examined. And as I studied the history of the creation of "The Eternal Jew" I came to realize that the film did have a fascinating and unusual evolution — one that was not as straightforward as the normal production process of script, shoot, edit and release. And by charting the making of the film there were truths to be learnt not just about the choices that Fritz Hippler had made, but also about the decisions that Joseph Goebbels and Adolf Hitler had taken as well.

The film originated from a request made by Goebbels in the autumn of 1939. He told Hippler, his head of newsreel production and a committed Nazi, to organize the filming of Jews in Nazi-occupied Lodz in Poland. This was because, Goebbels told Hippler, at "some foreseeable time" all the Jews were going to be "transported east".

The propaganda chief was obsessed with the power of film. "Goebbels thought that articles in the papers or what was said on the radio influenced the brain, the consciousness, the intelligence, the imagination," said Hippler. "The real primary forces of men are moved by the unconscious, that which he doesn't raise into his consciousness but which drives him on from beyond his consciousness. On these primary forces the moving picture works in a particularly insidious manner, and this medium he therefore wanted to use in a particularly pointed way . . . Each film, including the ones demanded by the state, was meant to be entertaining, not boring," continued Hippler, stating Goebbels's core belief, "because it makes no sense to make propaganda when the one who has to be captured by the propaganda goes to sleep."

It is hard to see at first glance how *Der ewige Jude* fits into this philosophy — even the most hardened Nazi would scarcely call it entertaining. But Goebbels did believe that "the Jew film" had the potential to excite emotional power and work on the "primary forces" of the audience. He worked with Hippler on various recuts of the film during November and December 1939. And, claimed Hippler, each time the film was recut it became more strident. On 10 December Goebbels recorded in his diary that "The Poland film [*Der ewige Jude*] turned out quite excellent. I am very happy with it." But only three days later he wrote: "Work long hours on films and the newsreel. The Poland film too had to be re-edited yet again at the Führer's wish."

And what exactly was the "Führer's wish" for the film? Fritz Hippler was certain he knew: "Hitler wanted to bring the 'evidence', so to speak, with this film that the Jews are a parasitic race within men, who had to be separated from the rest of men. As a consequence, Goebbels demanded rat scenes because rats were portrayed as a symbol for Jews."

There is clear corroborative evidence from Goebbels's diary that the film was recut at Hitler's instigation. And it is likely that any suggestions Hitler had to "improve" the film would have made it more radical — not just because Hitler's hatred of the Jews was even more visceral and excessive than Goebbels's, but because he and his propaganda minister had differing opinions about the best way to create powerful films, as an entry in Goebbels's diary from 5 July 1941 illustrates: "A few disagreements over the newsreel, the Führer wants more polemical material in the script. I would rather have the pictures speak for themselves and confine the script to explaining what the audience would not otherwise understand. I consider this to be more effective, because then the viewer does not see the art in it."

So it seems likely that any recuts ordered by Hitler would have been likely to make the film more "polemical" — and "polemical" is what the final product most certainly was. The film strives to make the audience loathe the Jews in the most unsubtle ways imaginable. Contrary to Goebbels's philosophy of film, every single viewer would certainly have seen "the art in it". For example, the final commentary intones: "The Jews are a race without farmers and without manual workers — a race of parasites!" And "Comparable with the Jewish wanderings through history are the mass migrations of an equally restless animal, the rat!"

As a direct consequence of its heavy-handed nature, the film was a failure. An audience-research study undertaken by the SD, the surveillance branch of the SS, concluded that: "The film was repeatedly described as being an exceptional 'strain on the nerves'."[1] And, as Hippler laconically put it, "The demand of the audience was not there. Whilst other films were sold out, the demand for this film at the ticket office was lacking."

Despite its lack of success with the German public, the film does offer us a window into Hitler's thinking at the time. Crucial is the date of the film's première — 29 November 1940. This was before the Nazis' "Final Solution" — the extermination of the Jews — had been ordered. In fact the film pre-dates the earliest moment that such an order was put into general effect by at least a year.

It is possible therefore to see in "The Eternal Jew" the certainty of Hitler's hatred before the manifestation of that hatred into action. Indeed, it could be argued that this film is evidence of clear genocidal thinking in Hitler's and Goebbels's minds months before the extermination of Europe's Jews was ordered.

Which still leaves us with the question of Fritz Hippler. I remember I asked him before we recorded the formal interview how he could claim not to be a rabid anti-Semite given the nature of the film. "I liked everything about Nazism with the exception of the anti-Semitism," he replied. "But I accepted that. It's a bit like finding yourself attracted to a beautiful, rich woman, but she has a hump on her back. You put up with the hump."

---

[1] Quoted in David Welch, *Propaganda and the German Cinema 1933–1945* (Oxford University Press, 1983), p.301

But this was at odds with the enthusiastic words he had spoken in support of anti-Semitism at the time. In an edition of the German magazine *Der Film*, published on 30 November 1940, Hippler wrote, "I can envisage that film audiences may feel that they have had enough of this subject. I can even hear the comments: 'Not another film about the Jewish problem!' But I must reply to this, and it is the intention of the film to stress the fact, that the Jewish problem only ceases to be topical when the last Jew has left the Völkisch fabric of all nations."[1]

And evidence of Hippler's central role in the creation of *Der ewige Jude* is given in Goebbels's diary. Take this from 17 October 1939: "Hippler back from Poland with a lot of material for the ghetto film . . . Never seen anything like it. Scenes so horrific and brutal in their explicitness that one's blood runs cold. One shudders at such barbarism. This Jewry must be eliminated." Less than two weeks later, on the 28th, Goebbels writes: "In the evening look at films. Rushes for our Jew film. Shocking. This film will be our biggest hit." And on 11 November he records: "I work on the Jew film, the script still needs considerable revision. Discussion with Hippler on the film's future form."

And, perhaps most tellingly of all, Hippler was perfectly happy to accept the credit of "director" of *Der ewige Jude* at the time. And even if Hitler and Goebbels did subsequently demand changes to the rough cuts he presented, Hippler was still "entitled" to the credit as

---

[1] Ibid, p.301

anyone who works in film or television today would confirm.

But in 1940 Hippler did not foresee that in only five years' time "The Eternal Jew" would become a problem for him. And, unlike many other people who can more easily dissemble, writers and film directors face a particular difficulty when political systems change — their own work stands as a permanent reminder of what they did at the time. Hippler died in 2002, but his work has outlived him. Nearly 70 years after it was created, *Der ewige Jude* still exists — marked prominently: "directed by Fritz Hippler".

NIGEL NICOLSON
AND DEPORTING YUGOSLAVIANS

I know some people who much prefer studying historical documents to questioning people who actually participated in historical events. "Interviewees can be so unreliable," they say. "Trust the documents." And whenever anyone says this, I think of one person — Nigel Nicolson. Because encountering Nigel Nicolson revealed to me the danger of believing that any historical source is inherently accurate; documents can dissemble just as much as people.

I met Nigel Nicolson in 1990 at his family home of Sissinghurst Castle in Kent. This Elizabethan mansion with a celebrated garden laid out by Nicolson's mother, Vita Sackville-West, is now administered by the National Trust. Nicolson showed me round, acknowledging the many visitors to the garden with the occasional proprietorial wave. He exuded the effortless sense of superiority you find in some members of the British upper class — not surprising really, when you consider his glittering CV. He had been born into the periphery of the Bloomsbury set, had known Virginia Woolf, had been educated at Eton and Oxford, had served in the elite Grenadier Guards during the war and had subsequently co-founded the publishing house of Weidenfeld and Nicolson. He had also found time to become a Conservative Member of Parliament and write a sensitive and best-selling account of his parents' relationship — *Portrait of a Marriage*. Nigel Nicolson was recognized as a man of principle and integrity. He had abstained, for example, in the vote of confidence for the Conservative government at the time of the Suez Crisis in 1956, and had subsequently lost his seat in parliament.

But I was interested in talking to Nicolson about only one tiny part of this distinguished career — the few weeks that he spent in Carinthia in southern Austria in the spring and summer of 1945. Earlier in this book (see pages 135–144) I discussed the role of British V Corps in handing over tens of thousands of Cossacks in this same area, but Nicolson, though a member of V Corps, was involved in another transfer of prisoners. As a 28-year-old intelligence officer with the 1st Guards Brigade he participated in the deportation of some of the 26,000 Yugoslav soldiers and their families who had sought refuge in southern Austria from the Communist Marshal Tito and his partisans.

Winston Churchill's policy on their fate was clear — they should not be handed over to Tito. Yet despite this, General Robertson, deputy to Field Marshal Alexander, the Allied supreme commander for the area, wrote these words in an order of 14 May 1945: "All surrendered personnel of established Yugoslav nationality who were serving in German forces should be disarmed and handed over to local Yugoslav forces [i.e. Tito's men]."

Once the Robertson order reached V Corps and its commander, Lieutenant-General Charles Keightley, it was "clarified" by his Brigadier General Staff, Toby Low (later Lord Aldington), in a series of other orders. The first, dated 17 May, called for "all Yugoslav nationals" in the area to be handed over to Tito. The second, of 18 May, defined "Yugoslav nationals" as "all non-Tito soldiers of Yugoslav nationality" and also included in the list of people to be deported "such civilians as can be classed as their camp followers".

Two points are significant about these orders. The first is that, as regards the soldiers to be sent back, there was an implicit extension from Robertson's instruction that only Yugoslavs "serving in German forces" should be returned to Low's "all non-Tito soldiers". This is because the struggle in Yugoslavia was complex, involving a number of different groups, some of whom could have argued (if they had been given the chance) that they had been fighting a civil war against Tito and had not been "serving in German forces" at all. The second point is that Low's order now extended to civilian "camp followers" — an extension that meant that many of the soldiers' families were also transported back to Yugoslavia. There had been no mention of civilians being handed over to Tito in the original Robertson order.

Another key part of Low's clarification order stated that the anti-Tito soldiers should not be told where they were being sent. As a consequence, Nigel Nicolson told me: "We had to invent the lie that we were sending them to Italy. And we told them that all through those ten days, and it was a matter of great agony . . . shame . . . to us to betray these people in this way and to lie to them, but there was no alternative if we were to carry out the orders we were given to send them back to Tito."

The anti-Tito forces in British hands were loaded into lorries and driven to the tiny station of Maria Elend, where they were told they would board the train to Italy and safety. But hidden away in the station building and behind nearby bushes were Tito's Communist partisans. As soon as the anti-Tito forces were safely locked in the carriages, the Communists revealed themselves. "And they [the anti-Tito soldiers] began hammering with their fists on the insides of the trucks and yelling imprecations," said Nigel Nicolson. "Not at Tito's partisans but at our guardsmen, accusing us, with some justification, of having lied to them and betrayed them. And that was the most terrible experience I had during the war, and it occurred not just once but twice a day for ten days until they'd all gone."

Part of Nicolson's duties as intelligence officer to the 1st Guards Brigade was to write a daily Sit Rep (Situation Report), and the one he recorded on 18 May, the eve of the forced repatriation, makes interesting reading: "About 2,000 Croats [i.e. non-Tito Yugoslavs] are being evacuated tomorrow morning from two large camps on the northern shore of the Wörther See . . . among whom are many women and children . . . The Croats have been given no warning of their fate and are being allowed to believe that their destination is not Yugoslavia but Italy until the actual moment of their handover. The whole business is most unsavoury and British tps [troops] have the utmost distaste in carrying out the orders. At the moment it is not known what higher policy lies behind the decision."

"I wrote those words in the Daily Situation Report," Nicolson told me, "which was circulated to our battalion and upwards to Division — that we had the utmost distaste in carrying out this order — and there was the most frightful row about that. I was sent for by the general or his chief of staff and told that whatever truth there was in this I should never have stated it in a public document, and further than that I was told — and it was more or less dictated to me — that in the next day's situation report I must deny what I'd written the day before and say that we have every reason to believe that they would be well treated once they got to Yugoslavia. That was totally untrue."

And so after a day of handing over the non-Tito troops to the Communists, Nicolson wrote this in his Sit Rep of 19 May: "The transfer was efficiently organised by 3 WG [the Welsh Guards unit involved] and the Tito major, the latter showing considerable tact in clearing away all Tito soldiers from the area with the exception of himself. First impressions of the reception accorded to the Croats was definitely good. They were kindly and efficiently handled and provided with light refreshments before continuing their journey by train into Jugo-Slavia. A Tito representative said that only the war criminals among them would be punished, and the remainder sent to work on their farms. We have every reason to believe that this policy, which accords with previous practice of Tito's men, will be faithfully carried out."

This Daily Situation Report of 19 May is a significant document. Nigel Nicolson told me that he had used deliberately ludicrous language in it — writing that the non-Tito troops had been provided with "light refreshments" and that they had been "kindly and efficiently handled" — because he thought it would be clear to anyone subsequently reading the document that it was a piece of fiction. After all, he said to me, who could possibly believe that Tito's bloodthirsty partisans would provide their enemies with "light refreshments"?

But Nicolson's subterfuge did not work. I know of at least one historian who took the document at face value and used it to try to prove that Tito's partisans had behaved responsibly when presented with enemy prisoners. It is a telling reminder of the need to treat all historical evidence — not only eye-witness testimony — with scepticism.

There is another reason why this document is important, of course, which is that Nigel Nicolson — a man of apparent integrity — agreed to write this collection of lies. Not only did he participate in deceiving the non-Tito Yugoslavs, he then put his name to a fictitious account of events. Yet this was an "honourable" man who had studied history at Oxford and was therefore more aware than most of the importance of an accurate historical record. When I met him he was clearly ashamed of what he had done, but there was no gnawing sense in him that he should have done something different at the time. His character, his education, his class, the discipline of the army, all pointed him in one direction — he should do what his superior officers told him to do, even if it meant telling outright lies and going against his "honourable" instincts.

The fate of many of the anti-Tito troops handed over to the Communists by Nicolson and the rest of V Corps was horrific. Thousands were murdered in the forest of Kocevje in Slovenia. I travelled there in 1990 just as the Communist grip on history was beginning to slip, and was able to witness first hand the pits deep in the forest where the bodies of the soldiers lay. Their graves were unmarked, and small pieces of human bone still lay scattered on the ground. It was evidence of a terrible war crime — a war crime, moreover, that had Churchill's wishes been followed would never have happened.

Just as with the handover of the Cossacks en masse, without any proper selection being made between those who had to be returned to Stalin (the Soviet citizens) and those who should not have been transferred (the non-Soviet citizens), so there is no certain explanation as to why military orders were issued concerning these Yugoslav prisoners that went against government policy. Most likely, as with the Cossacks, the Yugoslavs were handed over to their enemy just because at a time of administrative crisis senior British figures wanted to "get rid" of them as quickly as possible.

And we are lucky that Nigel Nicolson admitted before he died in 2004 that he had lied in his Situation Report about the "light refreshments" given to the non-Tito Yugoslavs. Because if he hadn't, then whenever this subject is studied in the future the precise nature and detail of this appalling action would be obscured. His fictitious report would rest quietly in the archives, ready to lie to future generations.

KARL BOEHM-TETTELBACH
AND THE CHARMING NAZIS

"He was a respectable person," Karl Boehm-Tettelbach said to me, talking of Adolf Hitler. "Charming as a host, not wild and shouting . . . He was very friendly . . . normal." I looked at him, bemused. This was *the* Adolf Hitler he was talking about? The one who presided not just over the Holocaust but over the destruction of his own country as well? The one who, from the first moment he came to power, espoused a policy of racial hatred? And he was "normal" and "charming"?

My encounter with Karl Boehm-Tettelbach at his flat in Cologne was to prove one of the most memorable of all my meetings. He had been born in 1910 in Portland, Oregon, and though his father was from the Rhineland his mother's family all came from the United States, so he was as much American as German. He had not been a member of the Nazi party, but had chosen to pursue a career in aviation. He had first flown as a pilot with the German air force, the Luftwaffe, and then, after the war, worked for Pan Am Airways. He was a striking man to meet: polite, hospitable and engaging. And his unusual insights into the senior Nazis he encountered could not easily be dismissed.

Boehm-Tettelbach had been selected in the mid-1930s to serve as Luftwaffe attaché to Field Marshal von Blomberg, the German defence minister. The fact that Boehm-Tettelbach was half-American did not count against him, as his German father had supported the right-wing Stahlhelm and was, as far as the Nazis were concerned, eminently respectable.

Working alongside Blomberg — whom he described as a "father-figure" — Boehm-Tettelbach met many of the top Nazis. Not just Hitler, but Goering, the head of the Luftwaffe, whom he remembered as a "jolly good fellow" who had the "proper language to talk to the pilots", and Goebbels, the propaganda minister, who always attentively asked the young man what films his boss liked, and promised to send over the latest entertainment pictures.

But Boehm-Tettelbach's most surprising memories are of two of the most notorious Nazis — Adolf Hitler and Heinrich Himmler, head of the SS. He described Himmler as "very normal' . . . He was a Bavarian, had a Bavarian accent, talked very nicely and he was not stiff . . . He could talk to everybody, he was sociable . . . He acted very friendly and I was not afraid of talking to him . . . I have to say, he was a very nice and agreeable guest because he involved even younger people such as me in a long talk with a cup of coffee or a glass of champagne or a glass of schnapps. And he enquired about the air force, how I was doing, how I was getting along and how long I would be with Blomberg; if I liked it, what I have seen on the last trip to Hungary — things like that — and was genuinely interested to hear

269

my opinion. You had the feeling you couldn't talk nonsense, you had to give him a good reason for your observations . . . so I always had a nice feeling when Himmler was around." This seemed an extraordinary remark. Himmler, after all, helped mastermind not just the Holocaust but also the ethnic re-organization of countries like Poland and the Ukraine. Few other individuals have brought more suffering into the world.

But Boehm-Tettelbach's judgement on the SS chief is confirmed both by contemporary documentary evidence and by other eyewitness testimony. SS documents show Himmler's fatherly, almost pernickety concern for his men: admonishing one for smoking and drinking too much, another for not spending enough of his leave with his wife. His private files even show how he carefully recorded his previous presents to his many godchildren so as to ensure that he never gave the same gift twice. (Favourite toys for boys were model tanks, planes or machine guns.) I also remember meeting one of Himmler's secretaries who revealed that as far as she was concerned Himmler had been a wonderful boss. He always asked after her, remembered her birthday, and was kind and punctilious. Himmler had great listening skills, she recalled. And she is not alone — several other people I met who worked closely with Himmler had broadly similar recollections. So Boehm-Tettelbach's memories fitted into a pattern, and mean that today we have to acknowledge that one of the greatest mass murderers in the history of the world was also, to those who worked for him, the perfect modern manager.

Boehm-Tettelbach's final meeting with Himmler is a confirmation of this judgement. In April 1945, in the last days of the war, when Boehm-Tettelbach was carrying secret messages to a field marshal in northern Germany, he stopped for the night at the estate of a millionaire Nazi supporter. On his arrival he was told that Himmler and his entourage were also there, like Boehm-Tettelbach en route to the North: "Himmler saw me, knew me and saw that I was really hungry and frozen, and he went into the kitchen with me personally to fry some eggs and give us tea . . . And then he noticed that I was in my summer underwear in just my short shirt, and he didn't like that and he said, 'Now, look here, you are going to Flensburg. In Flensburg there is a supply [depot] of the SS and you [go and] get a shirt and underwear for warmer days.'

"And I remember I went there when I arrived, and with Himmler's signature out of his notebook they gave me three shirts — good SS shirts. The button was not at the throat — it was at the shoulder. And there is still one shirt which my American daughter has available and wears when it's really very cold. That's from Himmler." Thus Boehm-Tettelbach placed in my mind the image of his middle-aged daughter visiting a shopping mall in the depths of an American winter, wearing an SS undershirt personally gifted to her father by Heinrich Himmler.

He had similar out-of-the-ordinary memories of his time with Hitler. In the mid-1930s he had stayed at the Berghof, the Führer's house at Berchtesgaden in southern Bavaria. Here Boehm-Tettelbach had an opportunity of observing the German leader at close quarters. He remembered that Hitler came across as a "respectable person . . . not wild and shouting". He "loved to talk" and also to watch films — particularly comedy pictures. Boehm-Tettelbach remembered Hitler sitting in an armchair at the Berghof, watching a German comedy, and laughing and slapping his thigh in enjoyment.

In 1944 Boehm-Tettelbach met Hitler in very different circumstances when he was posted to the Führer's wartime headquarters at the Wolf's Lair in east Prussia. Hitler had requested that "somebody [who had been] active in duty should report on the situation in the air. So they looked around and the only general staff officer still alive was Karl Boehm-Tettelbach. So, suddenly, I was forbidden to fly and I was transferred to the headquarters . . . Hitler knew me from Blomberg's time, and strangely enough he did not like new people. In my case he saw a face he remembered [and] he felt safer."

At the Wolf's Lair, Boehm-Tettelbach saw another side of Hitler — the dominating commander: "I never heard a conference where he did not win [the argument]. Years ago, when he started out, he had a computer memory, and if he heard something or knew something he registered that in his computer. So then if he saw somebody after a year he said, 'But then, last year, you said something else. You said you needed more steel — do you have enough steel?'"

Boehm-Tettelbach recalled how Hitler would get "mad" when his generals disputed what had been said at previous meetings, so he took to having shorthand notes made so that he could prove what had been agreed and "press" the other person into a corner: "That was his trick ... the other person who was reporting could not answer properly, so therefore he always won."

I asked Boehm-Tettelbach whether he "liked" Hitler at the time. "No, no, no, no!" he replied. "At that time I respected him. He impressed me, and he made me tense whenever I was near him. I was prepared in every respect to watch out."

Having met a number of people who worked with the Soviet leader, Josef Stalin, I was struck by the very different atmosphere of argument and discussion that Boehm-Tettelbach maintained existed in the presence of Hitler. Stalin tolerated no such debate — to question him was to put your own life at risk. Infamously, just before the war a reckless Red Army air-force officer had said in a meeting with the Soviet leader that his pilots were forced to use planes that were flying "coffins". Stalin had answered, "You really shouldn't have said that." And within a week the officer was dismissed. He was subsequently arrested and shot.

Nothing like that happened if you questioned Hitler — as Boehm-Tettelbach discovered. One day in the summer of 1944 he went to meet a field marshal who had flown in from Paris for a conference with Hitler. "I want to know his mood," said the field marshal to Boehm-Tettelbach, "because I'm going to give him hell. He should know what's going on in France." Then, according to Boehm-Tettelbach, "he really found some nasty words" to criticize Hitler.

But after his meeting with Hitler, the field marshal sought out Boehm-Tettelbach to say, "Boehm, excuse me. I was mad today, but I made a mistake. Hitler convinced me that it was justified and I'm wrong. I didn't know what he knows. So therefore I feel sorry."

"Therefore," concluded Boehm-Tettelbach, "he showed up angry and left enthusiastic and flabbergasted. Very strange. Very strange. But the flair Hitler had was unusual. He could [take] somebody who was ready for suicide, he could revive him and make him feel that he should carry the flag and die in battle. Very strange."

I pressed Boehm-Tettelbach on just how Hitler could have exercised such immense powers of persuasion, but he could explain it only by saying he felt Hitler possessed "antennae" that were "extremely fine". But on 20 July 1944 Hitler's "fine" antennae did not prevent a number of German army officers and sympathizers putting into action a plot to blow him up at the Wolf's Lair. Boehm-Tettelbach heard the bomb explode, but thought at first that the noise had come from one of the mines in the nearby forest, which must have been triggered by a rabbit. Then he saw SS guards running around and a plume of smoke rising through the trees, and realized that something serious had occurred.

I expected Boehm-Tettelbach's reaction to this attack to be the politically correct one — that Count von Stauffenberg, who had planted the bomb, and the rest of the conspirators were heroes. Boehm-Tettelbach, after all, was not someone who had been party to the atrocities of the regime. But I was wrong. In fact, Boehm-Tettelbach "didn't approve" of the plot to kill Hitler at all. And the reasons he "didn't approve" are intriguing. To start with, Boehm-Tettelbach felt that "I would approve if he [Stauffenberg] would have succeeded in blowing himself up in the air with Hitler. That's what the Palestinians do now." He believed that Stauffenberg was "incompetent" because he had placed the bomb and then escaped himself. "I was trained to make a perfect job — you have to be a perfectionist."

Boehm-Tettelbach became angry as he spoke about Stauffenberg — this was the only subject in the interview that provoked him. He felt that by not blowing himself up and ensuring that Hitler died, Stauffenberg had brought misery and suffering to his fellow officers.

He himself could not have been clearer when I asked him what he would have done had Stauffenberg approached him and asked him to participate in the plot: "I would have said, 'I'm going to report to Hitler that you want to kill him.' I had no other choice. If I would have stayed quiet they [Stauffenberg's supporters] would have put me down in that little book [containing the names of the conspirators] and I would be shot."

But, I put it to him, there was an alternative course of action open to him had he been approached. He could have joined the plot himself.

275

"Yeah, well, no," he replied, before coming up with the not entirely convincing explanation that: "To kill Hitler, that's not difficult to do, that's easy . . . but . . . Himmler must be replaced, Goering must be replaced and many, many other people. Because just blowing Hitler up is nuts."

Boehm-Tettelbach also revealed that uppermost in his mind had been the "oath" of allegiance he had sworn — along with every member of the German armed forces — to Adolf Hitler: "Nobody approached me because they knew that I wouldn't break my oath." The oath was something that Boehm-Tettelbach confessed he had taken "very seriously indeed". Bizarrely, he told me that this oath "accompanied me my whole life to the end. I mean oath is oath . . . I can't break the oath, otherwise I might [have to] commit suicide."

But, after interviewing him for some time, I suspected there was another — even simpler — reason Boehm-Tettelbach did not take part in the plot. He was loyal not just because his oath somehow bound him like an unthinking slave, but because in 1944 he still supported Hitler. After all, many of those who participated in the plot to kill Hitler had sworn the oath too.

By the end of the interview I had reached the conclusion that Boehm-Tettelbach was a decent man who had made wrong judgements — but who had also turned a blind eye to the evidence in front of him. When he learnt the full details of the horrors of Auschwitz he said he was shocked, but he had known the Nazis were violently anti-Semitic in the 1930s and had just looked the other way, preferring to live the glamorous life of a flyer during the day and "go to dances" at night.

What he still puzzled about was the monumental misjudgement he had made about the character of Adolf Hitler: "Strange that a person can show up and talk to me, like you are talking to me, and suddenly I hear that he killed three people at night. This is something you can't grasp. This is extraordinary. This is outstanding. It's something unusual, very unusual. Well, it's the same as the French Revolution. You know the people in the French Revolution, the leaders there? They wanted to do something good, and ended up killing the people."

So the lesson Boehm-Tettelbach took from his remarkable life was clear: "I met him [Hitler] as a normal man, and at the very end, when he was dead, he was a horrible man . . . So therefore you have to judge someone very thoroughly before you throw your life into his lap."

KRISTINA SÖDERBAUM
AND ACTING FOR THE NAZIS

In 1991 I met Kristina Söderbaum, the former pin-up girl of the Third Reich, at her plush little house in Zurich. And before we started the formal interview I suggested that we film her watching one of her old movies. So she sat on a cream leather sofa and leaned forward, gazing in a puzzled way at a video of herself in a 1944 epic called *Opfergang* ("Sacrifice"). As our own camera panned between her watching the video and her image on the television screen, there appeared to be no possible relationship between the two people. On the television was a young woman in a clinging swimsuit, the very image of the perfect Aryan maiden, all big blonde hair and prominent breasts. On the sofa was a little old granny with glasses.

Watching a sequence of herself riding a horse through the surf, she struggled to remember anything about the film. "It was very cold in the water," she said at last. "And we had to do that shot a number of times." She sighed: "Many fell in love with me, but whether that made me a sex symbol, I don't know. I lived in a golden cage. I saw very little of the war."

But seeing herself in the swimsuit also jogged another, clearly rather more painful memory: "Goebbels [the Nazi propaganda minister] said that I was not sexy, but that I was erotic. So, all right, I was not sexy, I was erotic."

Goebbels, the man who had made this judgement that still rankled with Kristina Söderbaum, controlled the German film industry as if he were an old-fashioned Hollywood producer. He slept with so many of the actresses that he was known as *der Bock von Babelsberg* ("the goat of Babelsberg"), referring to the suburb of Berlin where the studios were situated. But he does not seem to have found the Nazi "Aryan" ideal of womanhood particularly attractive in a mistress — perhaps because he had the perfect such specimen at home in the shape of his blonde, big-boned wife, Magda. For his extra-marital affairs Goebbels pursued dark-haired, Slavic-looking women (a racial type that his propaganda called "sub-human") like the Czech actress Lida Baarová.

But Goebbels recognized a useful propaganda tool when he saw one — and he certainly saw one in the form of the Swedish-born Kristina Söderbaum. And it was about her propaganda work on two of Goebbels's most influential films that I particularly wanted to hear from her.

Goebbels asked her to star in a film that came to symbolize his approach to anti-Semitic film propaganda — *Jud Süss* ("The Jew Süss"). Unlike *Der ewige Jude* ("The Eternal Jew"), which was released in the same year, 1940, *Jud Süss* was a sophisticated piece of work. It purported to be a drama based on a real historical story, that of a Jewish man called Joseph Süss Oppenheimer, who had worked during the eighteenth century for the Duke of Württemberg, but the facts were twisted to produce the result Goebbels wanted — that "the Jew Süss" had been a thief and a rapist.

Kristina Söderbaum played the part of Dorothea Sturm, the daughter of the chief minister of Württemberg. In order to have sex with Dorothea, Süss has her fiancé arrested and, in one of the most powerful scenes in the film, demonstrates how he can ensure that the man she loves is tortured in the nearby prison. The torture will only stop if Dorothea gives way to Süss's desire. And so she is raped. Afterwards, distraught at her loss of honour, Dorothea commits suicide.

But Süss doesn't get away with the crime, and the last scene shows his execution in the town square. Dorothea's father, Chief Minister Sturm, now solemnly announces that all Jews must leave the city; Württemberg was to become, in effect, "Jew free". Sturm then declaims: "May our descendants hold on to this law so that they may be spared suffering and harm to their lives and property, and to the blood of their children and their children's children."

The film's connection with contemporary events in Germany was obvious. Süss personified the danger that the Nazis claimed the entire Jewish population presented — one of selfish opportunism, criminality, blood lust and sexual defilement.

The film was a huge hit amongst both ordinary Germans and the Nazi elite. Himmler liked it so much that he ordered every member of the SS to see it. In his testimony at the post-war Auschwitz trial, SS man Stefan Baretzki revealed that the effect of the film on the SS garrison at the camp had been to make them increase their mistreatment of the inmates.[1]

Kristina Söderbaum's line on all of this — from which she would not deviate during the interview — was straightforward: "Today, we know so much more about the war. Then we didn't know so much. But now we know it from films we have seen, from terrible pictures of concentration camps and such like. Then it suddenly becomes much worse, and one says, 'For heaven's sake, I helped with this!' Then one didn't see it like that — one didn't know what it would lead to."

Not surprisingly, I didn't find this an entirely satisfactory explanation. Not only had evidence of the persecution of the Jews been all around her at the time, but she had been married to the director of the film, a committed Nazi called Veit Harlan. He had personally travelled to the Lodz ghetto to select 120 Jews to be used as extras in the film, and had then revealed in the German magazine *Der Film* that: "I am depicting authentic Jewry as it was then, and as it now continues unchecked in Poland."[2]

The only element of her account of *Jud Süss* that I thought was possible to take at face value was her explanation of why she had been asked to take part: "Well," she said, "they wanted me, this blonde, not very intelligent, nice Aryan girl." And in truth, talented actress as she undoubtedly was, she didn't appear to

---

[1] David Welch, *Propaganda and the German Cinema 1933–1945* (Oxford University Press, 1983), p.291

[2] Ibid, p.287

have given a great deal of thought to her actions at the time. Something that was certainly true of her participation in the single most extraordinary film ever produced in the Third Reich — *Kolberg*.

Anyone with any significant interest in Nazi mentality should study *Kolberg*. This historical feature, made in the last months of the Third Reich, encapsulates much of the nihilistic defiance at the core of Nazi thinking. Veit Harlan, who made *Jud Süss*, also directed *Kolberg*, and he confessed in his autobiography, that although the screenplay at the time was credited to both him and Alfred Braun, in reality Joseph Goebbels himself had written much of the dialogue.[1]

The film purports to be the story of the heroic resistance of the citizens of the Prussian town of Kolberg during the war against Napoleon in 1806. But, as with *Jud Süss*, since the real facts were inconvenient — in reality the town had eventually fallen to the French — history had to be rewritten so that the locals managed through their steadfast determination to repulse the invaders. One of the central points that Goebbels wanted the film to make was that ultimately it was up to ordinary people — not professional soldiers — to defend their homeland. This was a contemporary message that Goebbels was also relentlessly repeating in the newsreels of the period. He himself was a fanatical supporter of the Volkssturm, the people's army, a kind

---

[1] See Veit Harlan, *Im Schatten meiner Filme Selbstbiographie*, "In the Shadows of my Films: Autobiography", (Gütersloh, 1966). See also Welch, *Propaganda*, p.97

of German Home Guard, who were supposed to make a last-ditch attempt to keep the Red Army at bay in the final year of the war.

One of the many astonishing things about *Kolberg* was its scale. It was, at the time, the most expensive German film ever made, with a budget of nearly 9 million Reichsmarks. And, incredibly, tens of thousands of German soldiers were diverted from the front line to act as extras. In his interview with us, Wilfred von Oven, a close aide of the Propaganda Minister, revealed that "Goebbels even said to me that it was more important that the soldiers act in his film rather than fight at the front — which was no longer worth doing since we were in the middle of total collapse."

Goebbels was entranced by the film when he saw it. He even ordered a copy to be parachuted into a besieged SS garrison in France in order to inspire the troops, and told the German composer Norbert Schultze, who wrote the music for the picture, that, "The film *Kolberg* will survive us!"

In its most dramatic scene, Maria, the heroic village maiden (played by Kristina Söderbaum — a part for which Goebbels must have thought she was type-cast), is told by the leader of the town's citizen-defence brigade, Nettlebeck: "You have sacrificed everything you had, Maria — but not in vain. Death is intertwined with victory. The greatest achievements are always borne in pain." Words which perfectly encapsulate Goebbels's own propaganda of the time, in which he called for "Total War" and a "radical" struggle unto death. Surrender was something that Goebbels and the citizens of Kolberg could not contemplate — death was something they could.

In the last days of the war Goebbels spoke of the film to his own propaganda staff — it was an inspiration, he said, because one day a similar film would be made about them: "Gentlemen, in a hundred years' time they will be showing another fine colour film describing the terrible days we are living through. Don't you want to play a part in this film, to be brought back to life in a hundred years' time? Everybody now has a chance to choose the part which he will play in the film a hundred years hence. I can assure you that it will be a fine and elevating picture. And for the sake of this prospect it is worth standing fast. Hold out now, so that a hundred years hence the audience does not hoot and whistle when you appear on the screen."[1]

It is possibly the most revealing personal speech that Goebbels ever made. It's all here: his egotism, his nihilism, his belief that he had the chance to write his own film script by the manner of his last days, and his sense that film can be as real as life itself.

So, given this background, I was eager to get Kristina Söderbaum's take on all of this. After all, she had played the most important part in the film — and played it brilliantly. But this was her only comment on *Kolberg*: "I found it ridiculous to be filming when the enemy was coming nearer and nearer. One knew about

---

[1] Goebbels's speech made 17 April 1945, quoted in Rudolf Semler, *Goebbels: The Man Next to Hitler*, (London, 1947), p.194

the war and everything that was happening. Then to stand in front of the camera, I felt like a monkey."

It was a disappointing response, but whilst it revealed nothing about the artistic or propaganda purpose of *Kolberg*, it did expose quite a lot about her own mentality — an impression of resolute self-centredness that was reinforced by the words she spoke to me after the filmed interview, over a cup of tea.

"Honestly," she said, "I have tried since the war to read up on all the terrible things Hitler did. But it's very difficult, you see, because he had the most wonderful blue eyes. And, more than that, he was always terribly nice to me."

PART SEVEN

MASS SUICIDE

Japan is the country most associated with acts of suicide during the war, and to no one's surprise, I suspect, two of the three personal histories about suicide in this final section of the book recount different aspects of the Japanese experience. But the reasons behind the actions of these people were not what I had expected.

I had thought, before I went on my first research trip to Japan, that religious zeal had been to a large extent responsible for the mass suicides in the last year of the war. I had read how the kamikaze pilots, for example, had believed that after their deaths they would return and live as "gods" in a Shinto shrine in Tokyo. But religion did not turn out to be the key to understanding the Japanese. Whilst there were some devout Zen monasteries in Japan that conformed to my predetermined view, for the most part religion — as we recognize it in the West — seemed to play little part in most people's lives.

Shinto, the traditional religion of Japan, is more like a philosophy of behaviour than a religion. Shinto has no single founder, no single scripture. It is vague on the question of any after-life, vague on theology, vague on the role of the "gods". One of the few areas it is not vague about is the responsibility of the individual to the group. Morality is what the group decides. Thus state Shinto, during the war, was essentially a tool of political control.

Even the famed Japanese worship of their emperor during the war as a "god" has often been misconstrued in the West. It was not that every Japanese thought their Emperor was a "god" in the sense of possessing supernatural qualities. Within state Shinto the Emperor was seen as a special person who was "god-like" in much the same way as British monarchs until the seventeenth century were perceived to be ruling by "divine right". And if some of the kamikaze pilots did genuinely believe they would return as "gods" after their deaths and live in a shrine in Tokyo, it was only in the most abstract sense — like being part of the wind or the rain.

Religion was not a dominant factor in either of these Japanese suicide stories. And rather than encountering any exotic "separateness" in the Japanese experience, I was struck by the similarity between one of the personal histories from Japan and the one included here from a German, Waltraud Reski. Her own traumatic experience in the town of Demmin in northeast Germany has many factors in common with the story of Shigeaki Kinjou from the island of Tokashiki on the other side of the world. Of course there were — and are — significant differences in cultural attitudes towards suicide in Germany and Japan (something I discuss at the end of the essay on Shigeaki Kinjou on page 312), but I believe that in popular culture these differences are over-emphasized. Instead of a religious core, each of these three personal histories has at its centre something else entirely — desperation. It's no accident that all of these suicide stories are set towards the end of the war, and concern people on the two losing sides, Germany and Japan.

Before I met these three — Shigeaki Kinjou, Kenichiro Oonuki and Waltraud Reski — I had little sympathy for people who commit suicide. Of course, I felt, any individual can decide to kill themselves if they want to, but I believed it was a supremely selfish act. I had seen the effects of suicide on the perpetrators' surviving family and friends, who were often guilt-stricken, and I knew that the ripples of suffering continue to spread out for years. But I now realize the harshness of that judgement. Thousands of people during the war never contemplated suicide until their situation changed towards the end of the conflict. Hopefully we shall never be placed in such a situation. But if we ever are, can we be so certain that we shall never act as they did?

KENICHIRO OONUKI
AND THE LOGIC OF THE KAMIKAZE

On 5 April 1945, Kenichiro Oonuki flew towards the Allied fleet off the Japanese island of Okinawa. His mission was simple: to smash his fighter plane, laden with high explosives, into an Allied warship. In the process he would turn himself into more than a million pieces, and also, he was told, into a kind of god. For Kenichiro Oonuki was one of the most infamous and feared warriors of World War II — a kamikaze.

These Japanese suicide pilots were often called "madmen" by the Allied servicemen who faced them. It is an unsurprising judgement. In times of war the belief that one's foe is insane is a useful tool, uniting everyone around a common goal. There is no space for equivocation, no possibility of dialogue, no question that one's own quest is right. What else can you do when someone is mad and threatens you, but hunt them down like a rabid dog? But the kamikaze were not mad at all. A study of Japanese history reveals that, paradoxically, the only "inscrutable" Japanese were probably the tiny number who — when asked — did *not* volunteer to become kamikazes and smash their planes and themselves into pieces.

In the summer of 1944 it was clear that the Japanese were losing the war. In their long history they had never been defeated before, and so the collective sense of shame the nation now felt was almost unimaginable; especially since the Japanese of this generation had been taught since childhood that their emperor should be defended at all costs. Japanese soldiers had also been told, from the moment they joined the Imperial Army, that they were forbidden to surrender. This was an act that would bring the greatest shame on their families. And after enduring a basic training of extreme brutality, during which recruits were beaten and bullied, the vast majority of Japanese soldiers were prepared to follow orders at all costs.

When they had begun the war at Pearl Harbor less than three years earlier, the Japanese had possessed superior weaponry in a number of key areas, not least in the air with the excellent Zero fighter. But they had made a massive misjudgement about the likely response of the Americans to their sneak attack on 7 December 1941. They thought the Americans would swiftly negotiate a compromise peace after much of their Pacific fleet had been destroyed. Instead, the Americans fought on, utilizing the huge economic resources at their disposal, until by the summer of 1944 the Japanese superiority in weaponry had been eliminated and the Imperial Army was retreating on all fronts.

On 15 June 1944, the 2nd and 4th US Marine divisions landed on the island of Saipan. This was an event of great significance because the Japanese classed this island, which had been occupied by them under a mandate before the war, as home soil. More than 30,000 Japanese troops were trapped on the small island, and retreat was impossible. So that meant either surrender — in which case they would break the oath they had sworn to the emperor when they joined the Imperial Army — or death. And so, on 6 July, Lieutenant-General Yoshitsugu Saito, their commander, ordered what amounted to a suicide charge against the American Marines. In an action that marked a turning point in the behaviour of the Imperial Army during the war, almost all of the Japanese soldiers died.

Just a few weeks later, on 20 August, the airmen of the Ozuki fighter group were trying in vain to prevent American B29 bombers from attacking the home islands of Japan. Suddenly two Japanese pilots, out of ammunition and driven to distraction by the inability of their fighters to destroy the Americans, deliberately crashed their planes into the B29s in mid-air. The pilots who died in this spontaneous act of defiance were lauded as heroes in Japanese propaganda. It was proof, many Japanese thought, that individual qualities like courage and self-sacrifice counted for more than technical superiority. And the leaders of the Japanese forces drew an additional conclusion from this action — that perhaps airborne suicide attacks might have real military value. So now they began recruiting "volunteers" who were prepared to crash their planes into Allied warships.

It was as a result of this recruitment drive that Kenichiro Oonuki became a kamikaze. He had joined the Japanese air force in 1943 and his original motivation for wanting to become a pilot was simple — they were the elite, and he wanted to be a member of this exclusive club. He certainly did not imagine that he would later be called upon to fly his plane into the superstructure of an Allied ship and sacrifice his life.

But then, in the autumn of 1944, a senior Japanese air force officer visited Oonuki's base. He said he was seeking "volunteers" for a "special mission", and made it clear that anyone who did volunteer had no hope of surviving. Oonuki and his comrades were told to think over the proposal and then, next morning, give one of three responses: "No", "Yes," or "Yes, I volunteer with all my heart." (It is an intriguing detail in the story that there were two versions of "Yes" on offer. What volunteering "with all my heart" demonstrated, of course, was a valiant note of heroism behind the acceptance.)

The immediate reaction of Oonuki and his fellow pilots was predictable. They thought the proposal was "ridiculous". "We were taken aback," said Oonuki. "I felt it was not the type of mission I would willingly apply for." He was right, of course. Who could possibly agree to such lunacy? But then, as the night wore on, they started thinking about what might happen to them if they said "No". They might well be accused of cowardice and ostracized by the rest of their group; worse still, their relatives might be shunned by other Japanese families.

Apart from a brief period at the end of the nineteenth century and start of the twentieth, Japan had always been one of the most culturally insular countries in the world. And the military-dominated government that had come to power in the 1930s had explicitly called for a return to the "traditional values" that had existed before contact with the West. So now, in 1944, for any Japanese to be excluded from the single cultural group they had been told for years was acceptable would mean terrible humiliation.

Then Oonuki and his friends thought of another possible consequence of refusing to "volunteer". Those who did not come forward could easily be "isolated and then sent to the forefront of the most severe battle and meet a sure death anyway".

Surely, on reflection, the easiest course to take in these circumstances was to "volunteer with all my heart", as Oonuki and all the other pilots on his course did when asked the next morning. "Probably it's unthinkable in the current days of peace," he said. "Nobody wanted to, but everybody said, 'Yes, with all my heart' . . . That was the surrounding atmosphere . . . We could not resist."

It would have taken a truly exceptional person to withstand the awesome cultural, peer and emotional pressure that was swirling around those Japanese air bases in 1944. Japanese propaganda trumpeted that the kamikaze were heroes — once they had completed their mission they would receive a "promotion", so that their families would receive a bigger pension after their death. They were even promised that after they had made the ultimate personal sacrifice they would become a kind of god themselves, and their souls would return in some vague, mystical way and live in the sacred Yasukuni shrine in Tokyo, where the emperor would come and worship them.

Oonuki and his comrades now transferred to a "conversion" course and practised "nose diving" — which was hazardous in the extreme. "I saw many die during the training," he said, "and if you hit the ground it's very difficult to collect up the pieces of the bodies." They were preparing for the biggest kamikaze attack of the war, on the Allied fleet off the island of Okinawa. The Japanese leadership believed that if they could defeat the Americans as they attempted to capture Okinawa, perhaps they could still conclude some kind of compromise peace.

Oonuki's plane was not ready when the first sortie left for Okinawa, so he had to say a painful — and final — goodbye to half a dozen of his friends: "I went to my colleagues once their engines had already started and they were on the runway . . . The azaleas were in full bloom, and so I made a bouquet of azaleas and gave it to my pilot comrades. And one comrade said, 'I am going ahead of you. I wanted to meet my destiny with you. I'm sorry.' They were the saddest eyes I ever saw . . . It's often said that before one's death a person has that really sad expression in the eyes . . . So before they took off I gave each of them a bouquet of azaleas — every one of them. And everyone thought, I am going ahead of you, and nobody talked of death. Everybody had the same expression in their eyes, like a deep sea fish looking up at the blue sky above."

The actions of Oonuki's comrades did have an effect — though not a decisive one. American aircraft carriers with wooden decks were particularly vulnerable. One direct hit from a kamikaze could penetrate straight through to the hangars and fuel tanks in the depths of the superstructure. In total, around 200 American ships were damaged and 24 sunk off Okinawa. For many of the Allied sailors, facing the kamikaze was the most frightening experience of the entire war. There were even stories of American sailors jumping overboard in psychological torment as the kamikaze attacked.

On 5 April 1945, Oonuki himself took off and flew towards Okinawa to join in the assault. But en route he was attacked by American fighters and forced to land his damaged plane on one of the nearby Ryukyu Islands. He did not feel pleased he had survived the enemy attack — quite the contrary: "I felt it was dishonour, because the special attack mission means you must meet an honourable death. So as a soldier it meant mission unfulfilled if I survived." Just over a week later he was picked up by a passing Japanese ship and taken back to the home islands, where he was greeted with the words: "Why have you come back?" and then imprisoned. "We were all reprimanded and scolded. We were told, 'Don't you feel sorry and shameful and guilty in the face of all those that have passed away? You are a disgrace to those who died.' Every possible accusation was made against us by senior officers. It was just the weakness of our mind that we survived. And then I was beaten by a bamboo sword to the extent that I could not move at all . . . We couldn't even kill ourselves — we didn't have anything to do it with."

Until recently Oonuki would not talk about his experience with the Kamikaze lest it brought dishonour on himself and his relations, and when I met him in Tokyo in 1999 it was obvious that recalling this whole episode was still deeply painful for him. It is not so much that he believed he was a victim of injustice, as that he still felt a "deep sense of guilt" that he survived. "Whatever the reason, survival gave you the sense of a burden. Your colleagues, to whom you have a stronger bond than almost your family, have passed away — but you simply survived." Part of him still clearly felt that his body ought to have been scattered over the flaming decks of an Allied warship off Okinawa in 1945. He should not be alive — even though he believed that the whole idea of the kamikaze was "simply ridiculous".

Judged without knowledge of the background, Oonuki's experience as a volunteer kamikaze is a straightforward example of the insane behaviour of the Japanese during World War II. Yet on closer examination it is anything but: "The special attack troop [the kamikaze]," he said, "is described as the model of courage, or the Japanese soldier portrayed as reckless and fanatic. But rather we were very calm, and we went through a very calm, dispassionate process of analysis [before agreeing to take part]."

Indeed, as Kenichiro Oonuki saw it, sometimes the only sane choice is to take the option that others, who do not know the full story, will later consider "mad".

WALTRAUD RESKI
AND MASS RAPE IN DEMMIN

In 1945, between Tuesday, 1 May and Thursday, 3 May, the Red Army went on the rampage in the town of Demmin in northeast Germany. As a consequence, Waltraud Reski lived through what she described as "hell on earth". Waltraud was 11 years old at the time, and much that happened was strange to her. Down by the river Peene, together with her younger sister, mother and grandmother, she saw "whole families who had tied themselves together. And I was wondering — Why are they doing that? I kept seeing women holding children by the hand and they were running down towards the water. We were not supposed to see it, and my grandmother was always keeping us busy, telling us to help push the cart or look after our mother. But I could hear it. There is a sort of splashing sound when a person jumps into the water. And so I kept asking, 'Why are they jumping into the water?' And then my grandmother said, 'They are so unhappy, they want to take their own lives.' That's what she whispered to me. But I didn't understand any of it."

Waltraud also recalled "the sight of those who had gone into the water the previous night, those terrible sights, those bodies, reddish-blue and swollen. I didn't often look because I didn't want it to be true . . . And when my mum was with us again we walked a little further, until we were quite close to the water . . . And then she grabbed us and wanted to run to the river with us. We were both screaming, and my grandmother was behind."

Waltraud Reski told her story sitting on the bank of the river Peene with the church towers of Demmin behind her. It was a tranquil spot. Ducks swam in the sparkling water and the sky was clear and blue. It was hard to believe that nearly 1000 citizens of the town — men, women and children — had committed suicide here during the Red Army's visit in May 1945. But they had. It was equally hard to understand what could have driven them to this. Why would a mother want to kill herself and her own children?

It seems that the Red Army were given free rein in Demmin for several days, immediately after Hitler had committed suicide on 30 April. For the Soviet soldiers this was a kind of obscene rest-and-recreation period. And though rape and pillage were officially forbidden in the Red Army, there were countless cases where the senior commanders turned a blind eye to what was going on — in fact, many of the senior commanders were not averse to a spot of looting themselves. Marshal Zhukov, the most famous Red Army commander of them all, was reputed to have sent trainloads of booty back from the front line for his personal enrichment.

To begin with, though she was "full of fear and anxiety", Waltraud was calmed by her grandmother: "I always mention my grandmother, she kept the family going, because my father was away at the war and my mother was very ill. And she used to say, 'Of course the Russians are our enemies, but they are also human beings.' So she tried to reassure us, the whole family."

Waltraud heard the Red Army coming long before she saw them: "This noise — the tanks rolling in — it's a frightening noise. Whenever I see it in a film now this memory comes back to me — you probably know it, this clanking and roaring. And then we barricaded ourselves in our homes. We blocked the front door and the other doors with pieces of furniture and thought nothing can happen to us."

They were wrong, of course, because soldiers who had fought through the German lines and crossed the river Oder found such defences laughable. "When they realized that people were not letting them in they started kicking, and then they were there. We fled from one room to the next while they were turning everything upside down. They kept saying, 'Uri! Uri!' — they wanted watches and jewellery, and we gave them to them. And then they marched off, they went on to the next houses, so for the time being they were gone." Meantime the whole town had surrendered. White flags flew from the windows and the roofs. But it made no difference to the Red Army. They shot the town officials and started to set fire to the buildings: "Demmin was to burn for three days, probably as a punishment. And the women were fair game for three days too — they were free to be abused. In fact, we were really all supposed to burn to death."

As Waltraud sat with her family in her home, still shocked at the sudden arrival of the Red Army, she heard a crackling noise and realized the neighbouring houses were on fire. She looked out of the back window and saw that the flames had already reached their back yard and were spreading fast: "So we were screaming. We were frightened — what are we going to do now? What if we don't get out of this trap? It was again my grandmother who really kept her nerve. We had this little handcart and she quickly gathered everything she thought was essential and then we left through our neighbour's back yard."

Pushing their handcart, the Reskis hoped to escape the attention of the Soviet soldiers and reach relatives in a small town some 16 kilometres away. But the Red Army in Demmin were intent on raping any German woman they wanted — and they wanted Waltraud's mother: "All the women were disguised, but you can always see whether a woman has a good figure and somehow they found my mother again and again and treated her terribly." All around, amidst the roar of the flames, the Red Army soldiers were snatching women and raping them: "My sister, who is four years younger than me, and I, we always tried to shield our mother and screamed." But it was all to no avail as "they only spared those women who were carrying a baby . . . I would have hit them if I could — if my grandmother had not held me. You know, this feeling of helplessness and everything, this cruelty — even today I am unable to find words for it. And for a long time afterwards I had a very disturbed attitude towards men."

The flickering fire, the red glow on the faces of the Soviet troops, the collapsing buildings, the screams of desperate women and children, the lust and the suffering — surely Waltraud Reski is right, and those scenes in Demmin that night in early May were a literal "hell on earth". "We all thought we were going to burn to death," she said. "We had no hope for life, and I myself, I had the feeling that this was the end of the world, this was the end of my life." During that night their grandmother represented their only hope of survival: "Well, today I must say, if my grandmother hadn't kept her nerve we would all have died miserably in the flames."

Waltraud's grandmother led the girls and their mother out of the town centre and past the river, where they saw families committing suicide together — jumping hand in hand into the fast-flowing water. But at last, having hurried by the river, Waltraud thought they had evaded the attention of the Red Army and had made good their escape. But she was wrong. A group of Soviet soldiers spotted them. They advanced towards the women and robbed their handcart of "our very last possessions". Then they eyed up Waltraud's mother and, liking what they saw, led her away to a little copse near by. "We ran after them and screamed," said Waltraud, "but they pushed us away with a rifle butt." Once again it was their grandmother who comforted the distraught girls until eventually their mother reappeared. But that last gang rape was too much for Waltraud's mother. She grabbed her two little girls and ran for the river in an attempt to commit suicide.

And it was at this point that Waltraud's grandmother saved their lives for the last time. She restrained

Waltraud's mother and shouted, "Please don't do this! What are you doing? What am I supposed to tell your husband when he comes back from the war and you're gone?" As a result, said Waltraud, her mother "became calmer" and allowed herself to be led away from the river and thoughts of suicide. The next day they reached their relatives' farm and made a home for themselves in an attic room. But there was one final horror in store.

Also living in the house was a Polish woman who had worked for the family as a domestic servant. She had been brought as a forced labourer to Germany and now saw a chance of revenge. Spotting a group of Red Army soldiers near by, she told them that Waltraud's mother was hiding in the attic. "She [the Polish woman] had suffered," said Waltraud, "and maybe her parents and relatives too, and she just wanted to compensate for it this way. She had to do it."

And so Waltraud's mother was raped yet again: "In Demmin I had already seen things that I didn't really understand, but I knew that it was inhuman and an offence against human dignity, how they seized the women and humiliated them. And like all the other women my mother became completely withdrawn . . . It's impossible to imagine what it is like to be raped ten or twenty times a day. So that one is hardly human any more. And my mother, she became a completely different person after this for the rest of her life . . . For me, it was as if all of a sudden I had to grow up. And I didn't feel like living. I saw everything in the blackest of clouds . . . All I can think of is how strong my grandmother was. I've always been grateful to her. And there were many women during the war who were so strong, and she herself said she didn't know why but all of a sudden she felt this strength."

Those few days in Demmin in May 1945 were life-changing for all of Waltraud's family. Her mother suffered bouts of paranoia from this point forward. Her grandmother discovered that she possessed enormous reserves of emotional strength. And Waltraud and her sister faced the traumatic end of their childhood. For Waltraud there was an additional consequence — from that moment onwards she became a dedicated pacifist.

All of us who heard Waltraud tell the story of her suffering in Demmin were shocked. Not just, of course, because of the abhorrent nature of the story itself, but also because news of what happened in that small town was so fresh to us. Perhaps that was because until the fall of the Berlin Wall all the locations where these crimes took place — and many of the interviewees themselves — were inaccessible to Westerners. But I also thought that there were other reasons why in the West these atrocities have received such little attention. It is uncomfortable to think of our own Allies as being capable of such horrendous war crimes, and the media in Britain and the USA are still wary of portraying even entirely innocent Germans as "victims".

SHIGEAKI KINJOU
AND THE DEATH OF THE INNOCENT

I had known from the start of my work that questioning people who had participated in World War II would offer a degree of insight that could not be gained just from reading books or documents. But what I did not realize at the beginning was how much could also be achieved from visiting the locations where those experiences took place. It was not, for example, until I drove across the immense steppes east of Kharkov that I began to understand the exhilaration that the Panzer crews must have felt during the huge German advance of Operation Blue in the summer of 1942. And it was only a visit to the wilderness north of Murmansk on the Kola peninsula that made me realize just why Allied seaman had felt so isolated in the Soviet Union whilst waiting for a return convoy. But it was the Japanese island of Tokashiki that was the single most valuable historical location I visited.

The island is famous for its wild beauty — cliffs tower above the waves of the East China Sea, and the hills are covered in trees and lush undergrowth. I visited Tokashiki in 1999, and as I drove with my film crew up towards a ravine in the deserted mountains, I thought of the American Marines who had fought through this thicket of undergrowth fifty-four years earlier. It was no wonder that they had told me how much they hated this "island-hopping". Losses for the Americans could be appalling — as they were on nearby Okinawa. You couldn't see more than a few metres into the forest, and the defenders held an obvious advantage.

But in March 1945 the Japanese soldiers knew that these advantages counted for little or nothing. All they could do by fighting in the forests of Tokashiki was to put off the inevitable: the American superiority in weaponry and technical support meant that Japanese defeat was certain. But every soldier in the Imperial Army had sworn an oath not to surrender. And so, trapped on Tokashiki, they knew they were supposed to fight — and die — on the island.

The position of the soldiers was clear enough — but what about the civilians on Tokashiki? On the one hand, they had not sworn an oath to kill themselves, but on the other they believed they owed absolute loyalty to their emperor. For Shigeaki Kinjou, then 16 years old, it was clear what was expected of all the inhabitants of the island: "We were the people of the emperor. The Japanese belonged to the emperor as his babies. We were his babies, his children. So we worked in a family system with the emperor at the top. We had to sacrifice our lives for the emperor."

The kamikaze offered an example of how to behave, with Japanese newsreels glorifying their actions. One propaganda film of the period even explicitly shows the kamikaze receiving the emperor's blessing. A Japanese officer is seen reading a message to a group of kamikaze pilots who are waiting to leave on their suicide mission. "These words are from the emperor," the officer says. "Those who have attacked the enemy individually have done a great job and produced remarkable results. How brave they were to sacrifice their lives for their country."

"[At the time] I thought the kamikaze were doing very well," said Shigeaki Kinjou. "I believed that they were sacrificing their lives for their country. And [as] civilians, we should also be ready to sacrifice our lives for the country when the time came." The civilians on Tokashiki had also been told, he said, that "they wouldn't survive if they were taken prisoner by the Americans. We were informed that we would be killed if we were captured. I think that's one of the reasons why so many people were prepared to commit suicide."

After about 40 minutes' drive up into the mountains, we reached our destination. It was an isolated spot on this isolated island. Once I had climbed over the concrete snake barrier that surrounded the ravine (worryingly placed there, I realized, in order to keep snakes inside) I felt as if I were cut off completely from the rest of the world. On every side cliffs and forest towered above me. Jungle streams gushed down the rocks, and the sound was magnified into a roar by the enclosed, claustrophobic space.

Around 800 villagers gathered here on 27 March 1945. They were mostly old people, women and children, and their mood was desperate in the extreme. Many were nearly hysterical, believing that the Americans would kill them if they were captured — there was even a rumour that they would all be hideously tortured first. Suddenly an American bomb exploded close to them, and this one event appears to have acted as a catalyst. Abruptly, one of the village elders took up a branch of a tree and started to attack his family with it.

As soon as Shigeaki Kinjou and his 19-year-old brother saw what was happening, they knew what was expected of them: "We understood what should be done now — I mean killing your family. Usually the father acted the main part in killing the family. But we didn't have our father with us. He was missing." Shigeaki now felt that the burden of fulfilling the wishes of the emperor, of the Imperial Army and of the village elders — all people and institutions he revered — had passed from his absent father to himself and his brother. The two of them, he believed, had to kill his mother, together with their younger brother and sister: "We didn't discuss anything. No words were exchanged. It's like telepathy. We didn't say, 'Let's start now' or 'Let's die together' or anything like that. We were destined to die and pressured to die."

Around them was "absolute chaos" as in the confined area of the ravine families killed each other. Shigeaki and his brother turned first on their mother: "We tried to tie her neck with rope or many other things until we tried the last thing. We took a stone and bashed in her head. That's the brutal thing we did to our own mother. I couldn't stop crying out . . . I never cried out like that in my life again . . . Then we killed our brother and sister." Shigeaki and his surviving brother knew what they had to do next: "Thinking of my psychological state at the time, I knew that I had to die and that was my fate . . . It was the turn of my brother and me to commit suicide." But he admitted that he still had "some kind of resistance to death."

Whilst he and his brother were "discussing what to do next", a boy ran past them saying, "It would be much better to kill Americans — at least one — before we die." Shigeaki and his brother "hesitated for a moment" before agreeing that a suicide attack on the enemy would be preferable to killing each other. Together they climbed out of the ravine and charged towards the Americans, only to discover that their enemy — contrary to what the Imperial Army had told them — was not prepared to kill unarmed civilians. They were captured, and both survived the war. But around 320 Japanese villagers died in the ravine that day — either by committing suicide themselves or by being "assisted" to suicide by others.

When I met him in 1999, Shigeaki Kinjou was still trying to make sense of what he and his brother had done. "I didn't kill them out of hatred or anything," he said, speaking of his mother, younger brother and sister. "But I think we were dreadfully manipulated, and I have suffered and felt guilt since the war until today."

That Shigeaki Kinjou and his brother — along with all the other villagers who gathered in the ravine that day — were "manipulated" is without doubt. As we have seen, soldiers of the Imperial Army had deliberately spread the rumour that the Americans would kill all of them if they surrendered, and the villagers believed their emperor wanted them to commit suicide. But there were also wider cultural factors at work. Suicide has a long tradition in Japan as an acceptable — almost admirable — way of escaping a problem that appears intractable. That is something that has not changed with the democratization of post-war Japan. On this same Japanese filming trip I read in a newspaper about a student who had killed himself because his exam results had been disastrous, as well as a case of a teenage couple who had entered into a suicide pact because of opposition to their relationship from their parents. Currently around 30,000 Japanese commit suicide every year — more than twice the suicide rate of America or Britain.

The Japanese cultural predisposition to consider suicide a possible option under the severest emotional stress was clearly a major contributory factor towards the horrific events of 27 March 1945 on Tokashiki; as was the fear engendered by the Imperial Army that there was no possibility of the Americans treating Japanese civilians humanely. Yet when I had filmed an interview with Shigeaki Kinjou that morning in Naha, the busy capital of the island of Okinawa, neither of these factors had been sufficient to allow me to imagine how this appalling event could have happened. But as I stood in that ravine on the island of Tokashiki, where the mass suicide occurred, and felt the intense claustrophobia of the rock and forest all around, I began, for the first time, to experience a glimmer of understanding.

POSTSCRIPT

After all these years of thinking about human motivation and belief during World War II, two ideas preoccupy me. The first is the importance of remembering the impermanence of our lives and the world around us. Samuel Willenberg, Estera Frenkiel and many other people I met suddenly found their world transformed for the worst through no fault of their own. One minute life seemed settled, moving along a stable and orderly course. The next their lives were shattered. They discovered that nothing need be the way it currently is. Everything is fragile.

The second issue concerns the malleability of human behaviour and attitude. To what extent are we who we are because of the inherent qualities within us — our genetic inheritance — or the conditioning of the environment around us? Of course we are all a mix of both, but I now believe that many people are more shaped by the "situational ethic" — their upbringing and the culture around them — than we might like to imagine. I met many former Nazis, for example, who went on to have successful careers in post-war democratic Germany, and a number of former Communists who have recently embraced rampant capitalism. They changed when the situation changed. They ditched the ideologies they claimed had been fundamental to their belief system when they were no longer useful.

But I encountered the most dramatic example of the power of the situation to influence human behaviour in the early 1990s, when I was editor of *Timewatch*, the BBC's history documentary series. I commissioned and then executive-produced a film from producer Catrine Clay about a Polish child, called Alojzy, who was snatched from his mother by the Nazis during the war when he was four years old.

Heinrich Himmler, commander of the SS, was so obsessed with the Nazi idea of "race" that he wanted to "attract all the Nordic blood in the world and take it for ourselves". In pursuit of that goal he ordered that a selection be made of "suitable" Polish children. These Aryan-looking boys and girls would then be separated from their parents and taken away to be raised as Germans. "Many say, how can you be so cruel as to take a child away from its mother?" wrote Himmler. "To that I answer, how can you be so cruel as to leave a brilliant future enemy on the other side who will kill your sons and your grandsons?"[1]

Documents were created for Alojzy, which said that his mother had died in childbirth and that his father

---

[1] See *Timewatch: Stolen Child*, produced by Catrine Clay, first transmission BBC2, February 1993. See also Himmler's memo "Some thoughts on the treatment of the alien population of the East", May 1940. English translation in *Nazism 1919–1945*, J. Noakes and G. Pridham (eds) Vol.3 (Exeter University Press, 1988), p.933

had been an SS officer shot by the Poles. He was no longer to be a four-year-old Polish boy called Alojzy, but a four-year-old German boy called Alfred Binderberger.

Alojzy remembered nothing of his life in Poland. Instead, one of his first memories was of leaving the German orphanage where he had initially been placed and arriving at his new parents' house: "I came up the steps, beautiful flowers left and right. I felt I was in heaven. There stood my grandfather, my mother — everyone was happy, looking at me. The grandfather came in, turned me round like a recruit, and said, 'Yes, well-built lad.' He was satisfied."

Alojzy was now brought up as a typical Nazi child. His new father had been a party member for years and worked for the armaments firm Krupp. His new mother had a desk job with the German air force, the Luftwaffe. And they were all happy together. "My mother was the heart of the family," recalled Alojzy. "And the relationship between my mother and my grandfather was very close. She was the apple of his eye. And because I was the apple of my mother's eye, I was my grandfather's special favourite."

When Alojzy was seven years old, the war ended: "It upset me a lot, to see Germany defeated. Hitler was my idol. He was the man who made Germany great. Overnight, suddenly, white flags hung out of all the windows and I howled. I wept. But then we said, 'It's the Communists who did this — who surrendered.'"

With the war over, Alojzy's real mother was determined to find him. She managed to discover his new German name and frantically searched for him, writing to the Red Cross and contacting any other organization she could think of that might be able to help. Eventually Alojzy was traced to his new German family and she wrote to them, asking for her son to be returned. But they loved him and would not let him go. "The Binderbergers didn't want to give him up," she remembered. "I waited. For me, these were the worst years. You can imagine how it feels. That was the most difficult time."

Alojzy's mother faced a huge problem in her effort to get her son back. By 1948, when she had discovered just where he was, Allied policy had altered. The emotional needs of the child were now thought to be paramount. And, in any case, few in the West were keen to return a child to Communist Poland.

Nonetheless, when he was 12 years old the Binderbergers decided to break the news to Alojzy that he was not their real son: "I remember, I came back from school in a good mood. I came into the room and I was amazed. My grandfather was there, my grandmother, my mother and my father. And my father had a letter in his hand. He said, 'Alfred, we've been waiting for you. We have some information for you. This is a letter from your mother.'

"I said, 'Papa, don't be silly, Mama is sitting here.'

"'No, this is from your real mother.'

"'Come off it!'

"'From Poland,' he said.

"And then I went crazy! Me, from Poland!

"He said, 'Well, maybe she's a German who couldn't get out of Poland.'

"I said, 'Oh, forget it! Anyway, I'm definitely not Polish.'

"Let me explain something here. During the war we had a lot of foreign labourers, from eastern Europe. They were slaves, really. They shifted coal and things. My grandfather sometimes used to give them a few coins. But they looked terrible — unshaven . . . instead of shoes they had newspapers wrapped around their feet with string . . . badly dressed, dirty. And people said, 'Look at them — they're sub-humans, the Polacks.' "

Alojzy's mother had written a heartrending letter asking her son if he realized that she had been trying to get him back for years, and ending, "I beg you, as my son, to write me a few lines and send a photograph of yourself. I can't wait for the time when I can press you to my heart. Your loving mother." She also enclosed two photographs of herself, which Alojzy tore up in front of his adopted parents. "It turned out," he remembered, "that my grandfather had, for two years, intercepted her letters. The letters had been addressed to my father but my grandfather opened them and replied, forging my father's signature, and told no one a thing about it. This is proof of my grandfather's great love for me. He didn't want to lose me."

But Alojzy didn't yet know an even darker secret. His beloved adopted mother had cancer, and she died a year later. "My world fell apart," he said. "I don't think there can be a greater love between a son and his

mother as there was between my mother and me . . .
Hardly a day passes without me thinking of her. I can't
say more than that."

When Alojzy was 14 his father got married again.
But there were tensions in the family. Alojzy didn't get
on with his father's new wife, and she didn't get on
with him. And born of the stress of this fresh family life
was a new willingness from Alojzy to visit the mother
he could not remember in Poland. "I did this out of
resentment against my father," said Alojzy frankly. "I
wanted to annoy him, to hurt him. To my amazement
he said, 'OK, you can go.'"

So in 1953, when he was 15 years old, Alojzy set out
for Poland: "What did I know about Poland? I knew
that it's very cold there. That there are bears and wolves
there. And there's lots of forest. That the Poles sleep on
ovens. That they don't wash, and they wear furs. That
was Goebbels's propaganda." The first meeting, when
he arrived at Poznan station in the early hours of the
morning, was fraught with anticipation. "I kept
thinking what to say to 'my mother'," remembered
Alojzy. "In the end I decided I'd get off the train and
say, 'Here I am. I just wanted to see you once, and I'm
going back on the next train to Koblenz.'"

"He just gave me his hand. 'Good day' — nothing
else," remembered Alojzy's mother. "Nothing else. I
kept holding back my tears."

"She just kept looking at me," recalled Alojzy. "Such
a smile, such an angel face. My mother was — still is —
very beautiful. With those amazing blue eyes."

318

"He was a real Hitler Youth," said his mother. "A typical German . . . he said the Poles started the war. I said, no, this wasn't true, and he'd soon find out."

Alojzy simply didn't know how to talk to his mother: "At the beginning I was always anti, always against, always against. The worst was I didn't know how to address her. I kept trying to use the third person, the formal style. I avoided the informal 'you' and I avoided 'mother' altogether."

Once the holiday came to an end Alojzy faced a choice — should he stay with his newly found "real" mother, or return home to his stepfather and his new wife? In an instant he made up his mind. He dramatically walked into his mother's bedroom, called her "Mama" for the first time and announced, "Mama, I'm staying here."

The trouble was that Alojzy had once again acted on impulse: "It was exactly the same as that time with my father in Germany. Then I said something spontaneously out of anger. This time, out of pity. But what could I do? I just kept hoping that I'd find a way out of this mess. But then there was the political situation — when you came to Poland you had to give up your passport, and I had to sign something. And the man said come back in a week, so I went back the next week and he gave me another piece of paper to sign. I couldn't understand a word of it. My mother stood next to me and said nothing. So I signed and asked for my passport. 'What passport?' he said. 'You're a Polish citizen now.' And with that he put the passport back in the drawer. I couldn't go back for 16 years. Not to Germany, not to any other country."

Alojzy completed his education in Poland and went to Warsaw University. But he never felt fully accepted in the country of his birth and missed his German family — he was not even allowed to leave Poland to attend his grandfather's or his father's funeral. "When you look at it like that," he said, "it's an absolute disaster."

But he believed he had learnt something valuable from his extraordinary life: "I'm the best example that we can love and understand one another. That a Polish child can be loved by German parents. Put it like this. In Poland I felt I found my old mother from Germany again. It was the same thing — the same gentleness. Maybe my Polish mother was even more gentle. But basically it was the same thing. The same love, the same devotion to the son."

Alojzy's story also, of course, demonstrates the immense power of the situation to influence human development. Here was a four-year-old Polish boy who was transformed into a happy and confident German — a member of the Hitler Youth who believed Poles were "slaves". It is a powerful reminder of the fact that we are not born with a belief system of any kind — as children we absorb the values around us. Only 15 per cent of the children snatched from Poland by the Nazis ever returned to their original homeland. Many must be living somewhere in Germany today, wholly ignorant of their Polish origins — who knows, some of them may still look down on Poles as inferior to Germans.

And whilst the testimony in this book is more nuanced than Alojzy's story, it does still suggest that the question of what is "right" and what is "wrong" is to a large extent determined for many people by what society decrees at any time is "right" and "wrong". Or, as the novelist Samuel Butler put it more than 100 years ago: "Morality is the custom of one's country and the current feeling of one's peers. Cannibalism is moral in a cannibal country."

But I am not some kind of radical determinist. There is always an element of choice. And some exceptional human beings — like Alois Pfaller and Vladimir Kantovski — do choose to stand out against the prevailing mores. But I now suspect there may be fewer people like that in the world than we might want to believe.

What it means in practical terms is that, in order to have the best chance of creating the lives we want, each of us needs to focus more on the culture that envelops us; not just on our families and any other individual groups that we may belong to, but on the political system that surrounds us as well. The best protection lies in trying to ensure that the situational ethic of society as a whole conforms to the rule of law and basic principles of humanity — values that after World War II were enshrined in the Universal Declaration of Human Rights and the European Convention on Human Rights. Just pretending that bad things are not happening and only thinking of oneself is rarely a sustainable option. Ignoring the "little" abuses when they begin only makes it harder to stop the bigger abuses when they follow. Ultimately, the best way of not becoming a "cannibal" is to try to prevent the place where one lives becoming a "cannibal country".

If most people's character and beliefs are more susceptible to change with circumstance than we might think, it also follows that we have to consider the testimony in this book with humility. "That's the trouble with life today," one former Nazi once said to me, "people who have never been tested go around making judgements about people who have been tested." And whilst this sentiment did not stop me condemning this man's wartime actions, his words did make me think more carefully before confronting the question: "What would I have done?"

In the end each of us has to decide for ourselves how we might change were circumstances to alter. Maybe terrible adversity would bring out the best in us, or, just maybe, it would reveal the worst. What do you think? What would you have done?

Also available in ISIS Large Print:

Kitchener's Last Volunteer

Henry Allingham with Dennis Goodwin

Henry Allingham is the last British serviceman alive to have volunteered for active duty in the First World War. He vividly recaptures life in the Edwardian era and how it was altered irrevocably by the Great War, and the subsequent coming of the modern age. Henry is unique in that he saw action on land, sea and in the air with the British Naval Air Service. He was present at the Battle of Jutland in 1916 and went on to serve on the Western Front. In recent years, Henry was given the opportunity to tell his remarkable story to a wider audience through a BBC documentary, and he has since become a hero to many, meeting royalty and receiving many honours such as the Legion d'honneur — France's highest accolade.

ISBN 978-0-7531-8290-1 (hb)
ISBN 978-0-7531-8291-8 (pb)

To Hell and Back

Susanna de Vries & Jake de Vries

As a young soldier on the battlefields of Gallipoli, Sydney Loch witnessed the horrors of war firsthand. On his return to Australia, he wrote an account of all he saw, describing his work as fiction to evade censorship. As the war ground on abroad, Sydney's book, The Straits Impregnable, garnered widespread acclaim. But when the publisher revealed that it was a work of non-fiction, Australian military censors swiftly ordered it to be withdrawn from sale, and the book vanished.

Now, historians Susanna and Jake de Vries have unearthed Sydney's book for a new generation. To accompany it, they have written a biography of the remarkable life of Sydney Loch: from his early years in England and Australia to the war that shaped him and led to his work in Greece and Palestine helping refugees during World War II.

ISBN 978-0-7531-5689-6 (hb)
ISBN 978-0-7531-5690-2 (pb)

S. R.